HAM

AN OBSESSION WITH

HAM

THE HINDQUARTER

BRUCE WEINSTEIN

AND

MARK SCARBROUGH

PHOTOGRAPHS BY
MARCUS NILSSON

STEWART, TABORI & CHANG, NEW YORK

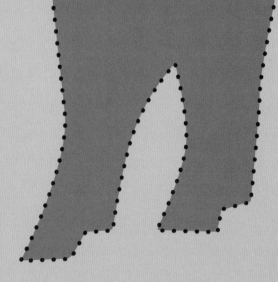

CONTENTS

THIS
LITTLE
PIGGY
WENT TO
MARKET

urs is a mixed marriage. I'm a Southerner from sharecroppers and Civil War soldiers; Bruce is a New Yorker from Torah scribes and kosher butchers. It all works because Baptists eroticize Jews and Jews eroticize ham.

It also works because after fifteen cookbooks together (not counting the ones for persnickety celebrities who insist on confidentiality agreements), we have a distinct division of labor: He cooks, and I write.

It's not that I don't cook. One look at me and you know I shan't starve. And it's not that we don't conceptualize the recipes together. Some of our best fights have been over brown sugar.

Look, I find it can add a cloying gooeyness to chocolate. Not always, mind you. Just sometimes.

And Bruce? The more brown sugar, the better.

So in the middle of concepting out the recipes for *The Ultimate Brownie Book*, right on the busy corner of 7th Avenue and 21st Street in New York City, we descended into a full-throttle yellfest that included such delights as "you don't understand a thing about baking" and "you never value anything I say."

Just as things were getting really dire, Bruce's seventy-something shrink walked by. (These things can *only* happen in New York.)

"You boys OK?" she asked.

We both nodded and took a breath.

"See you Tuesday," she said to Bruce as she crossed the street.

We paused a beat and went right back at it.

Anyway, our division of labor has come about because of our backgrounds: He once studied cheffery at Johnson and Wales, and I once taught freshman English at the University of Wisconsin, Madison.

So for the past decade, Bruce has been in the kitchen, trying out new ideas, new techniques—a steady stream of dishes. He likes to play with his food. And since nothing gives him more pleasure than roasting meat, this book was his joy: sweating joints all day long. He bustled through the recipes, humming and happy. Ever busy, he's the one with the Protestant work ethic. Don't get me started. I, a true son of the South, prefer to laze about on my ample ass reading novels.

One June morning, after a grueling session with Henry James, I walked into the kitchen to find him pan-frying a whole ham (for the results, see *Jamón del País*, page 39). Later, after spending an hour in a Flannery O'Connor chat room, I caught him trying to shove a twenty-four-pound ham into a ten-gallon tub. And around Thanksgiving, when I was putting together a series of highbrow Auden poems to read before the meal, I watched in horror as he shaved the mold off a country ham.

Perhaps I'm getting ahead of myself. Beyond writing, my other role in this culinary circus is to research our more arcane interests in food. And that innate curiosity is really how these two little piggies went to market to buy more hams than you can imagine.

It started like this: One afternoon in late winter, I found myself reading some fascinating websites about American country ham. (You toggle your browser fast enough between Eudora Welty and porn, and it'll happen to you, too.) To be honest, I hadn't thought much about ham. Sure, when I was a kid, it showed up at every holiday that marked the coming or going of the Messiah. But a ham was otherwise a blank centerpiece: sort of like a turkey but with more provenance, more Southern atmospherics, more cultural foofaraw, as well as an aggressive, in-your-face meatiness, proving all that pretension was nothing but folderol.

It wasn't that I knew zilch about ham. For one thing, I'd been on way too many press trips and always dreaded that moment when some PR shill

GLAZED FRESH HAM

would open her eyes really wide and say, "Now we get to taste the ham." It's always the climax of the prescribed food tour—and of almost every travel show, too, from Rick Steves's I'm-right-on-schedule adventures to Anthony Bourdain's slouched ramblings: "Ah, the ham of blah-blah-blah that's smoked over thus-and-such from pigs who only eat this-and-that."

And no wonder. Ham is succulent and sweet, an Easter lunch as well as a summer picnic, a winter dinner and a barbecue favorite, good on sandwiches, great on pizza. It's the subject (or object) of rifle shoots in New England, cook-offs in Kansas City, and a host of culinary fetishes—some written, some photographed, and some better left undocumented.

As I trawled the websites that afternoon, I was again struck by how ham is such global fare—a local icon, a national treasure, a talisman of *terroir*: Italian *prosciutto crudo*, Portuguese *presunto*, Basque *jambon de Bayonne*, Chinese Jinhua hams. By one count, there are more laws governing the production of the various *jamón* in Spain than there are those covering that nation's transportation network.

Soon enough, I scraped back my chair, roused the collie, and ambled into the kitchen, where Bruce was emptying the dishwasher. (Ah, marriage.) "What do you think about ham?" I asked.

"Other than liking it?"

"No, I mean, what do you know about it?"

Bruce launched into a discussion of brines, of curing—but soon got tangled up in smoked versus unsmoked, wet versus dry, nitrates versus not,

American versus European, and so forth.

"There's a lot to it," he finally said.

"I'd like to know more."

He nodded.

"Don't be scared," I added. I once told him I wanted to eat never-been-frozen shrimp, and we ended up on a 2,500-mile car trip to Newfoundland.

"I'm not."

"You used to be." Another time I told him I didn't want to sit around all summer in the East Coast heat, and we somehow landed in Morocco.

"After thirteen years together, I'm immune to it."

"They're giving shots for everything these days."

OK, he was game. But first things first. If we were going to get anywhere, we had to nail down a definition of ham. In general, that is. What is ham?

We frothed up a couple late-afternoon lattes, got down a shelf of culinary reference books, and hammered out this definition:

> Composed of four muscles, a ham is one
> back haunch (the butt cheek, if you will) and
> upper back leg down to the shank (the shin,
> in butcher parlance) of a pig, boar, shoat, or
> other porcine-ish animal. (For a diagram, see
> page 38.)

From this followed three immediate conclusions:

> Every pig or pig-ish animal has two hams.
> A ham need not be smoked or cured in any way.
> The haunch of any other animal is not a ham.

During the ensuing months, we came across other backsides referred to as "hams," but these seemed to violate the spirit of the word. Yes, you can make deer or elk prosciutto from their haunches, and you can make duck prosciutto from a duck breast, but you'd never call a duck breast a ham. The product does not define the producer. Otherwise, my parents would be gay.

We also committed to one self-imposed limitation:

> We're only dealing with pigs.

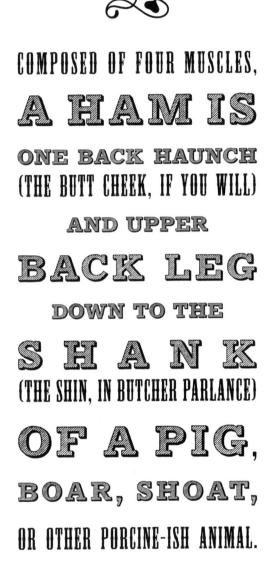

COMPOSED OF FOUR MUSCLES, A HAM IS ONE BACK HAUNCH (THE BUTT CHEEK, IF YOU WILL) AND UPPER BACK LEG DOWN TO THE SHANK (THE SHIN, IN BUTCHER PARLANCE) OF A PIG, BOAR, SHOAT, OR OTHER PORCINE-ISH ANIMAL.

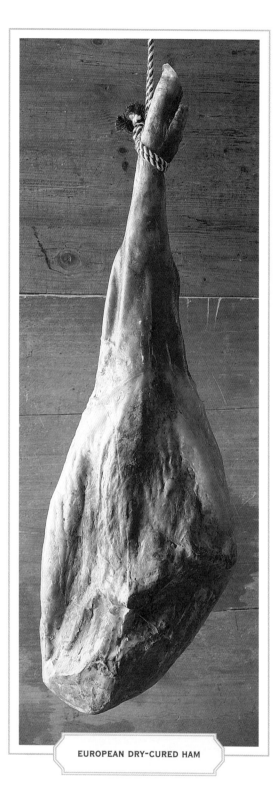

EUROPEAN DRY-CURED HAM

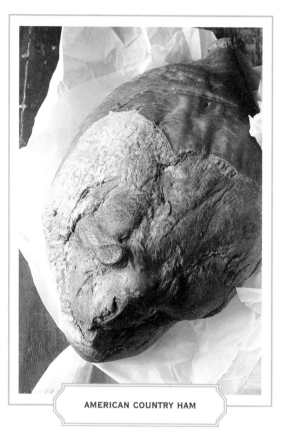

AMERICAN COUNTRY HAM

WET-CURED HAM

Yes, wild boars do produce hams. But when's the last time you saw a wild-boar ham in your supermarket? (Don't answer that if you live in New York City.)

And finally, this:

The front shoulder of a pig is not a ham.

These fatty quarters have recently been re-labeled "picnic hams," probably to get away from their less poetic (and equally confusing) tradi-tional name: Boston butts. They do indeed make the best pulled pork, but they are not hams in the strict sense of the word.

By "ham," we mean the hindquarter, the joint that becomes Italian *prosciutto crudo* and Span-ish *jamón ibérico*, the meat that comes to the table at a holiday meal—sometimes with those nasty canned pineapple rings and maraschino cherries stapled to it, sometimes tarted up with canned soda and unspeakable marinades, but many times just on its own: gloriously simple, smoked or not, cured or not—a large cut of pork, the ultimate roast.

Since that first fateful day, to uncover this hidden-in-plain-sight pleasure, Bruce and I have endured refrigerators full of ham leftovers, with hunks of pork being delivered by UPS every after-noon; I've been to northern Kentucky in the dead of freeze-butt winter; both of us have been to a ramshackle slaughterhouse in rural Massachu-setts; and we have borne witness to an enormous toe-on pig leg in our back refrigerator, a swarm of maggots in a French charcuterie, and a group of chic New Yorkers eating a quivering pile of ham in jelly. And we've both clocked a million miles on a treadmill trying to work it all off.

At the end of all that, we were finally ready to give ham its proper due—even if we had to start by killing a pig.

To call it an abattoir would be way too generous, about like calling a hedge fund manager a genius. It was just somebody's yard. Ed's. No last name given. He processed meat in a few outback buildings among the usual accoutrements of country life: a busted-out pickup, a doorless refrigerator, an upholstered couch on the back porch. And no amount of Michael Pollan–induced romanticism or Alice Waters localer-than-thou hype could make the place anything more than it was.

We got here the long way. That is, the idealistic way. When Bruce and I set out to discover what we could about ham, the first thing we decided was that we wanted to own a pig. What we failed to realize was that we'd have to kill it, too.

About four months before our trip to Ed's, we had approached Dan and Tracy Hayhurst, who run Chubby Bunny Farm, our CSA (Community Supported Agriculture). Every year, we buy shares in their farm, then all summer eat the organic harvest from their picturesque valley about twenty minutes from our house: raspberries in June, tomatoes in August, and tons of acorn squash by September.

Dan's a new breed of farmer. Organic, of course. Curly blond hair, vibrantly young. Does judo. And sports a wistful smile that says *You boys really want a pig?*

"We're writing a book," we explained.

He gave us that smile.

I'll be the first to admit that having someone else raise the beast was the easy way out. I'd grown up around farmers; I didn't idealize this rural America thing.

But our city friends did—and were horrified at the thought of watching our dinner grow up.

"You've gone native," one bottle-blond gym-rat told me on the phone. "I always suspected you liked nature. All those car trips to New Jersey."

"I told you we wanted to move to the country."

"Oh, let's not call it that. Let's call it a national park with cocktails. I've got to come up and see your . . . what is it?"

"Pig."

"Does it live indoors?"

"In the living room, last I checked."

"Cool."

His trek north began OK. He got out of New York in an after-work flurry, endured the Friday traffic crawl, but then things started to go wrong. There was the first phone call.

"How much farther?"

"Where are you?"

"Danbury."

"Another hour."

"My God. Do I need a passport?"

I talked him off this ledge by telling him there was a Starbucks at the next exit. "Get decaffeinated, OK?"

Twenty minutes later, the second call. "What's Southbury?"

"A town."

"What do they do there?"

"This is Connecticut. Whatever it is they do, they don't 'do.'"

By the time he got to Waterbury and headed into the hills on lonely Route 8, he was almost beside himself.

"Don't hang up," he said when I picked up. "I'm at mile thirty-seven. What's at mile thirty-eight?"

"More of mile thirty-seven. I'm sitting down."

"Because of me?"

"No, I'm finishing this glass of wine because of you."

In the end, I stayed on the phone for the next half hour.

"There's a Dunkin' Donuts *and* a McDonald's," he said when he got off the highway. "Looks like civilization."

"Just Winsted."

"What's that?"

"An old mill town. They used to make furniture."

"How do you know this stuff?"

"You're going to turn right on 183 just after the Citgo."

"You know the names of the gas stations?"

"Run by Bernie."

"I don't even *know* you."

Jaded urban sophisticates will apparently endure a lot to see a pig. Soon enough, his headlights swerved into our driveway, a quarter mile up the hill in the dark woods. He pulled down to the garage and got out, shell-shocked. "Do you know how much this land would cost in Westchester?"

"Do you know how much cookbook writers get as advances?" I picked at his heavy sweater. "It's summer, Nanook."

"I'm prepared." He looked up and blinked. "How's the pig?"

"Wilbur?"

"You named him? Charlotte and everything?"

"Sure. He's got these five-inch eyelashes. Bats them at you. We'll go over tomorrow."

Which we did. Wilbur was having a great summer in the Berkshires. He didn't live in a barn. He lived out in a field with the other pigs. He had a little metal structure, open on all sides, for protection against the sun and rain. Otherwise, he ran around and nuzzled the weeds—about like Dreydl, our collie, who also likes to show off in tall grass. Wilbur and his kin ate stale baguettes from a local bakery, as well as the vegetables Dan and Tracy couldn't sell.

When we called Wilbur, the whole herd rumbled out of the underbrush and tumbled down an embankment. They snorted around, nosed at us, and then went back to their porcine ways.

Despite frequent visits, Wilbur didn't seem to know us, although he seemed mildly disappointed that we had no food this time. He turned over a big bowl of water. And pissed on a post. But if this was the extent of his irritation, it wasn't much.

I stood watching him. He was a living creature. An animal. Doing his own thing. Minding his own business. And I felt it: a rattle in the floor boards of my stomach. The drama wasn't with our friend. That was all camp. The drama was with me. I was going to kill and eat an animal I had fed, seen, called, named. In cooking demos, I had always made this joke about being a carnivore: Pointing to my eye teeth, I'd say, "See these? Top of the food chain, baby." But what if I had to do what I threatened? What if I actually had to be the top of the food chain?

Our friend interrupted my angst. "Aren't we going to lunch?" he asked, scraping muck off his Prada boots with a twig.

That day I ordered a salad. And tried to forget what I'd felt.

But in early August, our gentlemanly ways of farming-by-proxy ran out. One otherwise glorious summer morning at the farm, I was filling a basket (yes, wicker) with kale and tomatoes when Dan slapped me on the shoulders.

"You ready for slaughter?"

I guess I looked as if I needed clarification.

"Your pig," he said. "He's good to go."

By now, Wilbur weighed about 250 pounds. Fighting shape.

"Oh, sure, sure," I said. "What can I do?"

"Help me get him to the slaughterhouse."

That wasn't exactly what I'd had in mind. I looked around for Bruce, but he was out feeding Wilbur. I always expect Bruce to have the answer to these things. Not that a slaughterhouse has come up all that often.

"Sure, sure," I said again. And then added, as if it made sense: "There are farmers in my family."

Dan smiled again. "Then you'll know what to do."

Later that afternoon, Bruce and I found ourselves in the muddy field. Aided by shouts and two-by-fours, Wilbur hauled himself into the trailer. He snorted, shook, and looked meaner than a pig should. Once the doors were closed, he jammed his nose aggressively through the crack. He'd never been caged; he didn't like it.

We tailed Dan up into Massachusetts. Although Wilbur banged on the trailer door, which bulged and popped with shocking force, we got to the so-called abattoir without incident. Dan backed his trailer up to the chute and opened the doors. Wilbur hesitated, looked around, and bolted into the keeping area.

I didn't know what to expect. A poker? A shotgun? I tried to put on a brave front. "What's next?"

"Forms," Dan said—and set off to get them.

It seemed this death would be like all the others in the modern world: bureaucratic.

Wilbur lay down on the dirt floor, groaning and snuffling. He calmed down pretty quickly. He stuck his nose through a gap in the boards, his big eye rolling this way and that. Damn it, there *were* eyelashes. I could see them, wiry but still wispy.

And so our whole stupid plan collapsed. Because we'd been playing at it. Playing with the notion of getting close to our food source. Like locavores at a New York City farmers' market.

I kneeled down next to Wilbur on the other side of the boards. Lightheaded, I was scared to death. No, of death. Scared of death. So I said to the pig the only thing that came to mind: "Forgive me."

I stood up, and Dan was back, prodding Bruce with Ed's clipboard. How do you want this bit cut? How do you want the ribs? Do you want the ears, the jowls?

"Ed will give a call tomorrow," Dan said, "to confirm all this before slaughter."

"It's not going to happen today?" Bruce asked, a familiar quaver in his vowels.

"We have to wait twenty-four hours," Dan explained. "The pig fasts. For a cleaner death."

We were off the hook. Except for our doubts. We drove home in silence.

"How are we going to do this?" Bruce asked.

"The pig?" I said.

"No, the book."

We did. It's in your hands. But we carried on with less bravado, with a healthy understanding that meat is, well, meat: muscle and ligament from a living creature.

Most of us have forgotten that lesson, living as we do in our faceless cities and suburbs. We buy ham in antiseptic packages, get it home, and cook it up. Yes, it's delicious. Nutritious, too. Neither Bruce nor I have stopped being carnivores.

But I do know this: We now have a different relationship with ham. It's Wilbur (or a pig like him). And it deserves our respect, our open-eyed knowledge and acceptance that we are indeed eating another animal. Emily Dickinson referred to maturity as a process of getting "wiser—and fainter, too."

Being a carnivore is an ethical stance. And as with all ethical stances, the older you get, the harder it gets to toe the line. Hell, to *see* the line.

Maybe that's the good news. I have a dear friend, Dot Wolfe, who's now in a retirement home in Texas. She and I were once talking about these sorts of things, about how the lines smudge the older you get, and she said, scotch in hand, "Baby, you've got to start life with lots of principles and then lose them one by one. Most people are trying to do it backward, and they're nothing but frustrated."

BIT OF A JOINT?

Roasting a fresh ham is the most elemental way to experience the meat: Nothing's cured, nothing's smoked, nothing's tarted up. You get a good, simple pork roast: juicy, tender, and toothsome.

And perhaps dining on a big roast is old-fashioned, too. When the Victorian middle class sat down to dinner, chances are they encountered a "joint"—that is, a piece of meat on the bone, usually roasted, but sometimes boiled. True, none of them sat down to a roasted fresh ham, mostly because pork was always cured in salt for long storage. But what Pip wouldn't have preferred this more modern version of his joint?

Most of the recipes in this first section are for roasts, with the exception of a couple of braises at the end. Because of its abundant connective tissue, a fresh ham performs well in the ambient heat of an oven or a grill. Yes, the Cacciatore (page 40) and the Tagine (page 42) are important exceptions, but by and large, a fresh ham is best when all that collagen and interstitial fat have melted and bathed the softening meat fibers.

Thus, these recipes are unabashed crowd-pleasers. Dorothy Parker once defined eternity as a ham and two people. To mitigate her cynicism (were it possible), we've shifted around the required poundages so every recipe doesn't serve 154 with leftovers. Some of these recipes make holiday fare; others, smaller roasts, are suitable for dinner parties. In any case, talk to your butcher: Tell her or him what you need and how you need it.

ROASTED FRESH HAM *WITH* A MAPLE-SPICE GLAZE

FEEDS 6 TEENAGE BOYS, 16 ADULTS, OR 26 TWENTYSOMETHING MODELS

After our existential ordeal with Wilbur, Bruce wanted to develop a recipe that honored the first taste of the meat by using the simplest preparation: roasted, not fussed up. So here's his basic recipe for a fresh ham. Yes, it requires several hours of slow cooking. Open another bottle of Pinot Noir and relax.

One 8- to 10-pound bone-in fresh ham, preferably from the shank end, any rind removed

1 teaspoon sugar

1 teaspoon ground cinnamon

½ teaspoon ground allspice

½ teaspoon ground cloves

½ teaspoon grated nutmeg

½ teaspoon salt

½ cup maple syrup

1. Put the Dickensian joint in a large roasting pan, preferably one that's shiny enough to reflect lots of ambient heat and not so flimsy that it tips willy-nilly when you pick it up. Set the oven rack as high as it can go and still afford the ham at least 2 inches of head space. Leave the roast in its pan out on the counter and fire the oven up to 325°F.

2. Mix the sugar, cinnamon, allspice, cloves, nutmeg, and salt in a small bowl. Wash and dry your hands, then smooth the spice mixture all over the ham's external surface. Work it down into some of the crevices, but be careful to avoid any deep-tissue massage. A ham is a complex structure of muscle groups—too much massage and they can come apart like Goldie Hawn in *Death Becomes Her.*

3. Cover the whole kit and caboodle with aluminum foil, shove it in the oven, and leave it alone for 3½ hours, while you go do whatever it is you do when a big, sweating hunk of meat is roasting in your oven.

4. Peel off the aluminum foil. Baste the ham with about half the maple syrup, preferably using a basting brush. Take it easy so you don't knock off the spice coating. Use small strokes—think Impressionism, not Abstract Expressionism. (Or just dribble the syrup off a spoon.)

5. Continue roasting the ham, uncovered this time, basting every 15 minutes or so with more maple syrup as well as any pan drippings, until an instant-read meat thermometer inserted into the thickest part of the meat without touching bone registers 170°F, about 1¼ hours. If it starts to singe or turn too dark, tent it loosely with foil, uncovering it just at the last to get it back to crunchy-crisp.

THE INGREDIENT SCOOP

In North America, **maple syrup** is sold in various state-sanctioned grades: A and B are the usual divisions, with A parsed into several finer demarcations. Basically, the lower the grade, the more intense the taste. Grade A Light Amber or Grade A Fancy would be fine for pancakes but bad for a long spell in the incinerator that is your oven. Better then to go with the lower, cheaper grades, like Grade A Dark Amber (our preference for pancakes, too, by the way) or even Grade B, usually reserved for baking. No matter what, don't swap a corn syrup–laced imitator for real maple syrup.

Eight pounds ain't **a whole ham** by a long shot. These things can weigh up to 24 pounds, maybe a tad more from those linebacker hogs. Because of their sheer size, most hams in the United States are halved for sale—or even cut into smaller sections. We've tried this roast with several cuts and prefer the shank end (see page 38).

6. Transfer the ham to a cutting or carving board and let it rest at room temperature for 15 minutes before carving into slices.

TESTERS' NOTES

Such a paltry little bit of spice rub? Indeed. We tried more, but it just got in the way. Frankly, the best roasted fresh ham has a thin crust and then lots of juicy meat, not a big glob of spices glued to the fat.

We've roasted hams in the broiler pan from our oven, in a flimsy aluminum roaster from the supermarket, and in a wallet-busting, heavy roasting pan from a fancy kitchenware store. You can just guess which did best. The 401(k)-emptier, of course. It gave the best crust, the best caramelization, and the best overall performance.

ROUND OUT THE MEAL

Now that you've roasted that big joint, you may want to have some other things on the table, lest your guests fall into a meat coma.

First, some roasted root vegetables. While the ham roasts, peel a few parsnips, a couple carrots, and a turnip or two; chop them into 1-inch pieces. Also peel, halve, seed, and chop a small butternut squash. Place everything in a large roasting pan, drizzle with a generous amount of olive oil, sprinkle with salt, and roast in a preheated 325°F oven for 45 minutes, stirring occasionally. Then add some small Brussels sprouts. Stir well and continue roasting for another 30 to 40 minutes.

Also a brown rice dish. Cook 2 cups long-grain brown rice with a little walnut or almond oil over medium heat for 1 minute, just until sizzling; then stir in 5 cups vegetable broth and 1 teaspoon dried sage. Bring to a simmer, then cover, reduce the heat to low, and simmer until the rice is tender and the liquid is absorbed, about 45 minutes. At the last, stir in some chopped dried cranberries and chopped pecan pieces, as well as a splash of balsamic vinegar, a little salt, and a few grinds of black pepper.

For dessert: In a large bowl, stir some pitted and halved plums in a little vodka, a couple teaspoons of sugar, and some finely grated lemon zest. Refrigerate for a couple hours to marinate. Serve the fruit and its sauce over scoops of purchased lemon sorbet.

MOROCCAN-STYLE ROASTED FRESH HAM

SERVES QUITE A FEW, UP TO 16

We almost cut this recipe, out of cultural embarrassment. Morocco and ham? Hmmm. But before the fatwa starts, let us say that this Moroccan-inspired spice rub was just too good to turn down. So here we go, cultural insensitivities notwithstanding.

2 teaspoons ground coriander

2 teaspoons ground ginger

2 teaspoons salt

1½ teaspoons ground cinnamon

1½ teaspoons ground cumin

1 teaspoon freshly ground black pepper

½ teaspoon turmeric

½ teaspoon garlic powder

¼ teaspoon ground allspice

One 6- to 7-pound bone-in ham, preferably from the shank end, any rind removed

1 tablespoon orange flower water

1. Use a fork to mix the coriander, ginger, salt, cinnamon, cumin, black pepper, turmeric, garlic powder, and allspice in a small bowl.

2. Give that big joint a rub-down with the orange flower water. Then sprinkle the spice rub evenly over the meat. Massage it a bit to get it even on all sides, but be careful: Because the meat is damp, the rub can ball up. Go slowly, deliberately, and cautiously.

3. Set the ham in a roasting pan, cover loosely with plastic wrap, and refrigerate for 12 to 24 hours.

4. Set the oven rack as high as it can go and still afford the ham at least 2 inches of head space. Get the oven heated up to 350°F. Leave the ham out on the counter while the oven preheats, about 15 minutes.

5. Take off the plastic wrap and cover tightly with foil. Put the whole thing in the oven and roast for 2 hours.

6. Uncover and continue roasting until an instant-read meat thermometer inserted into the thickest part of the meat without touching bone registers 170°F, about 1½ hours more. Leave the ham standing at room temperature for about 15 minutes to ensure that it's ridiculously juicy before carving it up, taking care—on peril of your life—that everyone gets some of that crunchy crust.

SLASH THE SHOPPING LIST

You can substitute 3½ tablespoons dried Moroccan spice rub or blend for the nine ingredients in step 1. Read the label: If the blend doesn't include salt, use only 3 tablespoons and add 2 teaspoons salt to the mix.

TESTERS' NOTES

Traditional Moroccan rubs almost always include ground dried rosebuds. If you're ready to take this baby over the top, you can find food-grade rosebuds from online spice suppliers and at many East Indian or Middle Eastern markets. Grind one or two rosebuds to a powder in a spice grinder, then add ½ to 1 teaspoon of the powder to this rub. Don't use rosebuds out of your garden—or your neighbor's. Pesticides make poor dinner accompaniments.

THE HIND  QUARTERLY

ISSUE NO. I   *We report food news whole hog.*   SECTION A

ALL ABOUT THE ★ RIND

IN CULINARY PARLANCE, the pig's skin is the rind. Lying over the thick layer of fat, it's tough and rubbery—they used to make footballs out of it. It's edible only with special preparation—see the cracklings recipe, page 30—not after normal roasting procedures.

If you've bought a fresh ham with the rind intact, remove it before you add any spice rub or glaze mixture. Why put the flavor on, only to remove it later when you slice off the rind after roasting?

Use a thin, sharp carving knife to take it off in strips from one tip of the ham to the exposed, cut section of the meat (not around the ham at its circumference). Leave behind as much fat as possible for flavor, self-basting, and pure decadence.

OK, yes, you can roast a ham halfway with the rind on, then take the rind off while it's hot, add the spices or glaze, and keep roasting until fully done. (Indeed, you have to go through that whole process for an American country ham, page 90.) But such belaboring seems pointless with a fresh ham because there's enough fat to protect the meat in the oven without the rind in place. Plus, these recipes don't necessitate that much protection, since we don't advocate incinerating the meat at 450°F or 500°F.

170°F THE INTERNAL TEMPERATURE GOAL FOR FRESH HAM

ALL ROASTED MEAT has two fundamental temperatures: the surface one and the internal one. If you were in chef school, you'd worry about both. For a home cook, the internal temperature alone is a great guide to (1) doneness, (2) juiciness, and (3) safety.

The USDA recently relaxed its internal temperature recommendation for cooked pork, down to 160°F. The meat has a pink, hot center without the fibers sharding into inedible garbage.

However, we've found that ham, unlike pork chops, is still a bit tough at 160°F. The reason? By 160°F, most of the natural juice has been squeezed out of the tightening planes of meat fibers, but that juice hasn't yet been replaced by collagen and connective tissue melt, both of which happen at just above 160°F. (Collagen is the main protein in mammals' connective tissue, accounting for up to a quarter of all the protein in meat.) Thus, we find that 170°F is a better marker: The collagen has melted, infusing those dry meat fibers again with juice, thereby yielding a more tender slice on the dinner plate.

CARVING A FRESH HAM

TO CARVE A SHANK-END HAM, make thin slices around the thigh bone, starting at the large end and cutting into the meat perpendicular to the bone. Of course, you'll never get a whole round slice off. Rather, slice a few thin slices from one side, then turn the ham over and slice a few more from another spot. Occasionally run your knife along the surface plane of the bone itself to loosen more meat from it as you carve.

In carving a butt-end ham, you'll end up with some slices but also with chunks and ends. Eye the larger sections of meat and slice down, creating thin slices, some of which may well fall apart because of the way the muscles are shaped. If it's falling into too many pieces, hack off that quadrant and cut it into thin slices and irregular chunks on a cutting board.

TUSCAN-ROASTED BONELESS FRESH HAM WITH POTATOES AND GARLIC

SERVES 6 TO 10, DEPENDING ON HOW MUCH PROSECCO EVERYONE'S HAD

Boneless hams have their place: They're sort of like gigantic pork loins. The taste of the bone is definitely missing in the roasted meat—so the attendant flavors have to be pumped up a bit to compensate. Just make sure the roast is properly tied first (see page 38).

4 minced garlic cloves plus 2 whole unpeeled garlic heads

½ cup olive oil

¼ cup chopped rosemary leaves

2 tablespoons chopped oregano leaves

1 tablespoon finely grated lemon zest

2 teaspoons salt

1 teaspoon freshly ground black pepper

One 3- to 3½-pound boneless fresh ham, tied with butchers' twine (see page 38)

4 or 5 large Yukon Gold potatoes, cut into quarters

1. Put the rack in the center of the oven and crank it up to 375°F.

2. Put the minced garlic, 3 tablespoons of the oil, half the rosemary, half the oregano, the lemon zest, half the salt, and the pepper in a mini food processor or a spice grinder—then give the stuff a whir until it's a paste. Don't have either of those tools? You can always grind everything in a mortar with a pestle—but chances are if you don't have a mini food processor, you don't have a mortar and pestle either. So failing all the above, finely mince the dry ingredients, put them in a small bowl, add the requisite olive oil, and mash everything repeatedly against the sides of the bowl with the back of a wooden spoon.

3. Rub the spice mixture all over the ham and set it aside for a minute.

4. Break the unpeeled garlic heads into cloves and scatter these in a large roasting pan. Add the potato quarters, the remaining rosemary, oregano, and salt, and the rest of the olive oil. Toss all this together till everything's shiny, then clear a space in the center of the mixture for the ham.

5. Set the ham in the pan and put the whole contraption in the oven. As the meat cooks, toss the vegetables every once in a while so nothing sticks. Roast until an instant-read meat thermometer inserted into the center of the meat registers 170°F, 2 to 2½ hours. The ham should stand at room temperature on a carving or cutting board for about 10 minutes so any juices seep back into those squeezed protein planes. Then slice off the butchers' twine and cut the meat into rounds and wedges.

TESTERS' NOTES

At the table, squeeze the soft garlic pulp out of the papery hulls and smear it on bits of crusty bread.

SMOKED FRESH HAM

FEEDS 8 TO 14, DEPENDING ON THE HAM'S SIZE

SLASH THE SHOPPING LIST

If you don't want to use all nine dried herbs and spices in step 1, make a rub from 1 tablespoon packed light brown sugar and 3 tablespoons plus 1 teaspoon bottled barbecue rub spice mixture.

THE INGREDIENT SCOOP

Nowadays, **smoked paprika** is practically synonymous with Spanish cooking. This wasn't always so. It was once a featured spice in dishes from Extremadura in western Spain, but because of complicated culinary politics and international obsessions, the smoky ground powder is now ubiquitous in Iberia. Smoked paprika comes in a bewildering variety of flavors, heats, and grinds. Suffice it to say that we always call for a finely ground spice that's mild but quite smoky. Look for it in the spice aisle of most large supermarkets—or from online spice purveyors.

Once Bruce had tested a fresh ham in the oven, it wasn't long before he had to tote one out to his testosterone-doped grill, which sits out on our back deck. So here's how you, too, can smoke a fresh ham at home. Pray for good weather.

1 tablespoon packed light brown sugar

1 tablespoon mild smoked paprika

2 teaspoons salt

1 teaspoon ground cumin

1 teaspoon dried oregano

1 teaspoon freshly ground black pepper

½ teaspoon ground allspice

½ teaspoon ground cinnamon

½ teaspoon garlic powder

¼ teaspoon celery seeds

One 5-pound boneless ham, tied with butchers' twine (see page 38); or one 7- to 8-pound bone-in ham, preferably from the shank end, rind removed

Wood chips for smoking, preferably hickory, pecan, or cherry, soaked in water for 20 minutes, then drained

1. Use a fork to stir the brown sugar, smoked paprika, salt, cumin, oregano, pepper, allspice, cinnamon, garlic powder, and celery seeds in a small bowl.

2. Rub this spice mixture over the meat, taking care to get some down into some of the crevices and indentations. Place the ham on a large baking sheet and refrigerate uncovered for 1 day—that is, 24 hours; no skimping.

3. Set up the grill for low-heat, indirect cooking. In other words, build a low-heat, well-ashed charcoal bed in a charcoal grill, then rake the coals to the perimeter or to one side—or heat half a gas grill to about 300°F, so the ham can eventually sit on a section of the grate that's not directly over the heat source.

4. Fill a small, shallow aluminum pan with wood chips. Place this pan on the coals or one of the gas grill's burners. Set the ham on the section of the upper grate that's not directly over the heat source. Cover the grill.

5. And now comes the barbecue magic: You have to maintain a constant, low temperature, 250°F to 275°F, adding more wood chips as those in the pan turn to ash. With a gas grill, monitoring the temperature is no sweat: The gauge is right there, and you can adjust the burners so that the temperature stays within the range. But with a charcoal grill, it's a little more work. Hang an oven thermometer in the grill so you can check the temperature. Keep adding more coals to the bed, in small handfuls each time, so the temperature remains fairly constant. And don't forget to replenish the wood chips as necessary. In either case, settle in and stick around. Continue barbecuing until an instant-read meat thermometer inserted into the thickest part of the meat without touching bone registers 170°F, 5 to 6 hours. Remove the ham from the grill and let stand at room temperature for 15 minutes before carving.

TESTERS' NOTES

Dried herbs? Shouldn't a proper foodie use fresh? In fact, no. Over prolonged heat, fresh herbs burn like Judas Iscariot. Dried herbs, already desiccated, can stand up to the heat like Shadrach, Meshach, and Abednego.

We're always amazed when people tell us their methods of cooking meat—7 minutes a side, 2 minutes this way then 8 that, or until it feels like the loose skin between someone's thumb and forefinger. Honestly, there's only one way to tell if meat is cooked properly: by taking its internal temperature. Use an instant-read thermometer, not one of those Ward-and-June-Cleaver probes that spear the meat during its entire adventure in the oven. Insert the instant-read thermometer right into the thick center (without touching bone) and hold it there until the temperature stabilizes. If more roasting is required, remove the thermometer and check the internal temperature in a different spot the next time.

We've always found we get the best smoke from wood chunks, rather than shards or splinters. To that end, we buy wood chips in clear packaging so we can see what we're getting. Dust and debris in the bag indicate chips past their prime.

OVEN-BARBECUED FRESH HAM

MAKES 12 TO 16 SERVINGS—FEWER IF PEOPLE HAVE BEEN SMELLING THE THING FOR A WHILE

SLASH THE SHOPPING LIST

Omit the twelve ingredients in step 4 and replace them with 4 cups bottled barbecue sauce, preferably a tomato-based sauce that's fairly wet and loose.

OK, let's say you really want the taste of barbecue but you don't have the patience to smoke a ham. Fake it. That is, roast the ham in the oven using smoky spices and flavorings that'll make people swear you were at the pit all day.

One 8- to 10-pound bone-in fresh ham, preferably from the shank end, any rind removed

2 tablespoons Worcestershire sauce

2 tablespoons mild smoked paprika (see page 24)

1 medium yellow onion, thinly sliced, those slices then separated into thin rings

One 28-ounce can tomato puree (do not use tomato paste or sauce)

½ cup apple cider vinegar

⅓ cup packed light brown sugar

2 tablespoons honey

1 tablespoon molasses, preferably unsulphured (see page 180)

2 teaspoons ground cumin

½ teaspoon ground allspice

½ teaspoon ground cloves

½ teaspoon salt

¼ teaspoon celery seeds

1 canned chipotle chile in adobo sauce (see page 182), stemmed

1 medium garlic clove, minced

1. Rub the ham all over with the Worcestershire sauce and smoked paprika. Set the thing in a large roasting pan, cover with foil, and refrigerate for 24 to 48 hours, depending on how deeply you want the smoky taste of that paprika to permeate the meat.

2. Uncover the ham and set it out on the counter for 20 minutes while you preheat the oven to 350°F.

3. Sprinkle the sliced onions on top of the ham and around it in the roasting pan. Cover tightly with foil and shove the whole thing in the oven. Leave it to bake for 3½ hours if it's an 8-pounder, 4 hours if it's a 10-pound monster.

4. Sometime before the stated roasting time is up, give the tomato puree, cider vinegar, brown sugar, honey, molasses, cumin, allspice, cloves, salt, celery seeds, canned chipotle, and garlic clove a whir in a large blender or a food processor fitted with the chopping blade until smooth, scraping down the sides of the canister once or twice to make sure everything is evenly pureed.

5. Take the roasting pan out of the oven. Transfer the ham to a cutting board, using two silicon roasting mitts or two large metal spatulas, plus lots of shoulder strength.

6. Scoop all the onions from the pan, put them on a second cutting board, and chop them into little bits.

7. Drain off the juice and fat in the pan—but into a disposable container, not down the drain, unless your spouse is a plumber.

8. Return the ham to the pan; sprinkle the chopped onions in the bottom of the pan.

9. Pour the pureed barbecue sauce over the ham, letting some of it drip down into the pan. Knock the oven temperature down to 325°F and continue roasting (uncovered this time) until an instant-read meat thermometer inserted into the thickest part of the meat without touching bone registers 170°F, about 1½ hours. While the ham roasts, baste it with the pan juices every 20 minutes or so. When done, let the ham stand at room temperature on a carving board for 15 minutes before slicing it.

TESTERS' NOTES

There's an unrelenting myth about marinades: that they somehow tenderize meat. But that holds true only if they contain some sort of acid, and only for about a quarter inch into the meat itself. If you have a ½-inch thick strip steak, a marinade that includes acid (vinegar, lemon juice, wine) may do some good—but not for this behemoth of a ham. The purpose here is merely to get a little flavoring into the exterior surface planes of the meat. The oven's heat, not the marinade, will "tenderize" the joint as it roasts.

ROASTED FRESH HAM
WITH APPLE-WHEATBERRY SALAD

MAKES ABOUT 8 SERVINGS (ADD STEAMED BROCCOLI AND IT'S A FULL MEAL)

I'll be the first to admit that I quickly reached a point in writing this book where I just needed a whole grain. Bruce's answer? Wheatberries. They're a tremendous nutritional kick, being the full grain of wheat (endosperm, germ, and bran) without the hull.

THE INGREDIENT SCOOP

A member of the onion (and thus the lily) family, the **shallot** is an aromatic vegetable known for its mildly sweet, slightly garlicky flavor. Most shallot plants produce a bulb with a small cluster of off-set lobes. We call for lobes in this book; separate a group into their distinctive parts, if necessary.

One 6- to 7-pound bone-in fresh ham, preferably from the shank end, any rind removed

1 tablespoon salt, plus additional to taste

2 teaspoons freshly ground black pepper

3 cups (about 20) peeled shallot lobes

4 medium-sized medium-tart apples such as Gala or Braeburn, peeled, cored, and cut into eighths

3 tablespoons walnut oil

½ teaspoon ground cinnamon

6 tablespoons frozen apple juice concentrate, thawed

2½ cups wheatberries

1. Heat the oven up to 350°F. Meanwhile, gently massage the ham with the salt and pepper, then place the joint in a large roasting pan.

2. Cover tightly with foil, slip into the oven, and roast for 2 hours.

3. Remove the roasting pan from the oven—be careful: it's ridiculously hot—and drain off all the liquid and fat. You can do this either by slurping it up with a bulb baster or by removing the ham from the pan and pouring off the juices. Make sure you also get out any scummy, half-gelatinous stuff that sits just around the ham or rings the pan.

3. Once the ham's in a dry roasting pan, toss the shallots, apples, walnut oil, and cinnamon in a large bowl. Spread this mixture evenly around the ham in the pan.

4. Place the whole thing back in the oven and continue roasting until an instant-read meat thermometer inserted into the thickest part of the meat without touching bone registers 170°F, about 1¹/₂ more hours, maybe 2. Every 20 minutes or so, baste the ham with 1 tablespoon of apple juice concentrate and stir the apples and shallots in the pan so they don't stick.

5. Meanwhile, put the wheatberries in a large saucepan and cover them with cool water so the water stands about 2 inches above the grains. Bring to a boil over medium-high heat; then reduce the heat, cover, and simmer slowly until the wheatberries are tender with still a little chew, something like al dente pasta, about 1¼ hours. The only way to tell? Taste one. Remove the pan from the heat, drain off any remaining liquid, and keep covered on the back of the stove.

6. Once the ham's at the right temperature, take it out of the oven, transfer it to a carving or cutting board, and let it stand for 15 minutes.

7. Scrape the apples, shallots, pan drippings, and juices into a large bowl, taking care not to mash the apples too much. Pour in the wheatberries and stir gently. Taste for salt—the mixture may need a little more. Carve the ham into thin slices and serve with the warm wheatberry salad on the side.

TESTERS' NOTES

This recipe may really just be an excuse to make a fine ham salad—at least with the leftovers. Chop a good portion of the ham into little bits, put these in a bowl, and add all the leftover wheatberry salad. Stir in a dollop of sour cream and one of mayonnaise, then season the mixture as you will. For a curried ham salad, add at least a teaspoon or two of bottled curry powder. For more heat, add some chopped, pickled jalapeño rings or ¼ teaspoon cayenne. Or mix in some chopped, stemmed fresh herbs: tarragon, thyme, oregano, and/or marjoram. Also stir in a teaspoon or two of lemon juice just before serving to brighten the flavors.

PORK CRACKLINGS

WELL, REALLY, THE SERVING SIZE SHOULD BE 0 BECAUSE YOU'RE NOT
SUPPOSED TO EAT THIS STUFF. BUT PLAN ON SERVING 6 TO 8, PROVIDED
THE CARDIOLOGIST ISN'T LOOKING.

Here's pure indulgence: fried pork skins. You'll need a fresh ham with the rind intact. You make these cracklings as the ham roasts (see page 19). But first, remove the rind as per the directions on page 22, and this time, split the fat difference between the ham and the rind. In other words, leave some fat on the rind as you slice it off in strips.

1. Lay these strips in the bottom of the roasting pan, all around the fresh ham, and roast together for the first 1¹/₂ hours as per the directions on page 28.

2. Use tongs to remove the rind strips from the pan; set them aside while the ham finishes roasting. (For safety's sake, consider refrigerating the strips while the ham roasts. Let them come back to room temperature for 15 minutes before continuing with step 3.)

3. Once the ham is done and on a carving board, dump the fat and other stuff out of the roasting pan and crank the oven up to 500°F. (If you like, tent the cooked ham with foil to keep it warm while the cracklings get crunchy.) Cut the partially roasted rind strips into 2-inch pieces and return them to the pan. Roast, stirring occasionally, until crisp and well browned, 15 to 20 minutes. Transfer them to a wire rack set over several layers of paper towel, which will catch any rendered fat as the pieces drain. Pop open a beer. Enjoy at will.

JERK-ROASTED BONELESS FRESH HAM

MAKES DINNER FOR 8 TO 12

A jerk seasoning paste or rub is a fiery Jamaican favorite. But wow, don't touch a thing after working with that habanero chile—not your face, not your kids, not the dog, not anything. Capsaicin, the chile's chemical burn, is not water-soluble. To clean up, use a grease-fighting liquid detergent and give your hands a good thirty-second scrub under lukewarm water. If you have any concern, wear rubber gloves when preparing the rub.

SLASH THE SHOPPING LIST

Substitute ¾ cup bottled jerk barbecue sauce or purchased jerk paste for all eleven ingredients in step 1. Do not use a jerk hot sauce or a dry jerk seasoning mix.

THE INGREDIENT SCOOP

Most **boneless hams** come from the butt end, since the shank end makes the standard, pretty presentation at the table. Buy boneless hams either already tied with butchers' twine or somehow loosely rolled up in the package. (You'll then have to tie it into shape at home—see page 38.) After roasting or grilling, a boneless ham is a breeze to carve. Just lay it flat on a carving or cutting board, like a football or a fat pork loin. Slice off one end and continue slicing off thin circles, working your way across the meat.

10 medium scallions, quartered

2 medium garlic cloves, halved

1 habanero chile, stemmed for sure and seeded if you want (or not, if you're a masochist)

1½ tablespoons peanut oil

1½ tablespoons minced peeled fresh ginger

1½ tablespoons packed dark brown sugar

2 teaspoons salt

1½ teaspoons ground allspice

1½ teaspoons ground cinnamon

1½ teaspoons ground coriander

1½ teaspoons dried thyme

One 5-pound boneless ham, tied with butchers' twine (see page 38)

3 tablespoons golden rum

1. Place the scallions, garlic, habanero, peanut oil, ginger, brown sugar, salt, allspice, cinnamon, coriander, and thyme in a mini food processor or a large food processor fitted with the chopping blade. Grind just until pasty, if still a little grainy. Or place them in a large blender but add 1 to 2 tablespoons water to help get everything rubbing together over the blades.

2. Rub this jerk seasoning mixture all over the ham, making sure to coat inside any cracks and seams but without weakening the fibers or loosening the twine. Set on a baking sheet, cover loosely with plastic wrap, and refrigerate for 12 to 24 hours.

3. Position the rack in the center of the oven and preheat the oven to 325°F. Meanwhile, take the ham out of the refrigerator and set it in a large roasting pan. Drizzle it with the rum, then let it stand at room temperature while the oven heats, about 20 minutes.

4. Cover tightly with aluminum foil and roast for 2 hours.

5. Peel off the foil and continue roasting until an instant-read meat thermometer inserted into the center of the meat registers 170°F, about 1 hour more. If desired, baste the ham occasionally with any pan drippings, taking care not to knock off the rub. Once roasted, the ham should stand at room temperature for 15 minutes before carving.

CONDIMENTS
☞ FRESH HAM

Big roasts of any stripe are best with a tangy or spicy condiment on the side. These whimsical versions are sure to perk up any dinner table.

◁ BLUEBERRY KETCHUP ▷

1 pint blueberries	1 teaspoon ground ginger
1 small shallot, minced	1 teaspoon lime juice
1 cup sugar	¼ teaspoon salt
⅓ cup white wine vinegar	¼ teaspoon freshly ground black pepper
¼ cup honey	⅛ teaspoon ground cloves

1. Dump everything into a medium saucepan and bring to a simmer over medium heat, stirring occasionally.

2. Reduce the heat to low and simmer slowly, stirring occasionally, until the sauce is somewhat thick, about like a loose tomato ketchup, 25 to 30 minutes. Pour into a heat-safe plastic or glass container, cover, and refrigerate for up to 2 weeks.

◁ CRANBERRY CHUTNEY ▷

8 ounces fresh cranberries	1 minced garlic clove
⅓ cup granulated sugar	½ teaspoon red pepper flakes
⅓ cup red wine vinegar	¼ teaspoon coriander seeds
¼ cup packed light brown sugar	¼ teaspoon mustard seeds
¼ cup orange juice	¼ teaspoon salt
2 tablespoons minced yellow onion	¼ teaspoon freshly ground black pepper
2 teaspoons minced peeled fresh ginger	⅛ teaspoon ground allspice

1. Bring all ingredients to a full simmer in a medium saucepan set over medium-high heat, stirring frequently.

2. Reduce the heat and simmer, stirring often, until the cranberries have begun to break down into a sauce, about 15 minutes.

3. Remove from the heat and cool for 10 minutes, then pour into a heat-safe plastic or glass container. Cover and refrigerate for up to 2 weeks. The chutney tastes best at room temperature, not right out of the fridge.

CUBAN *LECHON ASADO*

MAKES ABOUT **8** SERVINGS

Well, sort of Cuban. There are a million ways to make this luscious, citrus-laced Caribbean roast: some with bone-in cuts, some with the rind on, some with it off. Bruce adapted the technique a bit for a more modern meal, cutting down the servings so you don't have to wait for your next big get-together to try this delicious and decidedly decadent dish.

2 garlic cloves, smashed or put through a garlic press

1 tablespoon minced fresh oregano leaves

1 tablespoon dry sherry

1 tablespoon finely grated orange zest

1 tablespoon frozen orange juice concentrate, thawed

1 tablespoon lime juice

1 teaspoon ground bay leaf or 2 small bay leaves, ground in a spice grinder until about like very fine beach sand

½ teaspoon freshly ground black pepper

One 4-pound boneless fresh ham, tied with butchers' twine (see page 38)

2 medium yellow onions, thinly sliced, the rings not separated

½ teaspoon salt

1. Stir the garlic, oregano, sherry, orange zest, orange juice concentrate, lime juice, ground bay leaf, and pepper in a small bowl until it forms a paste. Pour this into a very large, zip-closed plastic bag.

2. Add the ham and seal the bag. Rub the paste over all of the ham by massaging it into the meat through the plastic bag.

3. Set the sealed bag in the refrigerator for 24 hours. Occasionally give the ham another rub through the plastic, just to make sure everything's coated.

4. Preheat the oven to 350°F. Lay the onion slices all across the bottom of a 9-by-13-inch baking pan. Take the ham out of the bag and place it on top of the onions. Use your hand to scrape out any additional paste still in the bag and pat it onto the ham.

5. Sprinkle the ham with the salt, then cover tightly with foil and roast for 1 hour.

6. Uncover the ham and continue roasting. About every 20 minutes, baste the ham with the juices in the pan and gently stir the onions so they don't start to stick. Keep on roasting until an instant-read meat thermometer inserted into the thickest part of the meat registers 170°F, 1½ or maybe 2 more hours.

7. Transfer the ham to a cutting board and let it stand at room temperature for 15 minutes before carving.

8. Meanwhile, skim the fat off the juices in the pan and pour them into a small gravy boat. You can use a gravy separator, a tool available at most cookware stores, or you can push a bulb baster down into the juices, below the surface fat, and slurp them up without also taking the fat. Serve the carved ham along with the pan juices and the roasted onions.

TESTERS' NOTES

Grate the orange zest with a microplane (originally developed to grate Parmigiano-Reggiano and other hard cheeses) or with the small holes of a box grater. Only use the orange part of the peel, not the white pith underneath. If the orange is thin-skinned, it may take more than one to get a tablespoon of just the orange stuff.

OK, a confession: This dish should be made with sour oranges—a Caribbean and southern European specialty, but not exactly an everyday item in our grocery stores. If you find them at a Latin American market near you, skip the tablespoon of orange juice concentrate and the tablespoon of lime juice in the recipe, and instead use 2 to 3 tablespoons fresh-squeezed sour-orange juice.

And of course use finely grated sour orange zest instead of that from a more "standard" orange.

GRILLED BUTTERFLIED FRESH HAM with AN HERB RUB

MAKES 8 TO 10 SERVINGS

Butterflying a boneless ham requires fancy knife work—mostly because there are so many parts of a 24-pound whole ham that can eventually become a 4-pound boneless one, with muscles lying this way and that in the cut. In the end, punt. Ask your butcher to butterfly a 4 1/2-pound rindless, boneless ham for you. It should end up a rough rectangle about 8 by 11 inches, and between 1 and 1 1/2 inches thick.

4 medium garlic cloves, thinly sliced

1½ tablespoons chopped fresh rosemary leaves

1 tablespoon chopped fresh oregano leaves

1 tablespoon chopped fresh sage leaves

1 tablespoon stemmed thyme leaves

1 teaspoon finely grated lemon zest

1 teaspoon salt

1 teaspoon freshly ground black pepper

3 tablespoons olive oil, plus additional for greasing the grill grate

One 4½-pound boneless ham, rind removed and discarded, the meat butterflied

1. Place the garlic, rosemary, oregano, sage, thyme, lemon zest, salt, and pepper in a little mound on a cutting board. Rock a large knife such as a chef's knife through the mixture, continually regathering it and rocking the blade back and forth until everything's finely mushed up, if still a little grainy.

2. Scrape the herb mixture into a small bowl and stir in the olive oil. Spread this paste over both sides of the butterflied ham. Place on a baking sheet, cover, and refrigerate for 24 hours. Don't shorten the time.

3. Take the ham out of the refrigerator while you prepare the grill. Either heat a gas grill to medium heat or build a medium-heat, well-ashed charcoal bed in a charcoal grill. A medium-heat fire is defined as about 375°F. Put another way, you can hold your open hand, palm down, six inches over the heat source for 4 or 5 seconds without having to pull it away.

4. Dab a little olive oil on a wadded-up paper towel, then grasp the towel with tongs and quickly rub the grill grate with the oil. Set the ham directly over the heat and grill, turning once or twice, until an instant-read meat thermometer inserted into the meat registers 170°F, about 35 minutes. Transfer to a cutting board, hold back the hungry hordes, and let the thing stand at room temperature for 10 minutes. To serve, make thin slices on the bias—in other words, angle your carving knife at a 45-degree angle and slice through the meat, thereby making a slightly wider slice than if you cut straight down.

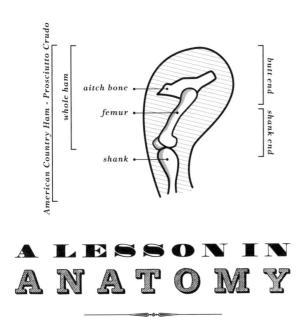

American Country Ham · Prosciutto Crudo

whole ham

aitch bone

femur

shank

butt end

shank end

A LESSON IN ANATOMY

As we said, a ham is the complete set of the four muscles, hip to shank. It can weigh from 12 to 28 pounds. However, most bone-in hams—and any you would use for these recipes—have been cut through the bone, resulting in two halves:

☞ The shank end has the thigh bone running right through the center of the meat. This cut looks like the traditional Normal Rockwell ham: a tapered, bone-in piece of meat, sort of like a rounder, fuller leg of lamb. The cut is easier to carve but the meat is also a little chewier, since these muscles get a workout hauling the pig around all day. Interestingly, the shank itself (sort of like the pig's shin) is not part of the shank-end cut; the shank sits just beyond the tapered part of the meat.

☞ The butt end includes a small piece of that thigh bone plus the more complicated structure of the hip's ball and socket, including the aitch bone. This cut is much more difficult to carve, thanks to all those bones, but the meat is more tender and definitely porkier, thanks again to all those bones.

TIE IT UP

Meat roasts more evenly if its shape is held with butchers' twine (also called cooking twine), a food-safe, dye-free, cotton twine available at high-end markets, most cookware stores, and their online outlets. In a pinch, beg for a yard at your supermarket's meat counter.

For a bone-in ham, tying is related to the type of cut. If you're working with the shank end (see left), it isn't really necessary to tie anything, since the muscle groups lie in fairly compact planes around the bone. Still, it can't hurt to tie it up—just the way it isn't necessary but can't hurt with a leg of lamb. Wrap the twine in several separate, knotted loops around the meat, imagining the bone as the center of those circles.

A butt-end ham, however, should be tied. There's no strict rule here; it depends on where the thigh was cut to make the two ham halves. Basically, you have to examine the cut you've got, then tie it in several places so the meat holds together and the planes stay adjacent as the joint roasts. Several loops in different directions, each loosely knotted, should do the trick.

For a boneless ham, first mound it into an oblong, footballish mass—not a long, thin thing like a tenderloin but rather a compact, rounded loaf. Begin at one end and make a loop around the ham with the twine, knotting it so the twine just rests against the meat's surface without pressing down like a corset. Continue making more loops every two or three inches, just so the ham will hold its shape as it relaxes in that warm, dry sauna called your oven.

In all cases, before carving, snip off and discard any and all twine.

JAMÓN DEL PAÍS

FEEDS 8, IF YOU'VE GOT SIDE DISHES LIKE BEANS AND RICE

This Peruvian specialty (Spanish, ha-MOAN dell pah-EES, "country ham") is really just a once-in-a-lifetime excuse to pan-fry a whole ham.

1 tablespoon ground annatto seeds

1 tablespoon minced fresh oregano leaves

1 teaspoon ground cinnamon

3 garlic cloves, smashed with the side of a knife or put through a garlic press

One 4-pound boneless fresh ham, tied with butchers' twine (see page 38)

About 3 tablespoons lard

1. Use a fork to mix the ground annatto seeds, oregano, cinnamon, and garlic in a small bowl until it forms a grainy paste.

2. Rub this stuff all over the ham. Put the ham in a large zip-closed bag, seal it up, and refrigerate for 24 hours.

3. Crank the oven up to 350°F. While it's heating up, pull the ham out of the bag and put the meat in a heavy-duty roasting pan. Let it stand on the counter for about 15 minutes so it's not ice cold when it goes into the oven.

4. Cover tightly with foil, then roast until an instant-read meat thermometer inserted into the thickest part of the meat registers 170°F, 2 1/4 to 2 3/4 hours—possibly a little more.

5. Remove the ham from the oven and the roasting pan; let the meat stand on a cutting board while you melt the lard in a large skillet over medium heat, until little waggles of heat swim across the melted fat in the skillet.

6. Put the ham in the skillet and fry on all sides until crisp and irresistible. It helps to have really big tongs to hold and turn the ham while it fries, especially if it tends to tip this way and that on an uneven edge. Once the ham is crisp—and don't stint on this; it can take 15 minutes— transfer it to a cutting board and cut into paper-thin slices.

THE INGREDIENT SCOOP

Annatto seeds come from a nasty-looking, hairy fruit native to tropical climates across the Americas. Their staining, pale red color is familiar from Brie and margarine, both of which get a slight nudge toward yellow thanks to a tiny pinch of this ground stuff. On their own, annatto seeds have a peppery-citrusy bite; they can now be found at many large grocery stores as well as almost all gourmet and Latin American supermarkets.

TESTERS' NOTES

Those annatto seeds can easily be pulverized in a mortar with a pestle, until the seeds are just a little grainier than talcum powder. Alternatively, they can be sealed in a zip-closed plastic bag and crushed with the bottom of a heavy pot or a heavy rolling pin. Don't whack; just press. You'll need about 2 tablespoons of seeds to give you 1 tablespoon of powdered stuff.

You needn't use store-bought lard. Before you rub the ham with the annatto mixture, cut off a little of the fat, maybe two 2-inch pieces. Melt these in a skillet over low heat, then pour the liquid fat into a small dish and save until you're ready to fry up the ham.

HAM CACCIATORE

MAKES ABOUT 6 SERVINGS
(OR FOR 2 RIDICULOUSLY INDULGENT FOOD WRITERS)

Here's the first of two braises for a fresh ham. Cacciatore is one of those peasant dishes that's gotten shellacked with culinary pretension. It's supposed to be hearty fare, made with what you have in your larder (as if you had a larder), or whatever your hunter husband (or wife, as in Alaska) brings home from the day's trek. Nobody really makes it with a fresh ham—which is an utter shame, because we sat around the kitchen and slurped this one down until there wasn't much left.

THE INGREDIENT SCOOP

Reduced-sodium canned tomatoes? Definitely. You need to be in control of the sodium content of your meal. You can adjust the salt in any recipe to your liking—but do so once you're done cooking, not somewhere midstream.

2 tablespoons olive oil

4 ounces strip bacon, preferably thick-cut double-smoked bacon, diced

One 4½- to 5-pound bone-in fresh ham, preferably the shank end, rind removed (see page 22) and tied (see page 38)

2 medium yellow onions, halved through the cores and then thinly sliced into half-moons

2 medium green bell peppers, seeded, cored, and chopped

2 medium carrots, peeled and chopped

2 medium garlic cloves, minced

12 ounces cremini mushrooms, thinly sliced

½ teaspoon salt

½ teaspoon freshly ground black pepper

1 cup dry white wine or dry vermouth

3½ cups canned diced tomatoes (about one 28-ounce can)

1 tablespoon chopped fresh oregano leaves

2 teaspoons chopped fresh rosemary leaves

1 teaspoon stemmed thyme

1. Heat a large Dutch oven over medium heat, then swirl in the oil. Add the bacon and cook, stirring often, until frizzled and ready to eat, about 4 minutes. Use a slotted spoon to transfer the bacon from the pan to a small plate.

2. Set the ham in the Dutch oven and brown it well on all sides, spooning up some of the fat in the bottom to baste it and turning it every once in a while, until all sides are well browned. Do not gray the meat—brown it. It should take approximately 15 minutes to get the job done. Transfer the ham to a cutting board and drain off all but about 2 tablespoons of the fat in the pan.

3. Add the onions to the pan and cook, stirring often, until softened and a bit translucent, about 3 minutes.

4. Stir in the bell peppers, carrots, and garlic. Continue cooking and stirring until everything's quite aromatic, about 3 minutes.

5. Add the mushrooms, salt, and pepper. Those mushrooms are packed with moisture in and around their porous cells; you want all that liquid (sometimes called the liquor) to fall out of suspension, coat the bottom of the pan, and then boil away to a thick glaze. You'll notice a definite pickup of moisture, then it will start simmering away. Stir and stir to keep everything from sticking. Depending on how long the mushrooms have sat on the grocery shelf, this will take between 4 and 7 minutes.

6. Pour in the wine and continue simmering until that wine has reduced by half, 3 to 4 minutes. Don't get out a measuring cup; just eyeball it to determine when about half the wine is left in the pan.

7. Add the tomatoes, oregano, rosemary, and thyme. Once the sauce is back at a simmer, return the bacon and any of its accumulated juices to the pan. Then nestle the ham into the simmering sauce, adding any juices that may be on the plate or cutting board.

8. Once the whole thing comes back to a real simmer, cover the pan and reduce the heat to low. Simmer slowly, turning occasionally, until the meat is tender when pierced with a fork, 3 1/2 to 4 hours. In this case, you needn't worry about the ham's internal temperature; rather, you want the whole thing to go long enough to produce full collagen meltdown so the meat is as tender as possible. In other words, it should be just shy of falling off the bone, or turning into some weird Italian riff on pulled pork. Carefully remove the ham with silicon mitts or a large metal spatula; let the meat rest on a cutting or carving board for 15 minutes while the sauce sits covered in the pan, off the heat. Then slice the ham and serve the pieces with the tomato sauce napped on top.

TESTERS' NOTES

You'll need a big, round Dutch oven or oval French casserole. Put the ham in it and set the lid on top. If the lid doesn't rest securely and tightly, you don't have the right equipment. Off to the outlet mall with you.

A ham this big will be too large to be submerged by more than half at any one moment. It's imperative that you turn it occasionally in the simmering sauce so that all sides stay moist.

HAM TAGINE

MAKES **6** SERVINGS

A tagine is a heavily spiced Moroccan braise, most often made in a shallow baking dish with a conical lid. You can find these culinary curiosities at most cookware stores, but a large saucepan or a medium Dutch oven with a tight-fitting lid will work in a pinch. This is the one recipe in this section that calls for the fresh ham to be cubed. (So in terms of technique, this recipe bridges to the next section—Asian dishes that use fresh ham, almost always cut up in some way.) Feel free to remove any inner blobs of fat. Serve this aromatic wonder over long-grain rice, couscous, or even wilted spinach.

SLASH THE SHOPPING LIST

You can omit the seven dried spices in step 1 and substitute 2 tablespoons bottled curry powder, provided you use a curry with saffron in the mix. Read the label carefully—do not use one that is simply a vehicle for too much cayenne. In any event, do not substitute a run-of-the-mill yellow curry powder that's just turmeric with a few additional spices. Look for blends that are loaded with spices, often brown, orange, or red. With curry powder, price is often a guide to quality.

THE INGREDIENT SCOOP

Very popular in Middle Eastern cuisine, **preserved lemons** are actually salted lemons packed in a juice brine. The soft rind is the prized part. The inner flesh is edible but can be depressingly mushy and so is usually removed and discarded.

2½ pounds boneless fresh ham, cut into 1-inch cubes

2 teaspoons ground coriander

1 teaspoon ground cinnamon

1 teaspoon ground cumin

1 teaspoon ground ginger

½ teaspoon freshly ground black pepper

¼ teaspoon saffron

¼ teaspoon ground cardamom

3 tablespoons mustard oil or peanut oil

1 medium yellow onion, sliced in half through the stem, the halves sliced into thin half-moons, these half-moons then separated into half-rings

2 medium garlic cloves, minced

½ cup chopped preserved lemon, rind only

¼ cup golden raisins

¼ cup shelled pistachios

1 tablespoon honey

3 medium carrots, peeled and sliced into 1-inch pieces

3 medium parsnips, peeled and sliced into 1-inch pieces

½ cup canned chickpeas, drained and rinsed

¼ cup sweet white wine, such as a Riesling or an Auslese

Salt to taste

1. Mix the ham cubes, coriander, cinnamon, cumin, ginger, pepper, saffron, and cardamom in a large bowl until all the pieces of ham are evenly coated in the spices.

2. Heat a tagine or a medium Dutch oven over medium heat. Swirl in the oil, then add the onions. Cook, stirring often, until softened and almost translucent, about 4 minutes.

3. Stir in the garlic and cook for 15 seconds. Then stir in the ham and all the spices in the bowl, scraping them out with a rubber spatula if necessary. Cook, stirring occasionally, until the meat has browned.

4. Stir in the preserved lemon, raisins, pistachios, and honey. Keep stirring over the heat until everything in the pan is well blended and evenly coated in the spice-and-juice mixture.

5. Sprinkle the carrots, parsnips, and chickpeas over the top without stirring them in. Drizzle the wine over the whole dish.

6. Cover, reduce the heat to low, and simmer at the barest bubble until the ham cubes are quite tender when pricked with a fork, 2 to 2 1/2 hours. The trick here is to keep the simmer low enough that you can count the bubbles as they appear—any faster and the mixture can stick. Plus, you don't ever want to stir in those vegetables sitting on top. They should cook in the attendant steam, retaining their color until the last minute, when you give them one stir just before bringing the thing to the table. By the way, at the very end, check the sauce for salt—the pistachios may have had some adhering to them and the preserved lemons are quite salty, but it still may not be enough for your taste. If you find the stew needs salt, start out by adding 1/2 teaspoon and take it from there.

TESTERS' NOTES

We prefer mustard oil for a tagine, but it's an esoteric ingredient, to say the least. Much favored in East Indian cooking, it's a pungent fat, sort of like a cross between toasted walnuts and cooked cabbage. Look for it at gourmet markets or from East Indian spice and condiment suppliers on the web. Since mustard oil is hardly a pantry staple, peanut oil makes a fine (if admittedly less aromatic) substitute. If peanut allergies present problems, go with pumpkin-seed or walnut oil (but not a toasted variety of either).

Section Two

THE ASIAN CONNECTION

To write of "Asian cuisine" is to write gibberish. In reality, there are myriad styles, tastes, and techniques across a vast continent, all shellacked for Western palates with a heavy pour of soy sauce. The mere notion of grouping recipes as "Asian" is as bogus as lumping dishes together as "European."

Except that it is indeed true that fresh ham has long been a favorite ingredient across Asia, probably more than in the West. For one thing, the texture of the meat is used for a wider range of effects. And (dare we say it?) its aroma is used in more innovative ways.

Western culinary traditions tend to focus on taste and minimize smell, despite the biological link between the two. Look at how we had to couch the mere mention of the smell of ham. And look at cake, that paean to Western culinary aesthetics. Over the centuries, we've morphed and masked its basic wheaty smell with a host of other flavors: almonds, chocolate, vanilla, and what have you.

In contrast, Asian culinary traditions often preserve and balance essential aromas. So these recipes offer many pleasures, taste being one.

That said, they will win no authenticity awards. They are our concepts, and Bruce has created them with the North American supermarket in mind. There may be a few ingredients you don't have in your pantry, but almost all are readily available without a trip to a specialty market.

FILIPINO TWICE-COOKED PORK

MAKES 6 SERVINGS

Here's a showstopper: The ham is first boiled in an aromatic mélange, then fried in lard until crisp. Serve the dish with a salad of cucumber "noodles" (see the technique in step 6 of Cold Fresh Ham in Garlic Sauce, page 55) and sliced, seeded red bell peppers, all dressed with a splash of rice vinegar. And have lots of beer on hand, of course.

3 pounds boneless fresh ham, cut into 2-inch pieces

½ cup rice vinegar (see page 52)

¼ cup soy sauce

1 teaspoon freshly ground black pepper

1 garlic head, the cloves separated but not peeled

3 kaffir lime leaves (see page 61)

2 cups reduced-sodium, fat-free chicken broth

1 tablespoon fish sauce

1 tablespoon lime juice

2 tablespoons lard or peanut oil

Cooked white rice

1. Mix the pork pieces, vinegar, soy sauce, pepper, garlic cloves, and kaffir lime leaves in a large saucepan until everything's well coated. Cover and refrigerate for 12 hours or overnight.

2. Pour in the broth and bring the contents of the saucepan to a simmer over medium-high heat, stirring often.

3. Cover, reduce the heat to low, and simmer slowly for 1½ hours. During the first 30 minutes or so, occasionally skim off any foam or impurities that might float on the broth.

4. Use a slotted spoon to transfer the pork pieces to a large bowl. Transfer the garlic to a separate bowl. Discard the kaffir lime leaves.

5. Stir the fish sauce and lime juice into the liquid in the pan. Set it over high heat and bring the sauce to a full boil. Continue boiling until the amount of liquid in the pan is about half what it was when it started boiling, 10 to 15 minutes, depending on how much heat your stove puts out.

6. Squeeze the soft garlic pulp out of the cloves and into the simmering sauce. Whisk well, until fairly smooth. Set the pan off the heat and cover it to keep warm while you fry the pork.

7. Melt the lard in a large skillet over medium heat. Add the pork pieces in batches and fry until crisp, turning on all sides to brown them well. Transfer the crisp chunks to a platter and keep frying more pieces. When you're done, ladle the sauce over the pork and serve at once over cooked rice.

THE INGREDIENT SCOOP

Fish sauce, a heady condiment from Southeast Asia, is made from fermented fish parts and salt (and, in better bottlings, a host of aromatics as well). Known as *nam pla* in Thailand, *nuoc mam* in Vietnam, *teuk trei* in Cambodia, *patis* in the Philippines, and *fish gravy* in Hong Kong, it has a notoriously rancid smell that mellows miraculously over the heat, providing a depth of flavor characteristic of many Southeast Asian dishes. If you have shellfish allergies or religious dietary concerns, check the label, since some bottlings include shellfish.

TESTERS' NOTES

For a more authentic Filipino taste, substitute coconut vinegar for the rice vinegar. Coconut vinegar can be made from either the sweet, sticky sap of the coconut palm or the water inside coconuts. In either case, coconut vinegar is cloudy, pungent, highly acidic, and a little yeasty. You'll most likely have to track down coconut vinegar at online suppliers of East Indian or Southeast Asian foods.

You can make this dish up to 2 days in advance. Prepare it through step 6, then refrigerate the sauce and the pork separately. When you're ready to serve, fry the pork as directed in step 7 while reheating the sauce over low heat, not until it boils, but just until it's hot.

STIR-FRIED HAM
WITH PRESSED TOFU

MAKES **4** SERVINGS WHEN SERVED OVER RICE WITH A STEAMED
OR SAUTÉED VEGETABLE ON THE SIDE

*We've long been fans of shredded pork and tofu, a takeout favor-
ite. In fact, ham's grainy texture beautifully counterbalances the
chewy texture of pressed tofu in the traditional dish. If you can't
find pressed tofu, make your own. Wrap each of two cutting boards
with a double thickness of paper towels, put 16 ounces of firm tofu
between them, weight the top cutting board with a can or a small
pot, and set the whole thing in the refrigerator for 48 hours so the
tofu drains and condenses. It won't be exactly the same texture as
the more chewy-cheesy pressed tofu sold in Asian markets, but it's
better than nothing.*

THE INGREDIENT SCOOP

Soy sauce isn't one thing but a multi-
tude. There are hundreds of varieties
from across Asia, all made from fermented, salted soy beans. In general,
they fall into three categories: light
(sometimes called "superior"), dark,
and flavored (such as mushroom soy
sauce). "Light" has nothing to do with
the sodium content. It is so labeled to
differentiate it from "dark" soy sauce,
which is highly aged and thus thicker,
sometimes like ketchup. All the recipes
in this book call for the light (that is,
the more standard) variety. You can
tell the difference between light and
dark or flavored sauces by the way
they coat the inside of the bottle:
Light barely does, but dark or flavored
will leave a thick film. Reduced-sodium
soy sauce is often labeled "lite."

2 tablespoons peanut oil

1 tablespoon minced peeled fresh
ginger

2 medium garlic cloves, minced

1 pound boneless fresh ham, shredded

8 medium scallions, cut into 2-inch
pieces

12 ounces pressed firm tofu, cut into
matchsticks 2 inches long and about
¼ inch thick

3 tablespoons soy sauce (regular or
reduced-sodium)

1½ tablespoons Shaoxing wine (see
page 49) or dry sherry

1 tablespoon Worcestershire sauce

1 teaspoon sugar

¼ teaspoon five-spice powder (see
page 50)

1. Heat a large wok or sauté pan over medium-high heat, swirl in the oil,
and add the ginger and garlic. Stir-fry for 30 seconds by tossing with two
wooden paddles or two heat-safe rubber spatulas, keeping everything
moving over the heat, up the sides of the wok and then back down into
its fiery center.

2. Add the ham and stir-fry in the same manner for 5 minutes, until
cooked through.

3. Drop in the scallion bits and the tofu. Keep stir-frying until very aromatic, about 2 minutes.

4. Stir in the soy sauce, Shaoxing wine, Worcestershire sauce, sugar, and five-spice powder. Stir-fry until the little bit of sauce comes to a simmer (almost instantly) and thickens a bit.

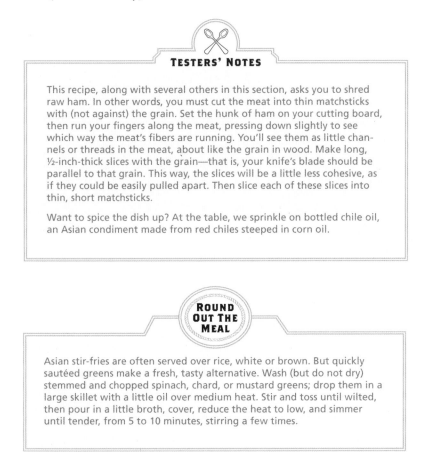

TESTERS' NOTES

This recipe, along with several others in this section, asks you to shred raw ham. In other words, you must cut the meat into thin matchsticks with (not against) the grain. Set the hunk of ham on your cutting board, then run your fingers along the meat, pressing down slightly to see which way the meat's fibers are running. You'll see them as little channels or threads in the meat, about like the grain in wood. Make long, ½-inch-thick slices with the grain—that is, your knife's blade should be parallel to that grain. This way, the slices will be a little less cohesive, as if they could be easily pulled apart. Then slice each of these slices into thin, short matchsticks.

Want to spice the dish up? At the table, we sprinkle on bottled chile oil, an Asian condiment made from red chiles steeped in corn oil.

ROUND OUT THE MEAL

Asian stir-fries are often served over rice, white or brown. But quickly sautéed greens make a fresh, tasty alternative. Wash (but do not dry) stemmed and chopped spinach, chard, or mustard greens; drop them in a large skillet with a little oil over medium heat. Stir and toss until wilted, then pour in a little broth, cover, reduce the heat to low, and simmer until tender, from 5 to 10 minutes, stirring a few times.

RED-COOKED FRESH HAM & CHESTNUTS

MAKES 6 TO 8 SERVINGS

"Red cooking" is a Chinese braising technique using a mixture of soy sauce, rice wine, broth, and spices, particularly star anise. Good-quality soy sauce, when long braised, will take on a deep red cast—thus the name. Trim some of the ham's exterior fat for a leaner dish.

2 cups reduced-sodium, fat-free chicken broth

¾ cup soy sauce (regular or reduced-sodium)

¾ cup Shaoxing wine or dry sherry

⅔ cup julienned peeled fresh ginger (see page 57)

1½ tablespoons honey

12 medium scallions, cut into 2-inch pieces

4 medium garlic cloves, sliced into thin slivers

Four 4-inch cinnamon sticks

2 or 3 star anise pods

One 4½- to 5-pound bone-in fresh ham, rind removed

4 cups jarred roasted chestnuts

1. Stir the broth, soy sauce, Shaoxing wine, ginger, honey, scallions, garlic, cinnamon sticks, and star anise pods in a large saucepan—large enough to accommodate the ham and still be covered tightly, but not so large that the ham sits too far out of the liquid, which should come about a third of the way up the meat.

2. Set the ham into the broth mixture, then bring it all to a low simmer over medium-high heat.

3. Cover, reduce the heat to low, and simmer slowly for 2½ hours, turning the ham in the liquid about every 30 minutes. During the first hour, skim off any foam or impurities that might scum the broth's surface.

4. Skim the sauce one more time; then toss in the chestnuts, cover, and continue simmering slowly until the ham is meltingly tender, 1 to 1½ hours more, turning the ham every so often so the meat stays moist. An instant-read meat thermometer inserted into the thickest part of the ham without touching bone should register 170°F.

5. Transfer the ham to a cutting board and let it stand at room temperature for 15 minutes. Discard the cinnamon sticks and the star anise pods. (Some pods may have broken apart, so you'll have to go fishing.) Cut the ham into thin slices, then serve in bowls with the broth and vegetables spooned over the slices, about like a soup with ham slices in it.

THE INGREDIENT SCOOP

Shaoxing wine (绍兴酒, *shahow-shing jiu*, sometimes Romanized as "shao shing" or even "hua tia") is a mass-produced Chinese rice wine, one of many *huangjiu*, or "yellow wines," from China. It's available at most high-end grocery stores, in all Asian markets, and from online suppliers. Some bottlings are red, not from aging but because of the red yeast used to ferment the rice. Time was, Shaoxing wine was served as a beverage, but few bottlings of this quality ever make it to North America. In a pinch, substitute dry sherry.

TESTERS' NOTES

The simmer in steps 3 and 4 should be quite low, with just enough bubbles at any moment that you can count them as they form. Too many and you'll start to lose the sauce through evaporation.

Try the dish in a slow cooker. Dump everything in step 1 into the cooker, stir until the honey dissolves, then add the remaining ingredients all at once. Cover and cook on low for 8 to 10 hours, until the ham is tender and an instant-read meat thermometer inserted into the thickest part of the meat without touching the bone registers 170°F.

CHINESE-STYLE BARBECUED BONELESS FRESH HAM

MAKES 6 TO 8 SERVINGS

Chinese barbecue isn't about smoke. It's about the sweet, sticky glaze, often garishly red (but not necessarily so, as here). You'll need a rack to lift the ham up so this more authentic glaze doesn't dissolve in all those porkish juices. It's definitely a Chinatown favorite, although a host of corn syrup–laced, overly sticky, bottled glazes have swamped any authenticity at many establishments. Maybe such time-saving short-cuts are inevitable, given that so much of Chinese cooking is already "condiment-based." Still, it's easy to resist the trend when you do it yourself.

⅓ cup hoisin sauce (see page 160)

¼ cup soy sauce

2 tablespoons packed light brown sugar

1 tablespoon minced peeled fresh ginger

½ teaspoon five-spice powder

3 medium garlic cloves, put through a garlic press or smashed repeatedly with the side of a heavy knife

One 3- to 4-pound boneless fresh ham, tied with butchers' twine (see page 38)

1. Stir up the hoisin, soy sauce, brown sugar, ginger, five-spice powder, and garlic in a small bowl. Slather this all over the ham, then set it on a lipped baking sheet, cover loosely with aluminum foil (so the foil doesn't rest on the marinade), and refrigerate for a full 24 hours.

2. Preheat the oven to 350°F. While it heats up, uncover the ham and let it sit on the counter for 15 minutes.

3. Check the ham to see which side has the thickest layer of fat. Lift the ham up, put a rack underneath it on the baking sheet, and set the ham fatty side down on that rack. You can also use a V-shaped roaster, often used to roast chickens. Roast for 1½ hours.

4. Use silicon mitts or a couple of large, metal spatulas to turn the ham fatty side up. Continue roasting, basting often with pan juices. The ham and its juices may start to burn a bit, but remember that the point here is to get that glaze dark and crisp. If you find that it's getting too dark, tent loosely with foil. Keep roasting until an instant-read meat thermometer inserted into the center of the meat registers 170°F, between 1½ and 2 hours more. Cool the ham for 15 minutes on a cutting or carving board before slicing into paper-thin pieces.

The required rack can be the type on which you cool cookies, but it can't have rubber feet—these will melt in the oven. You want to lift the ham just out of its rendered fat, which will be copious. So also use a lipped baking sheet, or you'll end up with burning ham fat on your oven floor. A broiler pan and its rack will do in a pinch, but its construction may not allow proper air circulation and doesn't drain off the rendered fat as well as a wire-mesh rack on a shallow, lipped baking sheet. Or, as stated in the recipe, try one of those specialty, V-shaped, chicken roasters.

ROUND OUT THE MEAL

Serve this ham alongside bowls of rice, either the more standard long-grained or sticky short-grained rice, as well as some quickly steamed greens—like bok choy, Chinese water spinach, or Chinese flowering broccoli—drizzled with bottled oyster sauce, a thick, salty-sweet condiment found in the Asian aisle of almost all supermarkets.

STIR-FRIED VINEGARY POTATOES ⟪WITH⟫ HAM AND HOT CHILES

MAKES 4 TO 6 SERVINGS

Potatoes in a stir fry? Indeed. China is now the world's largest producer of spuds; they are all the rage, particularly in the country's northern parts. In Bruce's interpretation of what's becoming a classic stir-fry, the potatoes should remain a little crunchy, with a little more tooth than al dente pasta.

THE INGREDIENT SCOOP

Rice vinegar, sometimes called rice wine vinegar, comes in two forms: seasoned and not. A perfect pantry has both, but a well-stocked one has the unseasoned variety. "Seasoned" simply means there's sugar in the mix—the bottle is usually marked "seasoned" on the label, even in tiny type. Unseasoned is never marked in any way—nor indeed called "unseasoned" in this book, except in this one paragraph where the differentiation matters. All our recipes call for the unseasoned variety—or simply "rice vinegar." If you're in doubt about what you've got, look at the ingredients listed on the label. You don't want to see sugar or any other sweetener. By the way, if you ever need seasoned rice vinegar but only have the regular stuff, use the amount required but add ⅛ teaspoon granulated white sugar for every ½ teaspoon unseasoned rice vinegar.

1½ pounds yellow-fleshed potatoes (such as Yukon Golds)

¼ cup peanut oil

1 pound boneless fresh ham, shredded (see page 47)

6 medium scallions, cut into 3-inch lengths, each of these then sliced into thin strips the long way

¼ cup julienned peeled fresh ginger (see page 57)

2 medium garlic cloves, cut into thin slivers

8 to 16 dried thin Chinese red chiles or 2 to 3 serrano chiles, thinly sliced

¼ cup rice vinegar

2 tablespoons soy sauce

1. Peel the potatoes, then turn them into thin threads. Most authentically, use a turning slicer (such as one available from Benriner), a Japanese kitchen tool that makes long threads of vegetables by twisting them over a very sharp blade. (Those threads may be familiar from the nests of daikon and carrot often found on sushi plates.) Or use a mandoline to make shoestring potatoes by running the potato repeatedly over the appropriate shoestring blade. Or run the peeled potatoes the long way over the large holes of a box grater, thereby making the longest pieces possible. In any event, set these threads in a large bowl, cover with cool water, and set aside.

2. Heat a large wok over medium-high heat until smoking. Pour the oil along the rim of the wok so that it drizzles down to the center. Toss in the pork and stir-fry until cooked through, about 2 minutes.

3. Add the scallions, ginger, garlic, and chiles; continue stir-frying until softened, about 2 minutes. One warning: Those chile oils can volatilize and burn your eyes. Have the vent on high or open a window.

4. Pick up the potatoes by handfuls, squeeze dry, and toss them into the wok. Work quickly but efficiently. Stir-fry until crisp-tender, about 3 minutes. (The only way to tell is to taste.)

5. Add the vinegar and soy sauce. Stir well, then continue stir-frying until 90 percent of the liquid in the pan has been absorbed, about 2 minutes. Serve hot right out of the wok, over steamed or braised mustard greens or even over raw, very thinly shredded, stemmed baby bok choy (which will cook just a bit if the hot potato-and-ham stir-fry is ladled right on top of it from the wok).

TESTERS' NOTES

Don't use baking potatoes for this dish; their extra starch will needlessly cloud the suace.

The potato threads will indeed remain crunchy, perhaps not to everyone's liking. If you want less tooth, drop the threads in boiling water and cook for 1 minute over high heat. Drain in a colander set in the sink, then add these threads in step 4, as indicated in the recipe.

COLD FRESH HAM
🍖 GARLIC SAUCE

MAKES ABOUT 10 SERVINGS—OR MANY MORE FOR A NIBBLING PARTY

The Chinese name for this dish is something like "Crystal Boiled Ham"—which actually doesn't sound much better than our more pedestrian title. In the end, this is buffet fare, something to make ahead and serve at a cocktail party along with other things for nibbling.

THE INGREDIENT SCOOP

Sichuan peppercorns are not pep-percorns at all; they're the little pods of a small citrus fruit grown across Asia. They have a peppery bite and a bizarrely tongue-numbing quality. Look for them in Asian markets and from suppliers on the web. Use them whole in these dishes—no grinding required.

One 3-pound boneless ham, tied with butchers' twine (see page 38)

10 medium scallions, 6 halved length-wise and the remainder cut into 1-inch sections

1 large ginger knob, peeled and sliced into coins (about 1 cup)

2 large, thick orange-peel strips (take them off with a vegetable peeler)

Two 4-inch cinnamon sticks

2 star anise pods

1 teaspoon Sichuan peppercorns

½ cup soy sauce

1 tablespoon Asian red chile oil or sambal (see page 62)

1 tablespoon sesame oil (see page 159)

1 tablespoon rice vinegar (see page 52)

1 tablespoon minced peeled fresh ginger

6 garlic cloves, quartered

4 medium cucumbers, preferably quite cold

1. Place the ham in a saucepan just large enough to hold it comfortably and be covered tightly. Add the 6 halved scallions, the ginger, orange peel, cinnamon sticks, star anise pods, and Sichuan peppercorns. Fill the saucepan with just enough water to cover the ham.

2. Cover and bring to a low simmer over medium heat. Reduce the heat to medium-low and continue simmering until an instant-read meat ther-mometer inserted into the center of the ham registers 170°F, about 1 hour.

3. Set the covered pan with the ham off the heat for 45 minutes, then put it in the refrigerator and chill overnight, liquid and all.

4. Place the soy sauce, chile oil, sesame oil, vinegar, ginger, garlic, and the 4 cut-up scallions in a large blender or a food processor fitted with the chopping blade. Blend or process until fairly smooth, the vegetables minced but not turned to mush. Pour this sauce into a gravy boat or some other serving vehicle, cover, and refrigerate overnight as well.

5. Just before serving, transfer the ham from the poaching liquid to a cutting board. (Discard the liquid and all the aromatics and spices.) Remove the butchers' twine and slice the ham into very thin rounds.

6. Peel the cucumbers, then use a vegetable peeler to make long, thin strips of cucumber, about like noodles. Run the peeler the length of the vegetable each time and catch the noodles in a large bowl. Keep turning the cucumber to work on all sides, but stop once you've got just the seed core in your hand. Toss out that core and start in on another cucumber.

7. Mound all the cucumber noodles on a platter. Lay the ham slices on top. Pour some sauce over the ham and cucumbers. Pass the remaining sauce on the side so everyone can doctor theirs to their liking.

ROUND OUT THE MEAL

This aromatic ham needs a side of creamy peanut noodles. To make an easy, no-cook sauce for the noodles, whir all of the following in a food processor until smooth: ½ cup creamy peanut butter, 6 tablespoons vegetable broth, 2 tablespoons toasted sesame oil, 2 tablespoons soy sauce, 2 tablespoons rice vinegar, 2 teaspoons Shaoxing wine or dry sherry, ½ teaspoon sugar, and several dashes hot red pepper sauce. Toss this dressing with cooked and drained noodles, preferably dried Chinese egg noodles.

CHINESE NOODLES WITH HAM AND CASHEWS

MAKES 4 SERVINGS

This is sort of like lo mein, the popular Chinese takeout dish, except there's a bit more hammy heft with fewer noodles in the mix.

6 tablespoons reduced-sodium, fat-free chicken broth

3 tablespoons soy sauce

1½ tablespoons hoisin sauce (see page 160)

1½ tablespoons Shaoxing wine (see page 49) or dry sherry

1½ tablespoons rice vinegar (see page 52)

1½ teaspoons sugar

1½ teaspoons sambal (see page 62) or another hot Asian chile sauce

3 tablespoons sesame oil (see page 159)

1 small shallot, minced

1½ tablespoons minced peeled fresh ginger

12 ounces boneless fresh ham, shredded (see page 47)

6 medium scallions, cut into 1-inch pieces

1 jarred roasted yellow or red pepper, shredded

½ cup roasted unsalted cashews

12 ounces Chinese egg noodles, cooked until al dente and drained

1. Whisk the broth, soy sauce, hoisin sauce, Shaoxing wine, rice vinegar, sugar, and sambal or its substitute in a small bowl. Set aside.

2. Heat a large wok or sauté pan over medium-high heat until smoking. Swirl in the sesame oil, then add the shallot and ginger. Stir-fry until fragrant but not in any way browned, about 20 seconds.

3. Add the ham and continue stir-frying until cooked through, about 3 minutes. Keep the ingredients moving over the heat—up the sides of the wok and back down into its hot center, over and over again. The best tools for the task? Two wooden spoonlike spatulas or flat paddles.

4. Toss in the scallions, pepper, and cashews. Stir-fry until aromatic, about 1 minute.

5. Add the cooked noodles all at once. Break them up; then stir-fry quickly, just to get them heated through, no more than 45 seconds.

6. Pour in the broth mixture; bring to a simmer. Keep stir-frying until that liquid is about three-quarters absorbed. Turn off the heat and toss once more for good measure.

TESTERS' NOTES

Cook the noodles just until they still have the slightest bite at their centers. Overcooked, they'll turn to mush as they're tossed with the vegetables and meat. Drain the noodles in a colander set in the sink and immediately rinse with cold water to stop any cooking. Yes, you'll lose some of the starchy coating that can pick up the sauce, but it's better than letting the noodles continue to steam in the colander and so turn flabby and unattractive. As to those noodles themselves, they can be fresh or dried. The fresh are sometimes found near the fresh pasta in or near the produce section of your market. The dried are often sold wound into little nests in their packages.

THE HIND  QUARTERLY

ISSUE NO. I   *We report food news whole hog.*   SECTION C

TENTING, COVERING, ★ ★ ★ ★ AND ★ ★ ★ ★ COVERING TIGHTLY ★ WITH FOIL ★

HERE ARE EXPLANATIONS FOR THREE COOKBOOK CLICHÉS:

☞ **TO TENT A HAM WITH FOIL,** use a large piece of aluminum foil and crease it the long way at about its middle. Lay this over the ham with the crease at the top, so the foil hangs down over the meat, like a Cub Scout tent. (The horror.) The tent doesn't need to be tucked in, but it can curve a bit at its bottom to keep it in place.

☞ **COVERING WITH FOIL** is basically tenting the meat, but with those bottom edges tucked in a bit more—not all the way—so that you have a little air flow without losing much moisture.

☞ **COVERING TIGHTLY WITH FOIL** means you're creating a steam/roast chamber. You'll need a very large piece of foil, possibly two or three seamed together. To create a seam, lay two equivalent sheets side by side lengthwise; then bend, roll, and crease the adjacent edges together, pressing down to seal tightly. The foil should create a sack over and around the ham, but it shouldn't be so tight that it rests on the meat. Tuck it in tightly at the edges so no steam can escape. Indeed, the foil must not rest on any spicy or acidic marinades to thwart any potential chemical reactions.

PREPPING THE GINGER

WHEN YOU BUY FRESH GINGER AT THE SUPERMARKET, choose chunks that smell sweet (no sour or acidic aroma), are firm to the touch (no mushy parts), and have a delicate, papery skin (no desiccated bits.)

In Chinese cooking, there are basically two ways fresh ginger is prepared: minced or julienned.

In either case, you must first peel said ginger. Use a vegetable peeler and go cautiously; the tastiest bits are found just under that papery skin.

To mince the ginger, cut the peeled piece into thin coins, then cut these into little strips. Gather them together on a cutting board and rock a heavy chef's knife through them, never lifting the blade off the cutting board but continually seesawing it through the pieces while turning it in a half-moon arc. Gather the bits together and do it again, until the ginger is about like coarse sand.

If that's too much trouble, buy preminced ginger in the produce section of the supermarket. It should be pale beige—never brown—and certainly not waterlogged, signs of having sat on the shelf too long. And read the ingredient list. The bottle should only contain ginger, no sugar. Store it in the refrigerator for several months—but beware: It can ferment. Always check before using.

To julienne ginger (that is, to cut it into Lilliputian strips), cut that peeled piece into two-inch segments, then slice these into thin strips the long way. Stack a few together and again slice them the long way, into thin matchsticks about as thick as sturdy sewing needles.

STEAMED HAM BUNS

MAKES 16 BUNS (GOD ONLY KNOWS HOW MANY WILL
MAKE IT OUT OF THE KITCHEN)

Admittedly, this is not an everyday recipe. If you want to make the buns ahead, complete the recipe through step 7, then put the buns on their baking sheet in the freezer; after 8 hours, transfer the frozen-hard pucks to sealable plastic bags and store in the freezer for up to 3 months. Don't thaw; just use them right from the freezer, adding 5 minutes to their time in the steamer. Most traditional buns (包, baow, "bun") are made with barbecued pork (叉燒, chahr siew, "fork roasted"—aka, roast pork); these are instead stuffed with an aromatic ham mixture that's actually lighter but just as flavorful.

1½ cups warm water, between 105°F and 115°F (use a meat thermometer to make sure)

5 tablespoons sugar

One ¼-ounce package or 2¼ teaspoons active dry yeast

5 tablespoons peanut oil, plus additional for greasing the bowl and the steamers

4¾ cups plus 2 tablespoons all-purpose flour, plus additional for dusting just about everything in sight

1½ pounds boneless fresh ham, cut into little-bitty cubes, about ¼ inch on every side

2 cups reduced-sodium, fat-free chicken broth

5 tablespoons hoisin sauce (see page 160)

3 tablespoons rice vinegar (see page 52)

1½ tablespoons soy sauce

1 tablespoon honey

1 tablespoon ginger juice (either bottled, or fresh peeled ginger juiced through a garlic press)

2 teaspoons five-spice powder (see page 50)

1 medium garlic clove, minced

1½ cups thinly sliced scallions

2¼ teaspoons baking powder

1. Put the water in a large bowl, add the sugar and yeast, and stir gently. Set aside until pretty foamy, about 5 minutes. If it doesn't get foamy, either the water was at the wrong temperature or the yeast had gone bad—so start again.

2. Stir in the oil and the flour until a soft dough forms. Dust your hands and a clean, dry work surface with flour. Gather the dough together, set it on the prepared surface, and knead until the mass is firm but quite smooth, about like a baby's cheek. As you knead, push the dough away from you with the heel of one hand while digging the heel of your other hand into the part near you, gently twisting your hands in opposite directions as you do so. Gather the dough together, twist it a quarter turn, and do that again. And again. And again. For about 10 minutes.

3. Oil a large bowl with peanut oil dabbed on a wadded-up paper towel, then gather the dough into a ball and put it in the bowl. Turn the dough over so it's got a thin coating of oil, cover the bowl with plastic wrap, and set aside in a warm place until doubled in bulk, about 2 hours.

4. Meanwhile, stir the ham, broth, hoisin sauce, rice vinegar, soy sauce, honey, ginger juice, five-spice powder, and garlic in a large saucepan over medium heat. Bring to a boil; then cover, reduce the heat to low, and simmer until the ham is tender, about 30 minutes. Uncover, raise the heat to medium, and boil away, stirring a lot, until the liquid in the pan has reduced to a shellac-like glaze. Stir in the scallions and set aside off the heat, uncovered.

5. Jam your fist into the dough, then lightly dust your work surface with flour and turn the deflated dough onto it. Knead in the baking powder, then cover the dough with a kitchen towel for 5 minutes.

6. Divide the dough into 16 balls. Each should be a scant $1/3$ cup. To be obsessive, each should weigh $2\,3/4$ ounces.

7. Lightly flour a large baking sheet. Use a rolling pin to roll one of the balls out to a circle 5 inches in diameter. Place $1/4$ cup of the ham filling in the center of the circle. Bring the sides of the dough circle up to cup the filling, like a big bonbon. Pull the dough into a little neck right at the top, then give it a twist to seal the bun. Set aside on the prepared baking sheet, cover loosely with a paper towel, and make 15 more.

8. Lightly brush stackable bamboo steamers with peanut oil—or lightly oil some other steaming contraption, like a very large vegetable steamer. If you want to forgo the oil, line these devices with Napa cabbage leaves.

9. Bring about 1 inch of water to a boil in a saucepan that can accommodate whatever steaming contraption you're using. Line the buns in a single layer in the steamer(s) and place over the simmering water, making sure none of the water gets onto the buns. Cover, reduce the heat to low, and steam for 15 minutes, until the dough has firmed up and cooked through. Check once or twice to make sure the water hasn't boiled away. If it has, add a little more. Let the buns rest in the steamer for a few minutes before serving, just so the filling doesn't peel off the roof of your mouth.

INDONESIAN CHILE HAM SAUTÉ

MAKES ABOUT 1 ¼ CUPS

Indonesian cooking is famous for its sweet-spicy combinations, irresistible and tongue-spanking. This recipe has been adapted for the modern supermarket, eschewing the esoteric chiles and sugars normally used. For the best presentation, search out so-called "sweet rice," a sticky, short-grain rice, to go under the sauté on the plate.

2 dried New Mexican red chiles, stemmed and seeded

2 medium scallions, minced

¼ cup thinly sliced lemongrass, white and pale-green parts only

2 tablespoons packed light brown sugar

2 tablespoons fish sauce (see page 45)

1 tablespoon minced peeled fresh ginger

½ teaspoon shrimp paste (optional)

1 or 2 hot red chiles (such as Thai hots or serranos) seeded or not, at will

3 medium garlic cloves, minced

1 kaffir lime leaf (optional)

3 tablespoons peanut oil

2½ pounds boneless fresh ham, shredded (see page 47)

Cooked white rice

¼ cup cilantro leaves, for garnish

1. Place the New Mexican red chiles in a medium bowl and cover with boiling water. Set aside to soften, about 10 minutes.

2. Drain the chiles, then place them in a large blender or a food processor fitted with a chopping blade. Add the scallions, lemongrass, brown sugar, fish sauce, ginger, shrimp paste (if desired), fresh chiles, garlic, and kaffir lime leaf (if desired). Blend or process until grainy, scraping down the canister as necessary to make sure everything gets whacked by the blade. Set aside.

3. Heat a large wok or sauté pan over medium-high heat until smoking. Swirl in the oil, then the ham. Stir-fry until it's fully lost its pink, raw color.

4. Add the chile paste and bring to a simmer, stirring often. Cover; reduce the heat to low. Simmer very slowly, stirring once in a while, until the ham is tender, about 20 minutes. Serve over white rice sprinkled with cilantro leaves.

THE INGREDIENT SCOOP

Lemongrass is an aromatic herb favored for its citruslike nose. In the produce section of your market, look for pliable stalks without withered leaves or desiccated bulbs. Remove the wiggly roots before slicing the white and pale-green parts.

Shrimp paste is sold in a very pungent cake made from fermented, partially rotted, dried shrimp, sometimes buried in the ground for months but more often left in the sun to get good and stinky. Called *terasi* in Indonesian, *belacan* in Malay, and *mam tom* in Vietnamese, it's a crucial ingredient for an authentic taste here—but may well be beyond the bounds of most Westerners' palates. Use it sparingly until you acquire the taste for it. As a general rule, Chinese brands are less pungent.

Kaffir lime leaves are the bay leaves of Southeast Asian cooking. They offer a pleasant citrus bite, less sour than the taste of the tiny, wrinkled limes from those very kaffir trees. In a pinch, use ¼ teaspoon finely grated lime zest (with absolutely no white pith) for every kaffir lime leaf required

SAMBAL

MAKES ABOUT 1¼ CUPS

There's no more classic Indonesian condiment than this fiery tangle of chiles and spices—and no better match to ham, whether in these Asian preparations or simply as a condiment for a roast ham of almost any stripe.

THE INGREDIENT SCOOP

In Bali, **sambal** is spooned onto rice at breakfast, lunch, and dinner. It's so popular globally that it's now found in East Indian cuisine, Thai cooking, and even in traditional Chinese woks. At Asian markets and even in most North American supermarkets these days, the bottlings come in a dazzling variety: from pure chiles without much else to more aromatic blends (as in this recipe).

2 small Roma or plum tomatoes

¼ cup small red hot chiles (such as red serranos or Thai hots) stemmed but not seeded

2 medium shallots, chopped

1 medium garlic clove, minced

2½ tablespoons peanut oil

2 tablespoons water

1 tablespoon rice vinegar (see page 52)

1 tablespoon packed light brown sugar

½ teaspoon salt

1. Place the tomatoes in a small pot, cover with water, and bring to a boil over high heat. Cook for 3 minutes, then gently remove the tomatoes with a slotted spoon (keep the water in the saucepan). Run the tomatoes under cold water to stop the cooking and loosen the skins. Peel off skins, cut the tomatoes open, scoop out and discard the seeds, and place the tomatoes in a food processor fitted with the chopping blade.

2. Bring the water in the saucepan back to a boil over high heat and make the chiles take a dive. Boil for 5 minutes. Transfer the chiles to the food processor. (You can discard the water in the pan now.)

3. Add the shallots and garlic to the food processor. Lock on the lid and process until pasty but still a little grainy, scraping down the sides of the canister as necessary.

4. Turn the vent on so the chile oils won't bowl you over—or open a kitchen window and get a fan blowing through the area. Heat a large skillet over medium heat, then add the oil. Tip and tilt the skillet so its bottom is thoroughly coated, then add all the chile paste from the food processor. Fry this paste until exquisitely aromatic and a little thickened, about 5 minutes, stirring almost the whole time.

5. Stir in the water, vinegar, brown sugar, and salt. Reduce the heat a little and continue cooking, stirring often, until all the oil and water have been absorbed and the mixture is a fiery, thick condiment, about like grainy ketchup. Store in a glass container in the refrigerator for up to 2 months. (The sambal actually tastes best if it's allowed to ripen a few days before using.)

BLUEBERRY
KETCHUP (P. 33)

SAMBAL

2

DRY-CURED

HAM

IN THE OLD WORLD

2

To dry-cure a ham is to invite ruin. Had we only known.

By late summer, we had the necessary cut in hand—Wilbur's—a rind-on, toe-on ham. We knew we wanted to cure it with the bone intact—not like some boneless prosciutto they might slice up at the supermarket deli, but like those Spanish hams in tapas bars, with the feet still attached.

Even more importantly, we knew we wanted to cure the meat without nitrates, nitrites, or chemical chicanery. Only the most authentic, nostalgic, Old World cure would do for us. No Insta Cure, saltpeter (potassium nitrate), or other chemical shenanigans—just salt and ambient atmospherics.

Armed with nothing but intent, I blithely set out on the research. And what I read was a tad troubling. Harold McGee in *On Food and Cooking* mentioned such delights as *Clostridium botulinum* appearing in meats "insufficiently or unevenly salted." He claimed it could bring on what German scientists called "*Wurstvergiftung*, or sausage disease." Admittedly, it had been a while since I studied German in college, but as far as I could tell, the word was better translated "sausage *poisoning*"—and, thus, of a more immediate threat.

The remedy? Here's what the Centers for Disease Control had to say about the matter:

> Respiratory failure and paralysis . . . may require a patient to be on a breathing machine (ventilator) for weeks, plus intensive medical and nursing care. . . .

Now dogged by fear, I consulted other cookbook writers. How did they make a dry-cured ham? I soon came across this jewel:

> [Take] a metal skewer and insert it in the center remove [sic] and smell—it should have a cured aroma. This takes practice.

Bad grammar inspired about as much confidence in us as forbidding German. Besides, what in the world was a "cured aroma"? And what exactly should have one? The metal skewer? Or the meat? And while we're at it, what takes practice? The inserting or the smelling?

For answers, we turned to Chris Prosperi, chef of Metro Bis, one of Connecticut's best restaurants. He's a locavore and a do-it-yourselfer of the highest order. He makes his own vinegar, for God's sake.

"No clue," he said, sitting at a table in his restaurant on a sunny August morning before the lunch rush set in. "But I do know this: You gotta get it right. Otherwise, you'll die."

Finally armed with our mortality, we sought comfort—and a European, in the flesh. We reasoned these people had been curing ham for centuries.

We should have given it more thought.

He was French: a *charcutier*, a butcher, from a couple towns over.

"Sure I weell help," he said. He wrote out a quick shopping list: kosher salt, cognac, and a wooden crate.

Bruce nodded as if it made sense.

Not to me. "Cognac?" I asked.

"We weell have a leettle celebration after we clean up."

Ah, yes. There it was: that *je ne sais quoi*. So comforting.

"And the crate?" I asked.

"Wooden. Like for champagne."

Wooden crates are as rare in rural Connecticut as liberals are in rural Georgia. "Why wooden?"

He gave me that withering look, the one Frenchmen probably practice in the mirror to let you know that no matter how much you study their language, you'll never get the subjunctive right. "Because eet weell look good een zeh photos."

Which got taken one bright summer morning, while his shop was full of customers swilling coffee and eating baguettes. Some said they were honored to be present—like at a birth.

Then the horror set in, just as it would in a delivery room. Bruce and our charcutier snapped on plastic gloves, pried open hunks of muscle at the bone, and dabbed up the hemoglobin-rich fluid that spilled onto the counter.

Turns out, our butcher was going to use the cognac for more than a quaff. He said he needed to wash and sterilize the bone. "Contamination," he explained, wrinkling his nose as he liberally applied the VSOP. Rot could apparently spread up the rifts, particularly along the branching fault lines in the muscles. As we'd soon find out.

He gave the joint a good salting, and Bruce plopped it into the wooden wine crate.

"Now I weell put eet een zeh basement. Een two weeks, we weell see what we have."

And we did. Problem was, he didn't. Unbeknownst to us, he'd left for the beach. August, the French, vacation: You know the drill.

Not that we were blameless. We teach cooking classes on Holland America cruises. We dashed off to Copenhagen for a transatlantic run. But we assumed he would watch . . . someone would watch . . . the ham would be watched by . . .

Two weeks later, we went to the shop and found our charcutier schmoozing his morning customers.

"Shall we check on zeh ham?" he asked us.

The first bell went off in my brain. Shall *we* check? Hadn't *he*?

We walked around the building to the basement doors. The minute he released the lock, I knew something was wrong: a horrible funk, sort of like what comes out of your garbage can if you've forgotten to rinse it out before your summer vacation.

I glanced at Bruce. "What the . . ?"

He shrugged. He's used to these smells. He grew up in New York, a city that makes its own gravy when it rains.

We crept downstairs, the odor becoming more intense—a wet rot, somehow almost viscous.

Ahead lay our champagne crate: up on some boxes, at eye level.

"Out of zeh way of vermeen," our charcutier explained.

He lifted the wire netting—and let out an ear-splitting screech. In the blink of an eye, he was running up the stairs, his hands fluttering in the air, our macho French butcher suddenly morphed into a Parisian schoolgirl.

Our ham was alive with maggots: writhing, swarming.

"What now?" I asked, my hand over my nose.

Bruce hefted the tray and took it out to the dumpster. One tip and it was no more.

But I had to give it one more look. I can't explain why. Suffice it to say, for Wilbur. The apology I gave at the abattoir.

There the ham sat, flung among butcher-shop detritus: livid, pink, and rotten. A complete waste, a foolhardy experiment gone awry—and at the expense of a life.

Back in the shop, our charcutier was among his less odiferous customers. "Eet ees probably zeh last time you weell eat here," he laughed as we walked out.

We trekked south to a valley outside Salisbury, Connecticut, where Alan Cockerline runs Whippoorwill Farm, a grass-fed beef and pork establishment. Alan, a fifty-something hippie-turned-animal-herder, seemed like the voice of reason we needed. Forget blissed-out acid flashbacks; with all the patience of an aging linebacker, Alan summarily dispenses with culinary stupidity. He has this way of rolling back on his heels, crossing his arms, and looking up at the ceiling, as if to say *Are we really having this conversation?*

"First off, you can't leave curing meat unattended," he said. "I watch my bacon every day."

I stuttered something about not knowing about the beach and summer vacation, about assuming someone would . . . "I trusted the guy," I finally said.

Alan would have none of it. "You forgot rule number one: You weren't in control of your food."

I started to walk away. I wanted to blame someone else. Because it's always someone else's fault: liberals, conservatives, Mom, Dad, someone.

But I knew Alan was right. Losing control of our own food? It's pandemic in America.

"We won't next time," I said.

But Alan wasn't done. He grabbed my sleeve. "And temperature," he said. "I know this: You've got to keep a constant temperature."

"How constant?"

He rolled back on his heels. "I'm not making the stuff. You're the food writer. You find out."

I did. Over the next week, I placed phone calls to producers in Italy and the Midwest, looking for the answer.

Which was: "Very constant." The salt moves through the meat at about an inch per week when the temperature is around 40°F. A few degrees colder and the salt won't crawl over the fibers; a few degrees warmer and the meat rots before the salt gets to it. (So much for curing in August.)

Wiser—and fainter, too—Bruce and I went back to the drawing board. But without a pig's leg. We'd only had one of Wilbur's cut so the foot stayed intact. And getting a toe-on, never-been-frozen pig's leg can be quite a challenge. Ask for it at your supermarket and see what they say.

Ever the New Yorker, Bruce found a way around the niceties. He called a wholesale meat supplier. Selling to retail customers off the street is sort of a gray area, but Bruce talked himself into it with a blizzard of words.

By week's end, we had an even larger leg, a 27-pounder, sitting on the counter in our kitchen. Dreydl, our collie, went a little nuts. His tongue lolled to the side of his mouth.

But we had a bigger problem: that temperature thing. It was September 30th—autumn, maples ablaze in the back yard. Where would we get a constant 40°F, day in and day out?

The fridge, of course. Bruce cleared out the one in the back pantry—no mean task for a guy whose idea of economic stability is 127 containers of leftovers—adjusted the temperature control, and prepared to let the meat rest in salt.

It all went swimmingly—except for that damn toe. The leg wouldn't fit with the fridge door closed. Not without a lot of jimmying. And the meat had to lie flat in order to condense evenly as it drained. So picture this: two guys, a big ham, a collie on meat alert, and a refrigerator door that won't shut all the way because a pig's foot is sticking out of the crack.

Bruce had a brilliant idea: If we stood it up on its thick end, we could close the refrigerator door really fast and the ham would fall back down onto its baking sheet with the foot hanging over into one of those in-the-door condiment trays.

Perfect.

Almost. The first time we opened the refrigerator to check on our project, a tray of salty juice and a big ham with a toe came crashing to the floor. Dreydl's tongue lolled again.

We shut him in the basement, cleaned the mess up, and got everything settled, the toe once again caught in the refrigerator door. Oh, well, we thought. We'll have to be more careful.

We were. We watched it, poured off the attendant juices (nasty as they were), and resalted.

About three weeks later, our ham was in its prime. It had condensed, shrunk, lost lots of its "liquid." We were now ready for the next part: hanging. We again needed a constant temperature. This time, about 55°F—a little higher than our fridge can go.

Problem was, we were getting on toward winter. Nightly frosts were strafing the hills. We couldn't very well tie the ham from a garage rafter. First, those freezes would be deadly for the ham. And then there were the vermin. Everybody wants to come inside at that time of year.

So we used our wine cellar. It's in a basement storage room. We cleared out that case of Coffaro Block 4 we'd been saving—just had to drink it—removed the racks, and hung the joint from the toe.

It seemed like a good plan. Except curing hams need air circulation. Which is no problem in a barn in Italy's Po valley, but is of some concern in a basement in Litchfield County, Connecticut. To compensate, we left the door of the wine cooler open during the day and put a fan in the room so air would blow around the ham.

It went OK for the first week or so. But did I mention that our basement is finished? And that we watch TV down there most nights?

Dreydl started hanging out by the storage room door. Quietly at first. Then persistently: a pathetic whimper as he tried to jam his nose in the crack.

Maybe we should finally get that dog fixed, I thought.

And then we, too, noticed it. That slight funk. Not as bad as at the charcuterie. Not rotten this time, just down-at-the-center-of-living-things. Like when you fry a skillet of chicken gizzards. We laughed about it while watching TIVO-ed movies. How funny life has gotten to be! How strange to be curing our own ham!

Which started leaking. Dripping ugly bits of mucusy sludge.

I cleaned them up and put a plate under the ham. And threw the plate out two days later because of more dripped junk. Put another one down there. Threw it out, too. And another. OK, we're gay but we don't have *that* many dishes.

Meanwhile, the smell was getting more intense. Not bad, just very, very present.

"Want to read upstairs tonight?" I asked. "I'm sort of tired of TV."

Then one day, the ham leaked a lot. So much that it overflowed the plate and stained the wine cooler a snotty yellow.

We started reading in the bedroom every night, two floors away from the ham.

I also called and emailed people. Lots of people. *Jamón* producers, Italian trade boards, Romanian ham experts. "That smell—is it right?" I asked.

They all said the same thing: "Yep."

Then one day as I was leaving to run an errand, I gave Bruce a little hug—and noticed it in his clothes. He smelled like meat. And not in a good way. Oh, my God, I thought.

And then another, scarier thought hit me. "Do I smell like that?"

"I didn't want to say anything. Your hair, too."

"I washed it less than an hour ago!"

"Doesn't seem to make a difference."

And that was that. We threw in the towel. We also threw out the wine cellar.

I went back to Alan, my hippie-turned-sage. "People shouldn't make prosciutto at home," he said. "What gave you that idea?"

"Europeans. They've been doing it for centuries."

"What kind of Europeans?"

Well, OK, not the chic ones in Barcelona. Not the sneering ones in Paris. Not the rush-rush-rush boys of Rome.

"In Bulgaria . . ." I started.

"Peasants," he said. "People who have to risk everything to have something to eat. People who don't have modern conveniences."

"Like a grass-fed beef and pork farm just down the road?"

He thumped my chest. "Exactly. Prosciutto isn't pretentious. It's survival, food for the winter. Food writers made it otherwise."

So Bruce and I finally went with discretion, that vaunted part of valor: We bought *prosciutto crudo*, *jamón serrano*, and other bits of European, dry-cured hams for testing these recipes.

⟼ *Section One* ⟻

EUROPE ON A PLATE

The world of European dry-cured hams, smoked or not, is enormous—and ever-expanding as new regional producers apply for EU (European Union) demarcations, support, and control. Some countries, like Italy and Spain, have well-developed artisanal traditions, codified by bureaucrats; others, like Bulgaria and Romania, simply have traditions localized family to family, about the way curry blends are handed down in India.

All that said, there are a bushelful of dry-cured hams that have risen to note on a global scale. All are readily available in the United States—or soon may be after crossing various import hurdles. Here they are in alphabetical order, to dispel any whiff of prejudice.

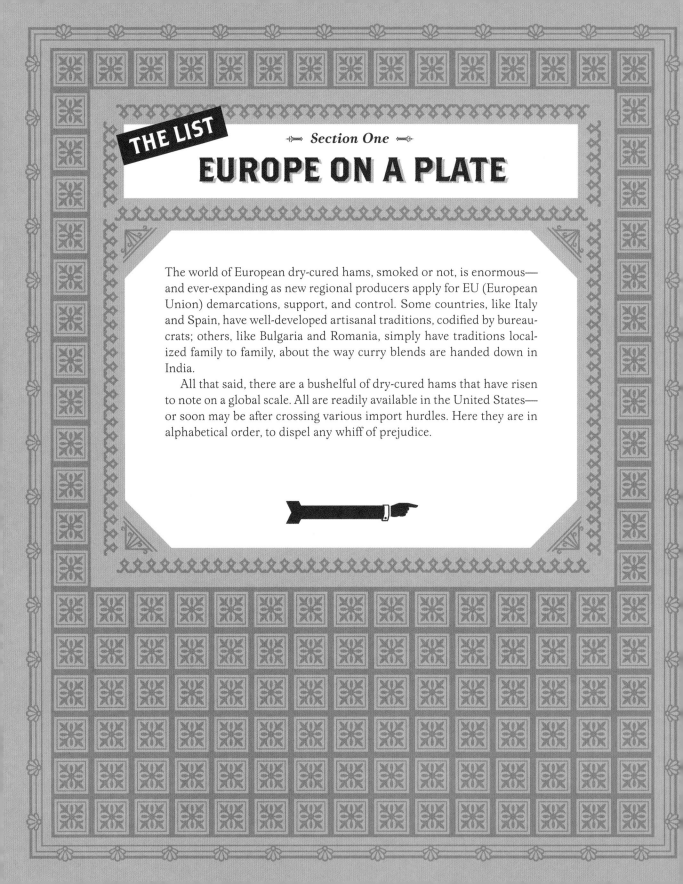

CULATELLO

Many consider this dry-cured ham (Italian, *KOO-lah-TELL-oh*, "little butt," but more vulgar, something like "asslette") the pinnacle of Italian ham-making. From a handful of producers in Zibello, Bussetto (the birthplace of Giuseppe Verdi), and surrounding Emilia-Romagna towns, all serried along the Lombardy border, *culatello* is made from only one part of the ham: the very hind thigh muscle. And only from pigs that have been bred to be much larger (and thus fattier) than those used for *prosciutto crudo* (see below). In traditional production, the meat is boned, salted, spiced, and tied up in a pig's bladder to hold its shape. It is then air-dried in curing sheds that are film-coated in various molds, dust, and grape must, all of which interact with the meat as the mythically deep, cool mists from the Po River drift through the windows. After curing, the hams are stacked in dirt-floored cellars and left to age at least another 10 months. The resulting meat is sweeter than prosciutto, certainly fattier, and mind-blowingly smooth. However, time is not on the side of culatello. Persnickety EU bureaucrats don't like the notion of mists, mold, must, and dirt. And warming weather patterns are tipping the entire region into the furnace. Perhaps as a harbinger of good news, an elite group of American producers have begun making culatello the old-fashioned way (but without those fabled mists). In any event, enjoy culatello in the simplest way imaginable: sliced paper thin. Screw the melon, figs, or any condiments. Just relish the meat.

ELENSKI BUT

This dry-cured ham (Bulgarian, еленски бут, *ay-LAYN-skee BYOOT*, "Elena leg") is a specialty from northern Bulgaria. Despite the nation's accession to the EU, the *elenski but* has not yet incurred various strictures and is thus still produced in truly artisanal fashion—which means quality varies. In traditional production, the hams are first singed to remove any hairs, then salted and summarily dumped in a *postav*, a barrel specifically made for the task. After about 40 days, the hams may be coated with a sour mixture of cornmeal and lime water (calcium hydroxide suspended in water) but are always stitched into bags (to protect against flies) and hung in the open breezes. They are sometimes also lightly smoked, a result not of culinary forethought but of their having been brought into the house at night and hung near the fireplace. The meat has a slightly sour taste with an aromatic, sweet finish.

JAMBON D'ARDENNES

Jambon d'Ardennes (French, *jzahm-BONE dahr-DEN*, "ham from the Ardennes") is a cured, smoked ham from the region of Belgium famous for the Battle of the Bulge. The hams are cured with a mixture of salt and herbs including juniper, thyme, and coriander; they are then smoked over beech or oak boughs until darkly colored. Finally, they are hung for many months, sometimes more than a year, yielding at long last a dense, chewy meat with a mineraly, herbaceous tang. Jambon d'Ardennes is particularly prized for its soft texture (originally a result of the cooler temperatures of northern Europe).

JAMBON DE BAYONNE

This dry-cured, not-smoked ham (French, *jzahm-BONE duh buy-UHN*, "ham from Bayonne") comes from the Basque region of southwestern France and has been a regional delicacy since at least Rabelais' time (around 1530), when he made it one of the meats at Grangousier's feast. The whole process is absurdly standardized: The antibiotic-free pigs must come from one of eight breeds, the pig must never be fed anything containing fish oil (an otherwise common practice along the coast), the meat must be cured near the Ardour River estuary with salt harvested from selected bays, and the curing must happen in conjunction with the weather—laid in salt from early November to late January or so, rubbed with a mixture of pork fat and flour (to retard the drying process) and hung until about May, then air-dried in the warmer summer months until July or so. (These days, some producers get the same effect through artificial climate control.) Sometime during the curing process, the hams may be rubbed with a pimento paste, which gives them their reddish translucence but also imparts a delicate sweetness to the meat that marvelously counteracts its fairly intense saltiness. In other words, all that standardization pays off big-time. Before sale, the hams are stamped with a "Basque cross" (sort of a flowery plus sign) and the word "Bayonne." The cured meat is usually sliced slightly thicker than, say, *culatello*, the better to experience the still tender but decidedly present chew, a texture achieved because of that earlier retardation of the drying process.

JAMBON DE VENDÉE

A bit of a rarity in the ham world, this boneless ham (French, *jzahm-BONE duh vawn-DAY*, "ham from the Vendée region") is first cured with sea salt, then rubbed with pear or plum eau-de-vie. It is lightly smoked over brush and herbs (often rosemary), resulting in a deep red color. The oblong meat is always sliced very thin and has a sweet, herbaceous flavor. Some French writers mistakenly refer to *jambon de Vendée* as a substitute for American bacon; it is in fact a more aromatic substitute for what we Americans call "Canadian bacon" (that is, smoked pork loin).

JAMÓN IBÉRICO

These hams (Spanish, *hah-MOAN ee-BAY-ree-coh*, "Iberico ham") may well be the sui generis of European cured meats. Since 2007, Spain has surpassed Italy in both production and consumption of dry-cured hams. Ibérico hams are made only from the famed *cerdo ibérico* (that is, a specific breed of black pig that thrives in the Dehesa, the vast forests of southwestern Spain) or from pigs that are three-quarters *cerdo ibérico*. These animals are sometimes mistakenly called "black pigs," even though not all are fully black and many other European pigs are black as well (the *noire de Bigorre* in France, for example). The meat is salt-cured for about one day per kilo of weight at slaughter, then washed and air-dried for two to four years (sometimes even longer). This produces a highly prized mineral tang that contrasts nicely against the sweet, nutty finish, with a fine, almost undetectable ghost of saltiness hovering in the well-marbled, deep-red meat. Imagine the texture (but not the taste) of really fine sushi tuna. The finished hams weigh 30 to 40 percent less than they did at slaughter, and the fat will have taken on a rich, golden hue from certain molds (like *Penicillin roqueforti*, the same stuff in the superior French cheese) activated in the protein during the curing process, which occurs naturally in drying rooms with windows that can be opened or shut, depending on the weather. These hams are sometimes colloquially called *pata negra* ("black hoof")—but the name is a bit inaccurate since there are other black-hooved pigs in Europe and not all *cerdo ibérico* have black hooves. Among the most important sub-categories:

- *Jamón ibérico de bellota*, from *cerdo ibérico* pigs fed only a natural diet (grass, roots, grubs) in the Dehesa during the spring and summer and then primarily acorns (*bellota*) from September to February (each pig needs four acres to get enough acorns—the ultimate free-range animal). The salted meat is subsequently air-dried for up to four years (sometimes more) to develop its complex, highly prized, nutty, even somewhat cheesy taste (found particularly in that glorious fat).

- *Jamón ibérico de recebo*, a slightly less dear ham cured from the legs of *cerdo ibérico* that do not gain enough weight from acorns and so are fattened up at the end with a diet of various grains.

- *Jamón ibérico de cebo de campo*, from *cerdo ibérico* that have been fed only a grain diet, no acorns; if the pigs are not allowed to be free-range, the hams are *jamón ibérico de cebo*.

JAMÓN SERRANO

The most readily available, cured, unsmoked ham from Spain, *jamón serrano* (Spanish, *hah-MOAN say-RAHN-oh*, "mountain ham") is made from the haunches of pigs fed a commercial grain diet and is considered inferior to the more precious *jamón ibérico*. The joint is first salted (but minimally, in order that the meat retain a sweet finish when cured), then stacked in much the way *prosciutto crudo* is cured, the resulting pressure on the hams forcing much moisture from between the intercellular layers. The hams are then washed and air-dried for six to eighteen months, often at a high elevation (thus the name). The result is a pale pink, soft ham—a delight on its own, atop a pizza, or in a creamy pasta sauce.

PRESUNTO

Like the Italian *prosciutto*, the word *presunto* (Portuguese, *pray-ZOON-toh*) simply means "ham." However, in English the term has come to demarcate a whole set of dry-cured hams from Portugal, similar to Spanish *jamón serrano* but with more chew, a slightly saltier flavor, and a little tang that's a great match to hard, aged cheeses. Look for specific regional monikers like Chaves or Alentejo (the latter made from those famous *cerdo ibérico*—see above). Some *presunto* have even achieved the coveted but tangled EU designation "PDO" (Protected Designation of Origin)—an assurance of quality, to be sure, but often a bargaining chip among nations in the union, sort of like a Good Housekeeping seal administered by bureaucrats.

PROSCIUTTO CRUDO

Prosciutto (Italian, *proh-SHOO-toh*)—just means "ham"—so it's necessary to differentiate, as we do in this book, between *prosciutto crudo* (*kroo-doh*, "raw"—the cured but still technically raw ham, often sliced thin and draped over melon wedges) and *prosciutto cotto* (*COH-toh*—that is, cooked ham, often used as deli meat for sandwiches and a big part of Chapter 4). There are many regional designations of Italian *prosciutto crudo*: *di Modena, di Norcia, di Capegna* (from Modena, from Norcia, and so forth). The two most famous are *di Parma* and *di San Daniele*. *Prosciutto di Parma* comes from the Emilia-Romagna region, where pig-farming has a long history. Parma's thirteenth-century cathedral doors include a panel devoted to pig slaughter, representing the month of November. The pigs are often fed a diet that includes the leftover whey from Parmigiano-Reggiano production (see page 87); the meat is cured only with salt, left in an 80-percent humidity environment for about one week, then resalted and left again for a couple of weeks. It is then washed, hung, and dried, originally in the region's cool breezes, but in these days of global warming, more via environmental controls. Finally, the ham is coated in a paste of salt, pepper, and fat to slow down the dehydration,

JAMÓN IBÉRICO

then hung for about one year to concentrate into a pale pink, sweet-salty meat with a creamy, off-white fat. A *prosciutto di San Daniele* undergoes a similar transformation but is darker, sweeter, richer, and perhaps a little chewier. It is more highly prized among aficionados; the difference is the result of the salt coming from the Friuli region near Venice and the dehydration process in the less humid, higher-altitude microclimates of that region.

SCHWARTZWÄLDER SCHINKEN

This smoked, dry-cured ham (German, *SHVAHRTS-vell-der SHEEN-kuhn*, "Black Forest ham") comes originally from the hilly, forested region near the university town of Freiburg in southwestern Germany. Because the hams are cold-smoked, the process goes much faster than that for *jamón ibérico* or even *prosciutto crudo*. The meat is dry-cured with salt, garlic, juniper, pepper, and other spices. These spices are actually a modern substitute for an older practice of shellacking the hams in beef blood before smoking, resulting in the characteristically black surface of the hams. After two weeks in the cure, the hams are washed off and hung for another couple of weeks to concentrate the meat as the fibers collapse. The hams are then cold-smoked (at temperatures around 77°F) for several weeks over simmering fir limbs and their sawdust. The resulting meat is quite flavorful, pale red, and lightly marbled with pristine white fat; its taste is bold enough to stand up to a host of preparations (besides being lovely on its own with grapes and dried apricots). One warning: Many hams sold in the United States as "Black Forest hams" are actually just deli meat. While a fine substitute in recipes that call for wet-cured ham (beginning on page 169), these knock-offs bear no resemblance to the real thing.

SPECK

These boneless, smoked, dry-cured hams are a specialty of the Austrian and Italian Tyrol (pronounced *shpehk* or *spehk*, depending on which side of the national divide you buy it on). The hams are dry-cured with salt, crushed juniper berries, bay leaves, nutmeg, and other aromatic spices. The meat is cold-smoked (around 68°F) over beechwood for about a week. *Speck* has a slightly chewy texture and an intense smoky flavor, which makes it a far more luxurious substitute for bacon in many recipes. But the best way to have it may be the simplest: thinly sliced, with horseradish and pickles on dark rye. A word to the wise: in Austria, *Speck* sometimes refers to salted, cured ham fat, similar to Italian *lardo*, a wonderful if heart-stopping indulgence, best in small bites, not piled high on a sandwich.

ŞUNCĂ

These Eastern European hams (Romanian, *SHOON-kah*, simply the word for "ham") are the quintessence of the European artisanal spirit: still made individually, usually just for the farmer and his kin, and cured around Christmastime. The exact spices mixed with the salt differ from family to family; the hams are hung for six to eighteen months and lose about 25 percent of their original weight. Although Romanian *şuncă* is not necessarily smoked, it often in effect is, just by virtue of being hung near the fireplace in the family home. The resulting meat is quite salty, something like an American country ham (see Chapter 3), as well as a little grainy and chewy.

YORK HAM

This dry-cured English ham must be cured and crafted within two miles of the city of York. The smoking (over oak sawdust) takes a little more than two months and results in a grainy, somewhat coarse meat, full flavored but quite salty. Legend has it that the original hams were smoked over the sawdust left from the construction of York Minster, but culinary folklore is rarely a guide to truth, only to provincial jingoism. In truth, these hams are cured with saltpeter (that is, potassium nitrate)—and thus retain their pinkish hue despite the smoking process. They are ready to eat when finished but are often roasted or even boiled to be served with a buttery Madeira sauce.

THE FAMED IBÉRICO PIGS ON THE SPANISH DEHESA

THE BEST COCKTAIL PARTY EVER

Fortunately, Italian *prosciutto crudo* and the other cured European hams don't invite ruin at the table—although, at first blush, a party that involves a whole leg on a table might seem like something out of an early-sixties magazine spread with an off-kilter, Spanish galleon theme.

In truth, you don't have to camp it up. Instead, throw a cocktail party by letting a dry-cured European ham be the centerpiece. One way to go would be to have slices of the ham on a serving platter—Spanish *jamón serrano*, German *Schwartzwälder Schinken*, or French *jambon de Bayonne*. You'll find at least one of these at most high-end supermarkets, or perhaps an Old World deli. In a big city, it's no problem. There's a dizzying array at Dean & Deluca in New York or Central Market in Austin. But we've also found prosciutto crudo in more unlikely places, a telltale sign of its culinary dominance—places like Ardmore, Oklahoma, or Newport, Vermont.

A EUROPEAN HAM PARTY

MAKES 1 GREAT EVENING

Have the butcher cut the ham into paper-thin slices, placing them between layered sheets of wax paper or plastic wrap so they stay fresh. Once home, store the sealed packet in the refrigerator, because the meat's cut cellular layers can now invite airborne bacterial colonization. Since any dry-cured European ham tastes best at room temperature, leave the sealed packet out on your counter for perhaps 30 minutes before the party starts. Unwrap the slices only when you're ready to put them on a platter, preferably furled or delicately crimped so they're easier to pick up and stay moister than when prone. Consider holding back half the slices, still sealed in the packet, until the party really gets rolling.

Or go whole hog. That is, buy a whole dry-cured European ham, the full leg, sometimes with the toe (or hoof) still attached. You'll most likely have to special order the joint, so plan on at least a week's notice for your butcher or market. Also you can check out various online meat suppliers like dartagnan.com or tienda.com.

If you've gone this far, you'll also want a special ham rack for presentation: a wooden plank with a metal, viselike scaffolding to hold the leg in place at the proper carving angle. Screw the toe end of the ham into the vice on the scaffolding so that the meat sits with one thinner side pointing up. Use a long, thin, sharp carving knife to slice off a thin piece of ham along the uppermost surface plane—then take off several more slices of mostly fat to get down to the rich meat underneath. (Don't discard those fat slices; save them back in the freezer to be cubed and used in stews or braises in place of bacon.) Only remove the fat from the area you intend to carve; that fat is what seals and protects the meat.

Eventually, you'll make paper-thin, U-shaped cuts along the top plane of the meat, shaving off slices to stack on a nearby plate. Don't go nuts and carve too much—just a few slices at a time will keep the party going. And don't turn the ham over until you've carved all of one side; the other side should stay intact so the meat stays moist. And remember: the better the ham, the smaller the slice. Fine *jamón ibérico* should be sliced into paper-thin, two-inch bits, like squat rectangles; each piece should just fit onto your tongue so that you can feel the fat melt before you begin to chew. If you'd like to see a video detailing the proper carving technique, check out the one posted on our blog, www.realfoodhascurves.com.

OK, so you've got the ham, sliced or whole. What else do you need in order to make the party a success? Here are some suggestions:

CHECKLIST

✔ First off, invite Charlotte Rampling or Penélope Cruz. If they're not available, try for a few überchic Europeans. Why? When it happens, you'll know.

✔ Have thinly sliced rounds of baguettes or some other crusty bread on hand. For God's sake, don't serve anything soft. You need crunch to complement the meat's velvety texture.

✔ Get a wedge of a hard, aged cheese like Parmigiano-Reggiano (see page 87), an aged Gouda like Boerenkaas, or sheep's-milk Manchego.

✔ Offer lots of little bite-sized fruits like grapes and cherries. They go gorgeously with the meat. And don't forget dried fruits like apricots and figs. Moist, pliable sun-dried tomatoes are also a great addition.

✔ As for wine, try to match your choice to the ham's country of origin. For a German dry-cured ham, choose a sweet Riesling or a Gewürztraminer, a good accompaniment to the salty meat. Or try a Catalonian Cava (a sparkling wine) with *jamón ibérico*.

✔ Don't go nuts shaking cocktails. You'll spend your whole party tending bar. Instead, make pitcher drinks like the ones on the next page.

✔ Put out several condiments to smear on crusty bread (but never on the ham). In fact, the better the ham, the fewer the condiments. That said, these can help clear the palate and offer a little respite from all that meat. Find some to consider on the next pages.

⊲ SANGRIA ⊳

Make this pitcher punch by first bringing ½ cup water; ⅓ cup granulated sugar; 1 medium seedless orange, cut into eighths; 1 medium lemon, thinly sliced; and a cinnamon stick to a simmer in a medium pan over medium-high heat, stirring until the sugar dissolves. Once the mixture is at a boil, take the pan off the heat and cool to room temperature, about 2 hours. Pour the contents into a large pitcher and stir in one 750-milliliter bottle of red wine and ⅓ cup orange juice. Also stir in some pitted Bing cherries; halved, seedless grapes; and perhaps some cubed fresh pineapple—a total of 1½ to 2 cups fruit. Chill in the refrigerator for 1 hour, then serve over ice.

⊲ GINGER PEAR COSMOS ⊳

The ginger in this sweet drink matches perfectly with the cured meat. Stir 3 cups pear nectar; 2 cups vodka; 1 cup Cointreau (an orange-flavored liqueur); ⅔ cup lime juice; 2 tablespoons granulated sugar; and 2 tablespoons ginger juice in a large pitcher. Add ice to the pitcher—but serve the punch in glasses also filled with ice.

⊲ POMEGRANATE CAIPIRINHA ⊳

To turn this on-the-rocks drink into a pitcher punch, put ½ cup granulated sugar (preferably super-fine bar sugar) and 12 small limes, cut into eighths, in a large pitcher. Muddle the limes and sugar by pressing them together with a muddler or the back of a wooden spoon until the sugar has dissolved and the limes are crushed. Stir in 3 cups cachaça (Brazilian sugar-cane rum) and 2 cups unsweetened pomegranate juice. Add ice to the pitcher, but serve the drink in glasses also filled with ice (and, if desired, garnished with mint leaves).

⊲ PEPPERY CAPONATA ⊳

This Sicilian condiment—resembling a thick dip—is made from eggplant bits in a spicy tomato sauce with capers and olives in the mix. It's available jarred at most supermarkets and all Italian delis. But here's an easy version that adds some roasted red peppers to the mix for a little more zip. Cook and stir a cubed (not peeled) 1½ pound eggplant, 1 chopped medium yellow onion, and 3 minced medium garlic cloves with ¼ cup olive oil in a large skillet over medium heat until the eggplant and onion turn golden brown, about 8 minutes. Stir in 1¾ cups canned diced tomatoes; 2 diced, jarred, roasted red peppers or pimentos; 2 tablespoons red wine vinegar; ¼ cup chopped basil leaves; 2 teaspoons minced oregano leaves; 1 teaspoon ground cinnamon; and ½ teaspoon red pepper flakes. Cover, reduce the heat to low, and continue cooking, stirring often, until the tomatoes break down into a sauce and the eggplant is very tender, about 10 minutes. Season with salt and ground black pepper to taste. Serve warm; or chill, covered, in the refrigerator for up to 3 days.

◁| TAPENADE |▷

Look for this olive paste at the deli counter, on the salad bar, or jarred and sold near the olives in your market. If you want to make your own, whir about 2 cups pitted cured black olives, ¼ cup olive oil, a few drained capers, a small quartered garlic clove, a teaspoon or two of lemon juice, and a few grinds of black pepper in a food processor just until the mixture becomes a coarse, grainy paste. (The more traditional method involves rocking a chef's knife endlessly through these ingredients on a cutting board to produce similar results—slightly more toothsome but definitely more labor-intensive.)

◁| FIG GINGER JAM |▷

Mix 7 chopped and stemmed large fresh figs, 1¼ cups sugar, 2½ tablespoons water, 2 tablespoons minced peeled fresh ginger, 1½ tablespoons lemon juice, and a pinch of salt in a large saucepan over medium heat. Stir until the mixture comes to a simmer, then reduce the heat a bit and continue cooking, stirring often, until thick and jamlike, about 12 minutes. Pour this mixture into a glass jar or plastic container and refrigerate for at least 24 hours, or up to 2 weeks.

◁| PICKLED CIPPOLINI |▷

Cippolini onions are notoriously sweet little flattened disks that are often roasted with olive oil. For a ham spread, it may be more satisfying to offer them as pickles, like the Sephardic ones served at Passover. Fill two quart-sized, heat-safe jars with peeled small cippolinis. (The easiest way to peel them is to drop them in boiling water for 30 seconds, drain, and then pinch the onions out of their skins.) Add a peeled garlic clove and a bay leaf to each jar. Then bring 3 cups water, 3 cups white wine vinegar, ¼ cup sugar, and 5 teaspoons salt to a boil in a large saucepan, stirring until the sugar dissolves. Set off the heat for 1 minute, then pour this liquid into the jars, covering the onions. Seal the jars and refrigerate for at least 48 hours, or up to 2 weeks.

◁| CRANBERRY-WALNUT PESTO |▷

Although any pesto will do, we prefer one that errs on the side of a little sweetness. For this version, soften ¼ cup dried cranberries in very hot water for 3 minutes. Drain, then add them to a large food processor fitted with the chopping blade, along with 2 cups packed basil leaves, ½ cup walnut pieces, ¼ cup walnut or olive oil, 1 teaspoon salt, and ½ teaspoon ground black pepper. Process until a smooth, thick paste. If you find the mixture is just too thick, you can drizzle some water into the processor and keep working it until you get a spreadable consistency. Serve at once, or place in a medium container, pour a thin coat of olive oil on top to keep the basil from browning, and refrigerate for up to 2 weeks.

NOSHES

A few of these recipes call exclusively for *prosciutto crudo*; a couple, only for *jamón serrano*—but most can be made with either. Both are cured, unsmoked hams, and some of these recipes even stand up well to a little smoke, such as you'd find in a York Ham or a *Schwartzwälder Schinken*.

That said, it would be a waste to use anything rarer than *prosciutto crudo* or *jamón serrano* (or their North American counterparts). In general, the more money you spend, the more delicate the flavor and the more craft or care needed to create that artisanal ham. To cook with *jambon d'Ardennes* or *jamón ibérico* is frivolity and will squander the subtle, sophisticated flavors.

But even Italian *prosciutto crudo* has its cult, a group of acolytes who will prophesy ruin for those who dare cook with it. Perhaps such feigned horror is inevitable since the meat is still relatively new to the United States, only having returned to this country in 1990 after a 22-year hiatus induced by bureaucratic tangles, trade-talk niceties, and a misunderstanding about how raw *crudo* actually is (see page 110). As in the rest of life, the acolytes are actually neophytes with dictums aplenty: you mustn't heat prosciutto, you must only slice it this way, you mustn't look at its sideways.

But frizzled *prosciutto crudo* is a treat indeed. And *prosciutto crudo* roasted on a pizza gets a little chewy to the tooth, the better to contrast with a soft, melted cheese. Heated in the oven, it is indeed not the same thing as when thinly sliced and laid over melon slices. Nor should it be.

PIZZA QUICK BREAD

MAKES 1 LOAF

With prosciutto in the mix, this quick bread tastes like pizza—a great treat for the kids when they come home from school, or for weekend guests who've announced they intend to stay Sunday night rather than going home as planned.

6 tablespoons olive oil, plus additional for greasing the loaf pan

1 medium leek, white and pale-green part only, halved lengthwise, washed carefully to remove any grit, and very thinly sliced

2 medium green bell peppers, cored, seeded, and diced

1 medium garlic clove, minced

3 ounces thinly sliced *prosciutto crudo* or *jamón serrano*, diced

1½ cups canned reduced-sodium tomato sauce

2 ounces Parmigiano-Reggiano, finely grated (about ¼ cup)

2 teaspoons minced oregano leaves

2 teaspoons minced rosemary leaves

½ teaspoon salt

½ teaspoon freshly ground black pepper

2 large eggs, at room temperature and lightly beaten

1⅔ cups all-purpose flour

2 tablespoons sugar

1½ tablespoons baking powder

1. Set the rack in the middle of the oven; preheat the oven to 350°F. Then lightly oil the inside of a 9-by-5-inch loaf pan, making sure you get the interior corners well coated. (If you're using a glass loaf pan, reduce the oven temperature to 325°F.)

2. Heat a large skillet over medium heat. Add the oil, tilt the skillet this way and that to make sure its interior is well coated with the oil, and then add the leek and bell peppers. Cook, stirring often, until the vegetables have begun to soften, about 8 minutes. Add the garlic and cook for 15 seconds. Dump into a large bowl and cool for 10 minutes.

3. Stir in the diced ham, tomato sauce, cheese, oregano, rosemary, salt, and pepper. Once everything's pretty well blended, stir in the beaten eggs until just combined.

4. Add the flour, sugar, and baking powder. Stir just until there are no traces of flour left, then spread into the prepared loaf pan.

5. Bake until somewhat firm, rounded, and lightly browned, until a toothpick or cake tester inserted into the center of the loaf comes out with no crumbs attached, about 50 minutes. Cool on a wire rack for 10 minutes before unmolding. Either slice up to serve, or continue cooling on the wire rack for 2 hours, then wrap in plastic wrap and store at room temperature for up to 2 days or in the freezer for up to 3 months.

SERRANO TAPAS

MAKES 16 APPETIZER BITES

Tapas (Spanish, TAH-pahs, from the verb "tapar," to cover) are little appetizers, often served with a glass of sherry in a Spanish bar. Their origin is the subject of many culinary legends. In one, King Alfonso X of Castile (1221–1284) commanded wine drinkers to take a little food with their alcohol to maintain good health. In another, the little plates topped glasses of sweet sherry to somehow keep the flies out. (Wouldn't those pests be attracted to the food as well?) No matter: Tapas are a quick bite over drinks with friends. The real secret here is the sherry vinegar, a sweet-sour spark that brightens up the flavors.

8 ounces thinly sliced *jamón serrano* (16 slices)

8 ounces chicken livers, cut into 16 pieces

1 tablespoon olive oil

1 tablespoon unsalted butter

1 tablespoon sherry vinegar

1. Lay a strip of ham on your work surface and place a piece of chicken liver at one end. Fold over each of the long sides of the serrano strip by about ¼ inch, making a thin border on each side, then roll the whole thing up, starting at the end with the liver bit, all to create a neat packet. Set aside and repeat this process to make all the appetizer bits.

2. Heat a large skillet over medium heat. Swirl in the olive oil and melt the butter. Add all the ham packets and brown on all sides, turning often, until lightly golden, about 5 minutes.

3. Transfer the pieces to a serving platter and spritz the vinegar on top.

ROUND OUT THE MEAL

These little savory bites are also great as the protein in a main-course salad. Chop up some frisée (that is, curly endive), radicchio, and romaine, then add some quartered cherry tomatoes, a diced pitted peach, some rinsed canned chickpeas, and some thinly sliced celery or a few sliced radishes (or both). Avoid a creamy dressing or a fruity vinaigrette. Just toss the wrapped bites in the salad with extra virgin olive oil and a little more sherry vinegar, along with some salt and freshly ground black pepper.

SERRANO WRAPPED SCALLOPS

MAKES 36 PIECES IN TOTO, ENOUGH FOR 6 TO 8 FIRST-COURSE SERVINGS

This make-ahead appetizer really brings out the salty, luscious taste of jamón serrano, *paired with scallops in an intense vinaigrette. That said, since the ham is never cooked in this recipe, you could use a more precious version of a dry-cured European ham, even a smoky* Schwartzwälder Schinken *or* Speck.

12 large sea scallops (about 1½ pounds)

2 cups dry white wine

2 tablespoons sherry vinegar

2 tablespoons coarse-grained mustard

1 tablespoon minced shallot

1 tablespoon lemon juice

1 teaspoon mild smoked paprika (see page 24)

½ teaspoon freshly ground black pepper

½ cup olive oil

18 thin slices *jamón serrano*

1. Stand a scallop on its edge and use a very sharp paring knife to slice it into three poker chips. Repeat with the remaining scallops.

2. Bring the wine to a simmer in a large saucepan set over high heat. Reduce the heat so that the wine slowly simmers, then drop in five or six of the scallop disks. Cook until barely firm and opaque, just 1 or 2 minutes; then, with a slotted spoon, transfer from the pan to a bowl and continue poaching more of the disks, never crowding the pan.

3. Whisk the vinegar, mustard, shallot, lemon juice, smoked paprika, and pepper in a large bowl. Whisk in the olive oil in a slow drizzle to make a fairly creamy vinaigrette.

4. Add the poached scallop disks, toss gently, cover, and refrigerate for 12 to 24 hours, stirring gently on occasion to make sure the shellfish keeps getting mixed up with the vinaigrette.

5. Slice each strip of *serrano* in half lengthwise. Set one of those strips onto your work surface, place a scallop disk at one end, and then roll the strip up, encasing the scallop inside. Repeat to create the remaining bites.

BRUSCHETTA DRY-CURED HAM, PEARS, AND PARMIGIANO-REGGIANO

MAKES 12 APPETIZER BRUSCHETTE, TO HOLD 6 PEOPLE AN HOUR OR SO

The best bruschetta is made with slightly stale, crunchy bread. Cut 12 slices off a large baguette or Italian bread, then leave them out on the counter all day. Once they're a little stale, they'll accept the garlic rub without tearing and will also have better tooth when toasted.

Twelve somewhat stale, ½-inch-thick slices French or Italian bread

2 medium garlic cloves, each halved lengthwise

¼ cup toasted almond, walnut, or pecan oil

2 ripe Bartlett pears, cored and thinly sliced

3 ounces *prosciutto crudo* or *jamón serrano*, thinly sliced and then cut into 12 small pieces, each about ¼ ounce

2 ounces Parmigiano-Reggiano, shaved into thin strips with a vegetable peeler

6 tablespoons honey

1. Set the rack in the oven so that it's 4 to 6 inches from the heat source and preheat the broiler.

2. Rub one side of each bread slice with the cut side of one of the garlic cloves. Don't press down and tear the bread; rather, lightly rub the garlic onto the bread so that its oils get into the crumb. You'll notice that the garlic slivers begin to wear down as you rub them on the bread, so use a new one when each gets a little long in the tooth.

3. Drizzle the garlicky side of each bread slice with 1 teaspoon oil.

4. Lay the slices, oil side up, on a large baking sheet or the broiler rack. Toast under the broiler until lightly brown and crunchy, 2 or 3 minutes.

5. Remove the baking sheet or broiler tray from the broiler. Place a few pear slices on each piece of bread; top with a prosciutto slice, draping it over the fruit. Sprinkle some shaved Parmigiano-Reggiano over each piece, then drizzle each bread slice with 1½ teaspoons honey.

6. *Optional.* Return the sheet or tray to the broiler and continue broiling just until the cheese melts, no more than 1 minute. Don't let the cheese brown—just let it soften and run a bit. Remove the tray or sheet from the oven and transfer the bruschette to a wire rack to cool for a minute or so (if you leave them on the tray or sheet, they can get soft and gummy from condensing steam underneath).

THE INGREDIENT SCOOP

Nut oils come in two varieties: toasted and untoasted. The toasted versions are one of a pantry's best-kept secrets. They add a rich, roasted flavor to salads, meats, and even vegetables, drizzled on while still hot. They are quite delicate, so use them as you would toasted sesame oil—at most just a few moments over the heat, lest they volatilize and lose all their aromatic richness. Toasted nut oils can go rancid quite quickly. Always smell before using; they can be stored in the refrigerator for several months.

Parmigiano-Reggiano (Italian, *pahr-MIJ-ee-AHN-oh rehj-ee-AHN-oh*) is a hard Italian cheese, made from part-skim, grass-fed, raw milk produced between April 1st and November 11th of any given year. Its hard, shell-like rind should be stamped with the cheese's name and place of origin for authenticity. Buy a chunk from a larger wheel, a chunk with the rind still attached—but the thinnest part of rind possible to cut down on any extra cost. (Once most of the cheese has been grated away, that rind can be frozen in a sealed plastic bag for up to one year and then tossed into a bean or greens soup to make the broth richer.) Grate the cheese using a microplane, a cheese grater, or the small holes of a box grater.

The quality of the honey will directly affect this dish. Don't just go for standard honey. What about chestnut, oak, or other tree varietals? Or a lovely floral honey, such as ones made from eucalyptus and star thistle in California? (Check out www.marshallshoney.com.)

Remember the rule of thumb for pears, as for almost all fruit: If it doesn't smell like anything, chances are it won't taste like anything. You can ripen pears in a sealed paper bag on the counter for a day or two, but they still won't be as fragrant as ones that arrive at your store ripe because they've had a longer stay on the tree.

We went back and forth as to whether step 6 was necessary. As you can see, there it stands. (In this case, the writer won out over the chef—mostly because the chef doesn't deal with the manuscript. But he does deal with the photos—so the picture shows the recipe without step 6.) If you'd like a fresher taste, by all means skip step 6. The bruschette will certainly be less like a ham-and-cheese and instead have a more fragrant, simple appeal. Still, you'll miss out on all that cheesy gooeyness. Life is all about trade-offs.

QUESADILLA ᴡɪᴛʜ DRY-CURED HAM, BRIE, MANGO, AND ROASTED RED PEPPERS

MAKES 4 BIG QUESADILLAS

A nosh? Maybe. But with a salad on the side, you could easily make a meal out of these well-stocked tortilla sandwiches.

1 ripe, peeled and pitted mango, sliced into thin spears

1 jarred roasted red pepper or pimento, thinly sliced

4 ounces *prosciutto crudo* or *jamón serrano*, thinly sliced and then cut the short way into narrow strips

8 large flour tortillas

8 ounces Brie, at room temperature

4 teaspoons olive oil

1. Gently stir the mango, red pepper, and prosciutto strips in a large bowl.

2. Lay all the tortillas on your work surface. (Don't have that much counter? Work in batches.)

3. Peel the top rind of the Brie, revealing the soft, spreadable cheese inside. Spread each tortilla with one-eighth of this cheese, leaving a ¼-inch border around the perimeter of each tortilla.

4. Top 4 of the tortillas with one-quarter of the mango mixture. Now set one of the untopped tortillas, Brie side down, on each of the ones with the mango mixture. Press gently to seal.

5. Pour 1 teaspoon olive oil in a medium skillet and set it over medium heat. Slip one of the tortilla sandwiches into the skillet; cook until lightly browned, about 4 minutes, turning once halfway through cooking. Transfer to a wire rack to cool a bit and continue making more quesadilla, using 1 teaspoon oil in the skillet each time to heat them.

4. Cut each quesadilla into 4 or 6 wedges to serve.

A CULINARY SMACKDOWN:
PROSCIUTTO CRUDO VS AMERICAN COUNTRY HAM

BOTH ARE DRY-CURED. Both are hung. Both are aged. American country ham producers have long been arguing that their hams are a terrific substitute for *prosciutto crudo*. And so a culinary wrestling match has been brewing for years.

What's the main difference? Italian *prosciutto crudo* is not smoked; most American country hams are.

American country hams also typically use more salt than Italian *prosciutto crudo*. That higher concentration elongates and dries out the protein strands, separating them into threads—thus producing the more granular texture of American country hams. The result is a slightly chewier meat—less velvety, more rustic, and a terrific choice for the center of the table at your next holiday meal.

In the end, American producers shouldn't worry about what arrives from across the pond. Their product is a unique contribution to the global ham scene—and worthy of its own chapter (up next, in fact).

A CLOSER LOOK:
NITRATES AND NITRITES

FOR CENTURIES, salts have preserved hams—and not just that metal we call "table salt" (that is, sodium chloride), but in fact a host of salts, including one in particular: potassium nitrate (KNO_3—or "saltpeter," because medieval alchemists and philosophers found it in rocks: πετρος, *PEHT-rohs*, Greek for "rock"). By the 1600s, Europeans knew that saltpeter was an efficient tool for keeping meat bright, pink, and safe.

How does saltpeter do its work? Actually, the nitrate in the compound doesn't do much; it soon breaks down into nitrite (NO_2) and then into nitric oxide (NO) which binds with residual iron in the meat. This keeps the fat from oxidizing (that is, going rancid), gives the meat its appetizing pink hue, and sops up excess oxygen, thereby suffocating certain bad bugs (like that famed *Clostridium botulinum* we feared when we tried to make our own *prosciutto crudo*).

These days some ham producers forgo the nitrate-breakdown dance and inject the joints with nitrites alone, the quicker to preserve the meat. That said, long-cured meats are enhanced by the slower breakdown of nitrates into nitrites, as the molecules spin out other flavor compounds in the maturing (aka decaying) process.

But nitrites are pretty aggressive compounds and don't only seek out iron for a partner. In fact, they bond with a host of amines (found in the meat's protein), latching onto their molecular chains and producing nitrosamines, some of which are known carcinogens. The jury is still out on exactly how dangerous these compounds are—or whether they react in humans the same way they do in mice. Various governmental agencies remain mute. But a word to the wise may well be sufficient.

In the end, despite their long history in culinary praxis, it's best to limit your consumption of nitrates and nitrites. For dry-cured hams, seek out artisanally cured meats that use only salt and selected spices. It takes longer to produce these hams, but the payoff outweighs all expense and inconvenience.

CHILLED HONEYDEW SOUP WITH FRIZZLED HAM

SERVES 4—OR UP TO 16 IN SHOT GLASSES

This soup could well be the first course of a fancier meal, so Bruce also likes to serve it in shot glasses with a little bit of frizzled ham atop each. Although it's more economical to make those crunchy bits of ham with prosciutto crudo, he's had good success with smoky Schwartzwälder Schinken *and even* Speck. *Frying those little bits of dry-cured ham is a treat indeed—and it adds the perfect salty crunch to this refreshing chilled soup*

THE INGREDIENT SCOOP

Prosciutto crudo is *Prosciutto crudo*. Sounds silly, but in North America "prosciutto" has come to mean any dry-cured meat. We hope that from the long introductory section you've come to realize that *prosciutto crudo* refers only to the Italian dry-cured ham and not to the many other dry-cured hams scattered across the Continent. To be clear: in this book *prosciutto crudo* means only that—the Italian dry-cured ham, not a generic term for all comers. That said, there are American varieties—like the fantastic prosciutto made by Herb and Kathy Eckhouse at La Quercia in Iowa—that can stand in for the Italian *prosciutto crudo* in these recipes. But by and large, we mean one thing, not a category.

One 3-pound honeydew, seeded, rind removed, the flesh cubed

¼ cup packed basil leaves

3 tablespoons lime juice

¼ teaspoon salt

1 cup sweet white wine such as a Riesling, Auslese, or even a Spätlese, plus a little more if necessary

1 tablespoon vegetable oil

4 ounces thinly sliced, dry-cured European ham, either an unsmoked ham like *prosciutto crudo* or a smoky one like *Speck*

½ teaspoon caraway seeds, lightly ground in a spice grinder or crushed in a mortar with a pestle

1. Place the honeydew cubes, basil, lime juice, and salt in a large blender or a food processor fitted with the chopping blade and blend or process until fairly smooth.

2. Add the wine and continue blending or processing until smooth, scraping down the sides of the canister to make sure there are no lurking chunks.

3. Either cover and place the blender canister in the refrigerator for 6 to 12 hours, or pour the soup from the processor into a large bowl, cover, and place in the refrigerator for the same amount of time.

4. Heat a large skillet over medium heat, add the oil, tip the skillet to coat its bottom, and add the ham. Fry, stirring once in a while, until the slices are crisp and lightly browned. Transfer them to a cutting board and chop them into little bits.

5. Check the soup just before serving. Because of various enzymes, it may have turned foamy and thick. If so, stir it down and thin it out with a little additional wine.

6. Pour the chilled soup into serving bowls or shot glasses. Top each serving with some frizzled ham bits, then dust each with a little of the ground caraway seeds.

HAMMY REUBEN BITES

MAKES 4 PANINI, WHICH CAN BE CUT INTO LITTLE BITS AND SERVED AS PART
OF A BIGGER COCKTAIL-PARTY SPREAD

A reuben is a belt-busting deli sandwich with corned beef and sauer-
kraut. Here, Bruce has bred it with a panino, a classic Italian sand-
wich, to create this blowout sandwich, best in small bites. If you have
a panini maker, by all means use it (according to the manufacturer's
instructions). This recipe is written for the old-fashioned method:
pressing the sandwich down in the skillet with some sort of heavy
weight.

8 slices ciabatta; or 4 ciabatta rolls, halved as for a sandwich; or 8 slices thick-cut country-style bread

¼ cup deli-style mustard

8 thin slices Swiss cheese

8 thin *prosciutto crudo* or *jamón serrano* slices

1 cup purchased sauerkraut, preferably the stuff that comes in bags in the refrigerator or deli case of your market, squeezed dry

2 tablespoons olive oil

4 teaspoons unsalted butter

ROUND OUT THE MEAL

These hearty bites are great with a radish slaw. Shred 8 medium radishes and a cored yellow bell pepper through the large holes of a box grater and into a salad bowl. Add two thinly sliced celery ribs, then mix in 3 table-spoons mayonnaise, 2 table-spoons lime juice, and ½ teaspoon ground cumin, as well as some salt and ground black pepper to taste.

1. To build one of the sandwiches, put 2 bread slices or 1 halved roll, cut side up, on your work surface. Spread 1½ teaspoons mustard over each slice or each cut side of the roll; then top one slice of bread or half with a piece of cheese, a slice of prosciutto (folded to fit), and ¼ cup sauerkraut. Make a sandwich by topping with the other slice of bread or the top of the roll mustard side down, then set aside and make three more.

2. Put 1 tablespoon oil and 2 teaspoons butter in a large skillet, then set it over medium heat until the butter melts, tilting and turning the skillet to make sure its cooking surface is fully coated in fat.

3. Place 2 sandwiches in the skillet. Gently press down on them with the flat lid of another skillet, saucepan, or pot. Or wrap two bricks in aluminum foil and place one on top of each sandwich to weight it down. Cook for about 3 minutes, until nicely browned, then use a big spatula to flip the sandwiches and keep cooking and pressing for about 3 minutes more, until uniformly browned. Be careful: They aren't sealed, so they can fall apart when they're turned over. It's no big deal—just quickly rebuild the sandwich and get it back in the skillet. Transfer the panini to a wire rack to cool slightly and repeat steps 2 and 3 with the other 2 panini.

4. Once all 4 sandwiches have been made, use a serrated knife to slice them into wedges or bite-sized bits, to fit best on an appetizer tray.

HAM AND POTATO SAVORY PANCAKES

MAKES ABOUT A DOZEN FRIED PANCAKES

These savory, crunchy pancakes resemble Hanukkah latkes (if they were ever made with pork). If you want, garnish them with sour cream and even a little salmon caviar for a crunchy starter to a more formal dinner—or a terrific breakfast. Use the large holes of a box grater to shred the potatoes and apple.

2 pounds yellow-fleshed potatoes such as Yukon Golds, peeled and shredded

1 medium sweet apple such as a Gala, peeled, cored, and shredded

2 large eggs, at room temperature and lightly beaten

6 ounces thinly sliced *prosciutto crudo* or *jamón serrano*, diced

½ cup matzo meal

¼ cup minced chives or the green part of scallions

¼ teaspoon salt, plus additional as needed

Peanut oil for frying, 6 cups or perhaps more

1. Working in small batches, squeeze the potato shreds dry over the sink, getting out as much excess moisture as you can.

2. Place the shreds in a bowl and stir in the shredded apple, eggs, ham, matzo meal, chives, and salt.

3. Pour the oil into a large skillet until it's about $1/2$ inch deep. Heat over medium heat until the surface of the oil is wiggly with small ripples.

4. Scoop up about $1/4$ cup of the potato mixture and slide it into the very hot oil. The batter will flatten a bit in the oil. Add a few more pancakes, $1/4$ cup each time—but take care not to crowd the skillet.

5. Fry until golden on both sides, about 10 minutes, turning once. Transfer to a wire rack, season lightly with salt, and continue making more of the pancakes.

SERRANO FRITTERS

MAKES ABOUT 1½ DOZEN SMALL FRITTERS

There's no reason to get crazy when you're forming these popper-bites, just make little malformed bundles that fall off the spoon into the hot oil. Have a creamy dressing on the side for dipping—although we've also been known to serve them up with a little bowl of barbecue sauce or even sambal (page 62).

1 cup water

7 tablespoons unsalted butter, cut into several pieces

1¼ cups all-purpose flour

4 large eggs, at room temperature

8 ounces grated Parmigiano-Reggiano

3 ounces *jamón serrano*, minced

¼ cup chopped parsley leaves

1 jarred roasted red bell pepper or pimento, minced

6 cups peanut oil

1. Heat the water and butter in a large saucepan set over medium heat.

2. Once the butter has melted, add the flour all at once, then stir with a wooden spoon until the mixture forms a sticky dough.

3. Continue stirring over the heat to dry the dough out, until it leaves a thin coating on the insides and bottom of the pot, about 5 minutes.

4. Scrape the dough out of the saucepan and into a large bowl. Cool for 20 minutes.

5. Beat in the eggs one at a time with an electric mixer at medium speed. Continue beating until smooth, then scrape down and remove the beaters. Stir in the cheese, ham, parsley, and red bell pepper.

6. Clip a deep-frying thermometer to the inside of a large saucepan or a large sauté pan and pour in the oil. The thermometer's bulb should be immersed in the oil without touching bottom. Turn the heat to medium-high and bring the oil to 375°F.

7. Drop the dough by rounded tablespoonfuls into the hot oil, a few balls at a time. Fry until golden brown, about 3 minutes, turning occasionally with a couple metal spoons. Transfer to a wire rack and continue making more of the fritters, taking care never to crowd the pan, so that everything fries evenly and quickly. Also watch the oil's temperature and adjust the heat up or down to maintain a fairly constant 375°F.

BRUSCHETTA with DRY-CURED HAM AND ARTICHOKE PESTO

MAKES 12 APPETIZER BRUSCHETTE

Consider making a double batch of this aromatic, flavorful pesto and keeping some back in the fridge for a quick pasta lunch in the days ahead.

Twelve ½-inch-thick slices French or Italian bread

One 9-ounce package frozen artichoke hearts, thawed and squeezed over the sink to extract any excess moisture

½ cup packed basil leaves

¼ cup toasted walnuts

¼ cup extra virgin olive oil

2 medium garlic cloves, quartered

1 teaspoon salt

½ teaspoon freshly ground black pepper

3 ounces *prosciutto crudo* or *jamón serrano*, thinly sliced and then cut into 12 small pieces, each about ¼ ounce

1. Set the broiler rack about 4 inches from the heat source and preheat the broiler.

2. Lay the bread slices on a baking sheet or the broiler tray; broil until lightly browned and crunchy, perhaps 2 minutes. For even crunchier bruschette, consider turning the slices over and broiling the other side for 1 or 2 minutes. But be careful: If the bread is too crunchy (yes, apparently there is such a thing), the bruschette will be ridiculously fragile and will shard all over everyone's party clothes at first bite. Once toasted, transfer the bread slices to a wire rack so they don't steam as they cool.

3. Process the squeezed artichoke hearts, basil, walnuts, olive oil, garlic, salt, and pepper in a large food processor fitted with the chopping blades, scraping down the sides occasionally so that everything gets into contact with the blade. If you don't have a food processor, you can make the pesto in a large blender; put everything except the artichoke hearts in at first to get things moving over the blades, then blend those artichoke hearts in a few at a time, maybe adding 1 or 2 tablespoons of water if you notice things aren't getting ground up.

4. Top each bread slice with 2 tablespoons pesto.

5. Fold and crimp the ham pieces decoratively over the pesto on the bruschetta.

TESTERS' NOTES

To toast walnuts, place them in a dry skillet over medium-low heat for about 7 minutes, tossing occasionally so none get too browned.

If you're going to make extra and use this pesto for anything that requires it to be heated—say, as a pizza topping or spooned into a stew at the last second as a quick thickener—then forgo toasting the walnuts. The already toasted oils can turn quite bitter if overheated.

PROSCIUTTO BREAD

MAKES 1 LOAF

This bread will be the centerpiece of any brunch, provided you've got condiments like tapenade (page 81) and some deli mustard as spreads.

⅔ cup warm water, between 105°F and 115°F

One ¼-ounce package (2¼ teaspoons) active dry yeast

½ teaspoon sugar

1 large egg, at room temperature and lightly beaten in a small bowl

1 tablespoon olive oil, plus more as needed for greasing

¼ teaspoon freshly ground black pepper

⅛ teaspoon salt

2 cups bread flour, plus more if necessary

3 ounces thinly sliced *prosciutto crudo*, sliced into tiny threads

⅓ cup chopped, pitted cured black olives

1 tablespoon minced, stemmed rosemary leaves

1. Mix the warm water, yeast, and sugar in a large bowl or in the bowl of a stand mixer if you're going to use one. Set aside until the yeast turns frothy and foamy, about 5 minutes. If it doesn't, either the yeast had gone bad or the water was the wrong temperature—so throw it out and start again.

2. Stir in the egg, olive oil, pepper, and salt.

3. *If you're working with a stand mixer*, attach the dough hook, snap the bowl into place, and add the flour, prosciutto, olives, and rosemary. Beat at low speed until a thick but still pliable dough forms. Should the dough start crawling up the hook or appear too sticky, add a little more flour, in perhaps 2-tablespoon increments, just until the dough is soft and pliable. Continue beating with the dough hook for 10 minutes, until the dough is soft and shiny, about as smooth as a baby's cheek.

If you're working by hand, pour in 1 cup of the bread flour and stir well. Then add the remaining flour, the prosciutto, olives, and rosemary. Stir a few times, then get your cleaned hands in the bowl and start working the dough until it begins to cohere. Dust a clean, dry work surface with a little flour and turn the dough out onto it. Dust your hands with flour and knead the dough by digging the heels of your hands into the dough while slightly twisting them this way and that, refolding the dough repeatedly onto itself as you knead so its surface keeps changing and getting stretched. If you notice the dough's turning sticky, knead in a little extra bread flour, just until you can work the dough without its sticking to your fingers and palms. Knead about 12 minutes, working efficiently and unswervingly.

4. Dab a little olive oil on a paper towel and wipe it around a large clean bowl to oil the insides. Gather the dough into a compact ball and set it in the bowl. Then turn the dough over so that the oiled side is now up. Cover the bowl with plastic wrap or a clean kitchen towel and set aside in a warm (75°F to 85°F), draft-free place to rise until doubled in bulk, about 1 hour.

5. Grease and flour a large baking sheet. Then plunge your fist into the dough to punch it down and turn it out onto a lightly floured, clean, dry work surface. Shape it into a football loaf, tapered at either end and thicker in the middle, about 10 inches long. Set the loaf on the prepared baking sheet, cover with a clean kitchen towel, and set aside in that warm, draft-free place until again doubled in bulk, about 40 minutes.

6. Meanwhile, set the rack in the center of the oven and preheat the oven to 400°F.

7. Uncover the loaf and slash its top surface with three diagonals, using a razor or a very sharp, very thin knife.

8. Place the loaf on its baking sheet in the oven and bake until browned and hollow-sounding when tapped, about 40 minutes. Cool on the baking sheet for 2 or 3 minutes, then transfer to a wire rack to cool at least 10 minutes before slicing. To store the bread, let it cool to room temperature, then wrap it in a clean kitchen towel and leave it on the counter overnight—or else seal the loaf in a zip-closed plastic bag and freeze it for up to 3 months (thaw at room temperature on the counter before serving).

TESTERS' NOTES

One persistent problem with yeast breads: A mixing bowl is too cold from the get-go, thereby chilling off the liquid and causing the yeast to fail. Before you begin a recipe like this one, take the chill off the bowl up by filling it with warm tap water and then wiping it out.

Where in your house is this fabled warm, draft-free place suitable for bread-rising? In ours, it's in the boiler room near the hot-water heater. In yours, it might be the back of a pantry, or perhaps the corner of the kitchen near the stove, or even the floor near a radiator in the winter (provided you don't have a collie in your house).

MEALS

There are two ways to get *prosciutto crudo*, *jamón serrano*, and other dry-cured hams into main courses:

→ THE FIRST WAY ←

They're often used as the wrapping or casing of a dish: around a meatloaf or as a cup for shirred (that is, baked) eggs. Since the meat is cured and dried, it's durable, and a significant amount of internal fat will slowly melt and caramelize into a chewy crust.

→ THE SECOND WAY ←

They're also frequently chopped to be tossed into pasta dishes or onto pizza. Prosciutto in pasta doesn't meet with favor among all Italian cooks, but the culinary compromise was probably one of those things that happened first in America and made its way back to Italy in a kind of bassackwards crossculturalism. Italian-American chefs could only get mass-produced American prosciutto before 1990, so the stuff found its way into foods without the encomia of the European real deal. Once real *prosciutto crudo* made its way onto the American market, the techniques were already well established.

PASTA ✠ *PROSCIUTTO CRUDO, PEAS, AND PARMIGIANO-REGGIANO*

MAKES 4 SERVINGS

We've played around with a lot of dry-cured European hams, and this recipe has become one of those go-to lunches at our house. It's pretty much of a classic anyway. The one trick? Make sure the pasta is slightly underdone when first cooked—it will cook a little more in the sauce.

¼ cup olive oil

6 medium garlic cloves, minced

1 medium shallot, minced

1 teaspoon red pepper flakes

6 ounces thinly sliced *prosciutto crudo*, diced

2 cups fresh shelled peas or frozen peas (no need to thaw)

½ cup reduced-sodium, fat-free chicken broth

1 pound dry linguine or fettuccini, cooked and drained according to the package instructions

3 ounces finely grated Parmigiano-Reggiano (see page 87)

½ teaspoon freshly ground black pepper

1. Heat a large skillet over medium heat, then swirl in the oil. Add the garlic and cook just until frizzling well at the edges, no more than 30 seconds.

2. Toss in the shallot and red pepper flakes. Cook, stirring often, until softened and very aromatic, no more than 2 minutes.

3. Add the *prosciutto crudo* pieces and continue cooking and stirring until they're browned at the edges, about 2 minutes.

4. Pour in the peas and continue cooking for 1 minute. Then add the broth and bring the sauce to a substantial simmer.

5. Add the cooked pasta and toss well so that everything gets mixed up in the noodles.

6. Sprinkle in the cheese and pepper. Toss just until the cheese melts and coats the noodles.

THE INGREDIENT SCOOP

The history of **olive oil** could fill a book—and the current trade disputes, a bureaucrat's life. Suffice it to say that all olive oil is not equal. "Extra virgin olive oil" seems like a moniker that should assure quality. It does not. The United States recognizes only four categories of olive oil: fancy, choice, standard, and substandard. All other labelings are mere window-dressing stateside. What's more, even country-of-origin labels can be troublesome, since Spanish olives make up 40 percent of the world's production, are imported to Italy, and find their way into bottles labeled "Italian olive oil." Is there anything wrong with Spanish olives? Of course not. But with deceptive labels? Emphatically yes.

What, then, to do? A well-stocked larder should have two bottlings. One should be a fragrant, sturdy oil for sautéing, roasting, and braising: not of the highest quality, but certainly with the tangy, sweet perfume of olives. Avoid bottlings that use words like "from refined olives"—which means the oil was probably extracted chemically from fermented, rotten, or already pressed olives. The larder's second bottle should be a more precious oil, one that makes the same claims but is also far more aromatic—and, in general, more costly.

Look for bottlings that claim the oil is made from "hand-picked olives" or is "first cold pressed." And do a taste test before plunking down $20 or more for a bottle. Beyond that, know your supplier. The marketplace can be harsh and unforgiving.

SHIRRED EGGS
in *PROSCIUTTO CRUDO* CUPS

MAKES 6 SERVINGS

Shirred (shuhrd) eggs are baked in little cups until the whites are set. Problem is, the oven's heat can toughen egg whites dramatically. The solution? A little fat protects the delicate protein chains. With a salad and a glass of red wine, this easy entrée makes an elegant meal.

¼ cup heavy or whipping cream

2 tablespoons minced chives or the green part of a scallion

2 tablespoons minced rosemary leaves

Unsalted butter for greasing the muffin tin

12 paper-thin *prosciutto crudo* slices

6 large eggs, at room temperature

½ teaspoon freshly ground black pepper

TESTERS' NOTES

Unfortunately, there's no such thing as a "standard" muffin tin. The tin used here should have indentations that hold between ½ and ⅔ cup liquid. The prosciutto may puff up a bit as it bakes in step 4. Just press it back into place with a spoon before adding the cream and eggs.

1. Warm the cream, minced chives, and the rosemary in a small saucepan over medium heat just until little bubbles ring the inside of the pan, 3 or 4 minutes. Cover and set aside off the heat for 30 minutes to steep.

2. Meanwhile, set the rack in the middle of the oven and heat the oven up to 350°F. Lightly butter 6 indentations in a standard muffin tin, or six ½-cup oven-safe ramekins.

3. Line each indentation or ramekin with 2 *prosciutto crudo* slices, crimping and overlapping them to create the outline of the indentation as well as a little lip on each. If necessary, tear the strips so they fill the indentations without any gaps or holes.

4. Set the tin in the oven or the ramekins on a baking sheet and then in the oven. In either case, bake until the prosciutto begins to get crisp at its edges, about 15 minutes.

5. Transfer the very hot muffin tin or the tray with the ramekins to a wire rack and divide the cream mixture among the indentations, a scant tablespoon in each cup.

6. Crack an egg into each indentation, then top each egg with pepper. Set the tin or tray with its ramekins back into the oven and bake just until the eggs are set, about 8 minutes for a softer yolk and 12 minutes for a more set yolk.

PIZZA ⚒ DRY-CURED HAM AND CLAMS

MAKES 1 PIZZA

Ham and shellfish are a typical Iberian combination—although Bruce tested this recipe with Speck *and the results were quite brilliant. For the best taste, check out pasteurized, shucked clams at your supermarket's fish counter. Failing that, you can use the more readily available canned clams (a 6 ¹/₂-ounce can should do the trick), but the taste will be ever so much stronger with canned.*

2 tablespoons olive oil, plus a little extra for greasing the baking sheet

4 medium garlic cloves, minced

Up to ½ teaspoon red pepper flakes

About ⅔ cup shucked clam meat

4 ounces thinly sliced *prosciutto crudo, jamón serrano,* or even smoky *Speck,* diced

3 tablespoons red wine

3 tablespoons chopped parsley leaves

3 tablespoons chopped shelled hazelnuts

1 pound purchased pizza dough (if frozen, thaw overnight in the refrigerator); or one 16-inch prebaked plain pizza crust

2 ounces finely grated Parmigiano-Reggiano (see page 87)

1. Set the rack in the center of the oven and get the oven heated up to 450°F.

2. Set a large skillet over medium heat for a couple minutes, then swirl in the oil so that the skillet's bottom is well coated.

3. Toss in the garlic and red pepper flakes. Cook, stirring all the while, for about 30 seconds. Don't stand right over the skillet—those chile oils can volatilize and burn your eyes. To err on the side of safety, make sure the hood vent is on or open a window in your kitchen.

4. Add the clams and ham. Cook until the ham is very lightly browned and frizzled at the edges, about 2 minutes.

5. Pour in the wine and bring to a full simmer. Continue cooking until the wine has reduced to a thick glaze, about 1 minute. Stir in the parsley and nuts, then set the skillet aside off the heat.

6. Dab a little oil on a wadded-up paper towel and use it to grease a large baking sheet. Lay the fresh dough on the sheet; dimple it with your fingertips as you begin pressing and pulling it into an irregular rectangle, about 11 by 7 inches. If you're working with a prebaked crust, you can skip this step entirely—just set the thing right on an ungreased baking sheet.

7. Spread the contents of the skillet over the dough, leaving a $1/2$-inch border around the perimeter. Top with the cheese.

8. Bake until the crust is firm and lightly browned, about 18 minutes. Transfer the pie on its baking sheet to a wire rack and cool for 10 minutes before slicing into squares or irregular pie wedges.

ROUND OUT THE MEAL

A good pie needs a good salad—and this salad needs a healthy shot of vinegar among the chopped lettuce, shredded carrots, and cubed cucumbers. So we prefer to dress the mix with a sherry vinaigrette, a little more piquant and zippy than the standard balsamic or white wine vinegar dressing. In a small bowl, whisk together 1½ tablespoons sherry vinegar, ¼ teaspoon stemmed thyme leaves, ¼ teaspoon salt, ¼ teaspoon freshly ground black pepper, and 1 medium garlic clove, crushed through a garlic press. Whisk in ⅓ cup extra virgin olive oil in a slow, steady stream to form an opaque, somewhat thickened vinaigrette.

PIZZA 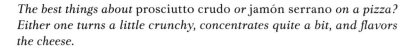 DRY-CURED HAM AND ARTICHOKES

MAKES 1 PIE (DOUBLE OR TRIPLE THE RECIPE IF YOU'VE GOT KIDS IN THE HOUSE)

The best things about prosciutto crudo *or* jamón serrano *on a pizza? Either one turns a little crunchy, concentrates quite a bit, and flavors the cheese.*

THE INGREDIENT SCOOP

To seed a **Roma or plum tomato**, first cut in half lengthwise. Holding it over the sink, run your finger into the chambers to dislodge the seeds and their watery packets. Why go to all this trouble? Those very packets will bog the pizza down, turning the crust into a gummy nightmare.

TESTERS' NOTES

If you're using a prebaked pizza crust, search for one without other spices or toppings, even grated cheese. The plainer the better for this pie, so the taste of the ham and the balance of other flavors are not overshadowed.

Olive oil for greasing the baking sheet

1-pound purchased pizza dough from the supermarket or a pizza parlor (if frozen, thaw overnight in the refrigerator); or one 16-inch prebaked plain pizza crust

2 ounces mozzarella, grated

2 small Roma or plum tomatoes, seeded and diced

10 basil leaves, shredded

One 9-ounce package frozen artichoke hearts, thawed and squeezed of all excess moisture

3 ounces *prosciutto crudo* or *jamón serrano*, thinly sliced and then diced

1 ounce finely grated Parmigiano-Reggiano (see page 87)

½ teaspoon dried oregano

½ teaspoon red pepper flakes

1. Set the rack in the middle of the oven and preheat the oven to 400°F.

2. Dab some olive oil on a wadded-up paper towel and use it to grease a large baking sheet. Lay the fresh dough on the sheet; dimple the dough with your fingertips as you begin to press it out into a rectangular shape to fit the baking sheet. Continue stretching and pulling the dough until it's a rough 6 ½-by-10-inch rectangle. If you're working with a prebaked crust, you can skip this step entirely—just set it right on an ungreased baking sheet.

3. Sprinkle the grated mozzarella evenly over the dough, leaving a ½-inch border around the perimeter. Top with the diced tomato and the basil.

4. Slice the artichoke hearts into halves the long way and sprinkle these over the pie. Top with ham; then sprinkle the Parmigiano-Reggiano, oregano, and red pepper flakes over the other toppings.

5. Set the pie on its baking sheet in the oven and bake until the cheese has melted and the crust is firm to the touch, about 18 minutes. Transfer the pie on its baking sheet to a wire rack and cool for 5 to 10 minutes before you slice it into squares or wedges.

COBB SALAD *SPECK*

MAKES ABOUT **6** SERVINGS

While we recommend a smoked German ham for this main-course salad (and Schwartzwälder Schinken *would work as well), you could easily use a not-smoked* presunto, prosciutto crudo, *or* jamón serrano *for a less complicated taste. The only caveat is this: The ham should be bought in somewhat thicker slices so you can cut it into cubes at home. Or try it with bits of leftover cooked American country ham (Chapter 3) or a cooked, wet-cured ham (Chapter 4).*

SLASH THE SHOPPING LIST

You can skip steps 2 and 3 if you buy a rotisserie chicken at your supermarket, remove the skin from over the breasts, and chop the meat of those breasts before adding it to the bowl. As an added bonus, you might find hard-cooked eggs on the salad bar at your market, too—thereby sparing you from making them yourself, as in step 1.

2 large eggs

2 medium garlic cloves

2 boneless, skinless chicken breasts

½ teaspoon salt

½ teaspoon freshly ground black pepper

1 tablespoon olive oil

Two ¼-inch thick slices *Speck*, diced

10 cups chopped lettuce

½ cup sun-dried tomatoes, chopped

One 9-ounce package frozen artichoke hearts, thawed and squeezed dry of excess moisture

2 ounces Parmigiano-Reggiano (see page 87), shaved into thin strips

1 tinned anchovy

¼ cup red wine vinegar

2 teaspoons Worcestershire sauce

1 teaspoon Dijon mustard

⅔ cup olive oil

1. Place the eggs in a medium saucepan, cover with water until it's 2 inches over the eggs, and bring to a boil over medium-high heat. Cook for 2 minutes, then cover and set aside off the heat for 7 minutes.

2. Meanwhile, slice 1 garlic clove in half lengthwise and rub the cut parts over the chicken breasts. Also season them with salt and pepper.

3. Set a large skillet over medium heat, add the oil, then slip in the chicken breasts. Cook, turning a couple times, until an instant-read meat thermometer inserted into the thickest part of one breast registers 165°F, about 8 minutes.

4. Transfer the chicken breasts to a cutting board and put the diced ham in the skillet. Cook, stirring often, until crisp, about 4 minutes.

5. Transfer the *Speck* pieces to a large bowl, then cut up the chicken breasts and add them as well.

6. Peel the eggs and roughly chop them. Add them to the salad bowl along with the lettuce, sun-dried tomatoes, artichoke hearts, and cheese.

7. Push the anchovy fillet and the remaining garlic clove through a garlic press and into a large bowl. Whisk in the vinegar, Worcestershire sauce, and mustard. Then whisk in the olive oil in a slow, steady stream to make a creamy vinaigrette. Pour the dressing over the salad and toss to serve.

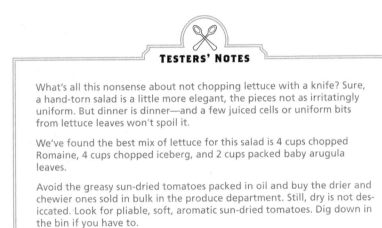

TESTERS' NOTES

What's all this nonsense about not chopping lettuce with a knife? Sure, a hand-torn salad is a little more elegant, the pieces not as irritatingly uniform. But dinner is dinner—and a few juiced cells or uniform bits from lettuce leaves won't spoil it.

We've found the best mix of lettuce for this salad is 4 cups chopped Romaine, 4 cups chopped iceberg, and 2 cups packed baby arugula leaves.

Avoid the greasy sun-dried tomatoes packed in oil and buy the drier and chewier ones sold in bulk in the produce department. Still, dry is not desiccated. Look for pliable, soft, aromatic sun-dried tomatoes. Dig down in the bin if you have to.

ORECCHIETTE WITH SAGE, ROASTED GARLIC, CAULIFLOWER, AND *PROSCIUTTO CRUDO*

MAKES 4 MAIN COURSES OR 6 FIRST COURSES OF A LARGER MEAL

Orecchiette *(oar-EHK-kee-AY-tay) are little bits of pasta shaped like small ears (*orecche* in Italian). You could substitute other pasta types, of course—*farfalle *(or bow ties) come straight to mind. The real stars of this dish are the garlic and cauliflower, roasted in a 9-by-13-inch baking pan until browned, caramelized, and utterly irresistible.*

1 garlic head, broken into its cloves without peeling them, the papery shell and inner core discarded

3½ cups cauliflower florets, cut into bite-sized bits

3 tablespoons olive oil

4 ounces thinly sliced *prosciutto crudo*, diced

1 tablespoon minced sage leaves

12 ounces *orecchiette*, cooked and drained according to the package instructions

2 tablespoons dry white wine or dry vermouth, maybe a little more

2 to 3 ounces finely grated Parmigiano-Reggiano (see page 87)

1. Preheat the oven to 425°F.

2. Place the unpeeled garlic cloves in a 9-by-13-inch baking pan and roast for 20 minutes.

3. Toss the cauliflower florets with the olive oil, then pour them into the baking dish and toss well. Continue roasting, stirring occasionally, until the florets are lightly browned and the garlic cloves are soft, about 20 minutes more. Transfer the baking dish and its vegetables to a wire rack and cool for a few minutes, just until you can handle those garlic cloves.

4. Squeeze the soft garlic pulp out of its papery hulls and back into the baking dish. Stir in the diced prosciutto and the minced sage. Set the pan back in the oven and continue roasting just until the prosciutto begins to sizzle, about 10 minutes.

5. Transfer the baking dish back to the wire rack and stir in the cooked pasta, wine, and cheese until the cheese melts. If you notice that the mixture is a little dry, you can add a splash or two more of the wine, just to make sure everything's moist but certainly not soupy. Serve the dish right out of the baking pan.

TESTERS' NOTES

To get the florets off a cauliflower head, remove the stems and leaves. (These, by the way, are fully edible but quite tough, so they're best in soups and stews.) Slice the florets off the base just where they meet the stem. Trim off any brown discoloration or squishy bits. Once the florets have been separated from the head, cut these into smaller bits so this pasta dish isn't a fork-and-knife affair—more like something that needs a big spoon.

We've also made this dish up to step 4, then stirred everything into a large saucepan of softened couscous for a very hearty side dish to steaks or a roasted chicken.

JUST HOW RAW IS "RAW"?

IN A WORD, VERY. *Prosciutto crudo, jamón serrano,* and other not-smoked European hams are indeed raw meat products. Cured, yes. But technically "not cooked"—therefore, raw.

So here's a puzzler you may have run across if you've been paying attention during your ham-purchasing events. At a supermarket in the United States, the person behind the counter will most often pull the *prosciutto crudo* or *jamón serrano* out of the refrigerator case and slice it up for you. But at a butcher shop in Rome, Paris, or Madrid, or at *tapas* bars in almost any city, the ham is never refrigerated, is set on its stand (sometimes draped with a towel), and sliced to order at room temperature.

What gives? According to Miguel Ullibarri, a *"jamón* passionate" who works with A Taste of Spain, one of the premier gastronomic tour companies in Spain, the difference may be cultural as well as culinary. "In Mediterranean countries, salted and air-dried meats are naturally viewed as preserved food," he told me, "a process that has proved efficient for centuries in this part of the world well before refrigeration was available." He contrasted this with "Anglo-Saxon countries" that identify cured hams as semiprocessed or even fresh meat, "thus requiring refrigeration."

OK, culture aside, what's the science? Bad microorganisms chow down in meat and other preserved foods only in the presence of available water—in culinary/chemical parlance, the "water activity level," written with the symbol "aw" and schematized on a scale of 0.0 to 1.0, the 0.0 being a water vacuum. A reading of 0.95 aw is considered bad news for spoilage (more water, more bacterial activity). Most salted, dried European hams have a surface reading of 0.80 aw and an inner-meat reading of 0.91 aw. In other words, close but not quite there.

So in a bid for safety, most Americans refrigerate salted, dried hams. But the fact of the matter is this: All of these hams taste best at room temperature when the various flavonids and peptide compounds can be volatilized and thus inhaled. To compensate, Spanish restaurants often cover the *jamón curado* (that is, "raw ham") with a thin coating of fat after the meat has been cut in order to seal out any airborne bugs and keep the joint moist when stored at room temperature for optimum taste.

All that said, sliced, dry-cured ham should be refrigerated, but tightly sealed to prevent the meat's further dehydration once the cellular layers have been cut and laid bare.

WHY ARE SOME DRY-CURED EUROPEAN HAMS PINK?

IT'S A FAR TRICKIER QUESTION than you might imagine, one that has puzzled culinary scientists for years. As we said, cured meats are often doped with nitrates or nitrites (page 90); the meat then stays a more appealing pink after curing, rather than an uglier, less-appetizing gray.

But there should be no nitrates or nitrites used in the cure for *prosciutto crudo* or any of the Spanish *jamón.* Yet the meat is pink.

Culinary sleuths have recently begun to solve the puzzle. Although San Daniele and Parma *prosciutto crudo* are cured only with sea salt, the salt itself contains naturally occurring nitrates and nitrites—but still not enough to keep the meat pink. Instead, the pink hue is likely caused by certain staph bacteria (*Staphylococcus carnosus* and *Staphylococcus caseolyticus*), which may further preserve the meat while tinting it.

STEWED MUSSELS WITH *JAMÓN SERRANO*, CHICKPEAS, AND SAFFRON

SERVES 2 BUT CAN BE DOUBLED OR TRIPLED

A big pot of mussels is dinner heaven! When Bruce first tested this recipe, we carted the pot to the coffee table, had a loaf of crusty bread at the ready so as not to miss a drop of the sauce, and put on a movie. OK, I admit a divine dinner had all the potential to be our carpet's damnation, but great rewards come from great risk.

1 tablespoon sherry vinegar

¼ teaspoon saffron

2 tablespoons olive oil

1 small onion, chopped

1 jarred roasted red pepper or pimento, chopped

2 medium garlic cloves, minced

2 ounces thinly sliced *Jamón serrano*, chopped

½ cup canned chickpeas, drained and rinsed

2 pounds mussels, cleaned and debearded

½ cup dry sherry

2 tablespoons minced oregano or cilantro leaves

1. Mix the vinegar and saffron in a small bowl and set aside for 15 minutes.

2. Heat a large pot over medium heat, then add the oil. Toss in the onion and red bell pepper. Cook, stirring a lot, until the onion softens and gets translucent, about 3 minutes. Add the garlic and cook for 20 seconds.

3. Stir in the ham and chickpeas. Stir over the heat just until the ham pieces start to brown a bit, about 1 minute.

4. Stir in the saffron and vinegar mixture, wait about 10 seconds, then pour in the mussels and dry sherry.

5. Bring the whole thing to a simmer; then cover, reduce the heat to low, and simmer slowly until the mussel shells open, stirring once in a while, about 7 minutes. Discard any mussels that do not open and stir in the oregano or cilantro leaves to serve.

THE INGREDIENT SCOOP

Mussels are a live food product and so should be kept cold in the refrigerator for no more than 1 day after purchase. They should be lightly scrubbed with a plastic brush or a clean sponge to get any residual sand off their shells. They also often have extruding, wiry filaments that should be pulled off no more than 5 minutes before the mollusks take the dive into the pot. Grasp those wiry bits and pull them along the shell's seam, ripping them out. Discard any mussels that will not close when tapped.

TESTERS' NOTES

There's no heat in this dish. If you like, add up to ½ teaspoon red pepper flakes with the chickpeas.

Mussels have a lot of briny saltwater still in the shells, so in tandem with the already salty *jamón serrano*, there's probably no need for extra salt. That said, have some to pass on the side for those who enjoy hypertension.

WHOLE TROUT STUFFED WITH *JAMÓN SERRANO*, ROSEMARY, AND FENNEL SEEDS

MAKES 4 STUFFED TROUT

Fast, easy, and elegant, this company supper cries out for a bottle of Spanish white from the Rueda region.

6 ounces thinly sliced *jamón serrano*, minced

⅓ cup fresh bread crumbs (see page 143)

1 tablespoon minced rosemary leaves

1 tablespoon crushed fennel seeds

1 medium garlic clove, minced

3 to 4 tablespoons dry white wine or dry vermouth

Four 1-pound cleaned, boneless, whole trout

2 tablespoons olive oil, perhaps more

3 tablespoons sherry or white wine vinegar

1. Preheat the oven to 450°F.

2. Mix the minced ham, bread crumbs, rosemary, fennel seeds, and garlic in a medium bowl. Add just enough wine to moisten the mixture, but not enough to make it wet and sloppy.

3. Divide this mixture among the 4 trout, stuffing it into their body cavities. Flap them closed.

4. Heat a very large ovenproof skillet over medium heat. (If yours can't hold all 4 trout, then heat 2 each over two separate burners, adding 2 tablespoons oil to each.) Slip the trout into the skillet and cook until crisp, about 7 minutes, shaking the skillet occasionally so the trout don't stick.

5. Use a large spatula to turn the trout one by one, then shove the whole contraption in the oven. Bake until cooked through, about 10 minutes.

6. Remove the very hot skillet from the oven and use that large spatula to transfer the trout to four serving plates.

7. Set the skillet back over medium heat and splash in the vinegar. Stir quickly to scrape up any stuff on the bottom of the skillet, then drizzle this sauce over the trout.

GROUPER FILLETS WRAPPED IN *PROSCIUTTO CRUDO* WITH A LEMON-BUTTER SAUCE

MAKES 4 LIGHT SERVINGS AND CAN EASILY BE DOUBLED

Although Bruce tested this recipe with grouper, you could use any variety of fairly thick, white-fleshed fish: snapper, rockfish, wreckfish, tilapia, or even hake. Fish sustainability is an ongoing issue and not easily resolved. If you're concerned, check out websites like www.fishonline. org or www.foodandwaterwatch.org.

THE INGREDIENT SCOOP

Dry vermouth is our go-to substitute for dry white wine. It's an aromatized wine, once made with bitter wormwood (thus the name—*vermout* [no "h"] is a French word from the German *Wermut*, or "wormwood") as well as nutmeg, juniper, marjoram, cinnamon, cloves, orange peel, and coriander. Vermouth may contain additional alcohol, but not for potency (as in a fortified wine), but rather for an enhanced flavor (thus the term "aromatized"). All that said, today's dry vermouth bears little resemblance to its far more herbal kin. But it still makes a great cooking alternative to white wine because it can be kept open on a dark pantry shelf for months. White wine, the cooking standard, begins to go bad within hours of being opened. Yes, you can keep it replugged in the fridge, but even so it begins to be compromised within a day. One warning: Vermouth comes in at least two varieties. A hypersweet version (often with a red label and definitely red in color, so sometimes called "red vermouth") is used in cocktails like Manhattans and Negronis. The somewhat drier if still sweet "dry vermouth" (also called "white vermouth" because it's clear in color, or even "French vermouth") is what's called for throughout this book. There are also other versions like "ultra dry," "semisweet," and "Punt e Mes," a very bitter vermouth. These are mostly liquor-store rarities and should not be used as a substitute for dry vermouth.

8 paper-thin *prosciutto crudo* slices

2 teaspoons Dijon mustard

Two ½-pound grouper fillets, skinned

8 sage leaves

3 tablespoons unsalted butter

1 tablespoon olive oil

2 tablespoons lemon juice

6 tablespoons dry white wine or dry vermouth

1. Preheat the oven to 400°F.

2. Overlap the prosciutto slices on your work surface in two batches— that is, 4 slices apiece, the slices overlapping each other to create a bed for the fillets in the next step.

3. Spread the mustard over the fillets, about ½ teaspoon on each side of each fillet. Lay 1 fillet on top of each set of prosciutto slices.

4. Top each fillet with 4 sage leaves, then roll and fold the prosciutto closed to create a wrapping around each fillet.

5. Melt 1 tablespoon of the butter with the oil in a large ovenproof skillet over medium heat.

6. Add the wrapped grouper fillets to the skillet and cook until the prosciutto has started to brown and crisp on one side, about 3 minutes. Turn the fillets with a big spatula, then shove the skillet in the oven.

7. Roast for 7 minutes. Remove the skillet from the oven and transfer the wrapped fillets to a serving platter. Pour off and discard any fat.

8. Set the skillet back over medium heat and add the lemon juice; swirl it around so that it picks up any little bits of stuff on the skillet's cooking surface.

9. Pour in the wine and bring to a simmer. Cook just until the amount of liquid in the skillet has been reduced to half its volume, about 2 minutes.

10. Remove the skillet from the heat and whisk in the butter just until it melts into a fairly smooth sauce. Pour over the fillets and serve at once by cutting each of those wrapped packages in half.

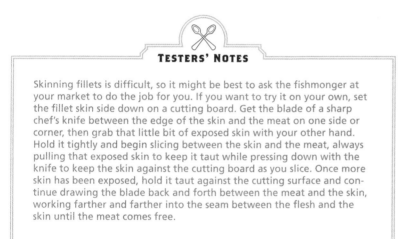

TESTERS' NOTES

Skinning fillets is difficult, so it might be best to ask the fishmonger at your market to do the job for you. If you want to try it on your own, set the fillet skin side down on a cutting board. Get the blade of a sharp chef's knife between the edge of the skin and the meat on one side or corner, then grab that little bit of exposed skin with your other hand. Hold it tightly and begin slicing between the skin and the meat, always pulling that exposed skin to keep it taut while pressing down with the knife to keep the skin against the cutting board as you slice. Once more skin has been exposed, hold it taut against the cutting surface and continue drawing the blade back and forth between the meat and the skin, working farther and farther into the seam between the flesh and the skin until the meat comes free.

SALTIMBOCCA-STYLE CHICKEN BREASTS

MAKES 4 HEARTY SERVINGS

Saltimbocca (Italian, sahl-tim-BOH-kah, "jumps in the mouth") is a classic Italian preparation that's arguably more popular in Switzerland, Greece, and the United States than it is in its country of origin. It's a terrific dish: The meat is wrapped in prosciutto, fried, and then sauced. This version adapts the famous "alla Romana" version that makes a sauce of mushrooms and Marsala for the wrapped cutlets.

THE INGREDIENT SCOOP

Throughout this book, we call for **grated nutmeg**, not ground. Nutmegs are the seeds of the *Myristica fragrans* tree, indigenous to southeastern Asia and Australia. Left on the tree to ripen, the seeds become a fruit that is made into jellies and candies in the Caribbean and Indonesia. But when harvested early, the nutmegs are pulled from their shells (which are ground to become mace). Invest in the seeds themselves, a few per bottle, and grate them with the small holes of a box grater or a small, fine-mesh cheese grater. The flavors will be more complex—sweeter and with saffron overtones—than those of preground nutmeg. However, if you insist on using ground nutmeg in these recipes, use half the amount required because its taste is more monochromatic, more pungent, and far less sophisticated.

Four 5-ounce boneless, skinless chicken breasts

8 paper-thin *prosciutto crudo* slices

32 basil leaves

¼ teaspoon grated nutmeg

2 tablespoons olive oil

1 tablespoon plus 2 teaspoons unsalted butter

8 ounces cremini mushrooms, thinly sliced

2 medium garlic cloves, minced

¼ cup dry Marsala or dry Madeira

¼ teaspoons salt

1. Spread a large sheet of plastic wrap on your work surface. Place the 4 breasts on it, spacing them several inches apart. Top with a second sheet of plastic wrap, then pound the cutlets to ¼-inch thickness using the smooth side of a meat mallet or the bottom of a heavy saucepan. This is not the time to take out your frustrations. You want to pound without whacking, firmly and insistently but not so violently that the meat tears. Peel off the top sheet of plastic wrap and set the breasts aside.

2. Place a piece of prosciutto on a cutting board. Lay 4 basil leaves on the prosciutto, then top these with 1 pounded chicken breast, laying it on the prosciutto so that the pointy ends of both match up. Lay 4 more basil leaves on the breast, then sprinkle with a pinch of nutmeg. Lay a second prosciutto slice over the breast in the same direction as the slice below, then press firmly to make a compact sandwich, folding various ends over and under so that the whole thing looks like a stuffed prosciutto pancake. Set aside and repeat this step 3 times.

3. Heat a large skillet over medium heat, then swirl in the oil. Add the wrapped chicken breasts and cook for 5 minutes on either side, until the prosciutto is lightly browned and even a little crisp and the chicken inside is cooked through. How can you tell if they're done? You can cut into one with a knife to find out. Or you can try to stick an instant-read meat thermometer right into the meat without the probe poking through and hitting the skillet beneath—in which case the temperature should read about 165°F. Transfer the packets to four serving plates.

4. Melt 1 tablespoon butter in the skillet, then add the mushrooms and garlic. Cook, stirring often, until the mushrooms give up their liquid and it boils down to a thick glaze, one that will hold its shape for a second when a wooden spoon is run through it.

5. Pour in the Marsala or Madeira and bring to a simmer. Continue cooking, stirring occasionally, until the amount of liquid in the skillet has been reduced to half its original volume, about 2 minutes. There's no need to measure it; eyeballing will do. You want enough sauce so that the chicken cutlets are nicely coated on the plates.

6. Remove the skillet from the heat and swirl in the remaining 2 teaspoons butter and the salt until the butter melts. Divide this sauce among the four serving plates with the cooked chicken cutlets.

TESTERS' NOTES

Bruce tells me he asked the butcher at Stop & Shop to pound the breasts for him. When I asked why, he said, "I was feeling lazy." Follow his indolent example at will.

PROSCIUTTO-WRAPPED MEATLOAF ᴡɪᴛʜ A VINEGARY TOMATO SAUCE

MAKES 6 HEARTY SERVINGS

There are two styles of meatloaf: in a loaf pan or on a pan in a shape like a football cut in half the long way, tip to tip—and what we refer to as "meatlump." We're unabashed fans of the latter; the loaf pan just lets the thing get too mushy and steamed, like a meat pudding. If you can't find ground veal, use ½ pound ground pork and increase the ground beef to 1 pound.

¾ pound ground veal

¾ pound lean ground beef

2 large egg yolks, at room temperature

1 medium shallot, minced

¼ cup milk (regular, low-fat, or fat-free)

1 ounce finely grated Parmigiano-Reggiano (see page 87)

1 tablespoon tomato paste

1 tablespoon stemmed thyme leaves or 2 teaspoons dried thyme

1 tablespoon minced rosemary leaves or 1½ teaspoons dried rosemary, crumbled

½ teaspoon grated nutmeg

½ teaspoon salt

½ teaspoon freshly ground black pepper

6 ounces *prosciutto crudo*, sliced paper thin

2 tablespoons olive oil

1 tablespoon unsalted butter

1 small yellow onion, minced

½ teaspoon ground cinnamon

3 tablespoons red wine vinegar

4 medium Roma or plum tomatoes, seeded (see page 104) and chopped

1. Mix both ground meats, the egg yolks, shallot, milk, Parmigiano-Reggiano, tomato paste, thyme, rosemary, nutmeg, ¼ teaspoon of the salt, and the pepper in a large bowl. You can start out with a wooden spoon, especially to break up the egg yolks and get them into the meat mixture—but you'll eventually want to use the best tool in the kitchen: your cleaned hands. Get in the bowl and gently mash the ingredients together, not so much that the meat loses all its coarse consistency and becomes pabulum, but so that the mixture contains the spices and other ingredients uniformly throughout.

2. Overlap the prosciutto slices (all going the same way) on a large, lipped baking sheet, or on the broiler pan—but in any case, use a lipped baking sheet, not the flat kind, sometimes referred to as a "cookie sheet." The fat rendered by the meatloaf will run all over your oven. You'll be less than pleased.

3. Gather the meat mixture together and lay it on the prosciutto strips, forming an oblong, slightly tapered, slightly flattened but still thick log with its ends perpendicular to the ends of the prosciutto strips.

4. Fold the prosciutto strips up and over the meatlump, overlapping them so they cover and protect the meat mixture. Pat the slices into place so they adhere, then turn the whole thing upside down so that the prosciutto "seam" is now against the baking sheet.

5. Brush the prosciutto slices with olive oil, then set the whole thing in the oven and bake until an instant-read meat thermometer inserted into the center of the thickest part of the meatloaf registers 165°F, about 45 minutes.

6. Meanwhile, melt the butter in a medium saucepan set over medium heat. Add the onion and cook, stirring often, until translucent and softened, about 3 minutes.

7. Stir in the cinnamon and the remaining ¼ teaspoon salt. Cook just until aromatic, maybe 20 seconds.

8. Add the vinegar and bring to a simmer. Continue cooking, stirring all the while, until the vinegar has reduced to a lacquered glaze, about 2 minutes.

9. Toss in the chopped tomatoes and cook just until they begin to break down, about 5 minutes. Reduce the heat to very low and cook slowly, stirring every once in a while, until the mixture becomes a coarse, thickened sauce, perhaps 20 minutes. Set aside, covered and off the heat.

10. When the meatloaf is done, transfer it on its baking sheet to a wire rack and cool for 5 minutes before slicing. Because of the lips on the baking sheet, it's helpful to transfer the meatloaf to a serving platter before slicing, although you'll need a super big spatula to get the job done—or perhaps the help of someone with a second spatula. (Just have a plan before you work together so you don't end up with an *I Love Lucy* moment, with the meatloaf in pieces all over the floor and counter.) Serve the meatloaf slices with some of the tomato sauce spooned on top.

3

DRY-CURED

HAM

IN THE NEW WORLD

3

ou don't have to cross the pond to find dry-cured hams. Truth be told, they're one of America's best artisanal products: country hams, often sold in canvas or netted bags, salty Southern behemoths in need of a soak before cooking.

As a child, I'd eaten them sliced and fried as steaks for breakfast on our obligatory travels to taste red-eye gravy and see the Civil War battlefield where my great-great-someone-or-other fell. As an adult, I'd tasted them in dribs and drabs from the hands of various publicists and locavores.

But I'll be the first to admit I was still leery. There they sat at the supermarket, often forlorn on a wooden shelf, a meat without any other meat around it, and unrefrigerated to boot. (The industry word for their ability to endure months without refrigeration didn't inspire a lot of culinary confidence: "shelf stable.") Yet I often heard words like "Smithfield" or "Virginia ham" whispered among the cognoscenti.

"Oh, didn't you eat it all the time when you lived in the South?" one asked me.

She was born and bred in New York. I didn't ask if she visited the Empire State Building all the time. "Oh, no, you know, we ate other things. It wasn't a big deal."

She backed up, a bird-thin woman. "Well, you'll never get one in Connecticut. For years, I've been teaching people they need to discover the local products that . . ."

I'm sure I dozed off—but wasn't deterred by geographical ineptitude. Bruce and I traversed the web, found producers across the ham belt (Virginia, West Virginia, North Carolina, Georgia, Tennessee, Kentucky, Missouri, and northern Alabama), sent our credit card numbers into the ether, and got country hams delivered to our door over the next few weeks.

Come early November, Bruce fixed our first one

for a dinner party with a couple who were former-sixties-protestors-turned-upper-management, as well as a bank VP whom we'd known for years as a married man, and his current boyfriend. Sometimes I think back to my days in the Baptist Student Union and my head hurts.

It had been a strange journey for the ham, too: the meat hard as a rock when it arrived via UPS, covered with a green-and-white mold that had to be washed off, the whole joint then soaked in a tub of water for a few days before being roasted until shimmeringly golden, a crunchy crust of fat over the meat.

I found bliss at first bite, while everyone else discussed something unimportant like national politics: the meat delicately chewy—not tough, just compact—salty but sweet, too. I'd never had anything like this. The country hams I'd tried before had been glazed and shellacked, like a rube who comes to the city, gets tarted up, and turns into a desiccated hack. But this ham was different: tender, rustic, sophisticated, and homey all at once. Good grief, it didn't need two bottles of Dr. Pepper as some unspeakable marinade painted on while it baked. It just needed to be itself.

Over the next few weeks, I lived in a paradise of country hams—and quickly learned that they're not all the same. There are state-by-state differences, region-to-region differences, even farm-to-farm differences. Hell, one producer tried to convince me there are hog-to-hog differences. "You ever seen two alike?" he asked.

I don't meet a wide range. Still, I became something of a maven, tasting the craft of various producers, increasingly surprised by the range of flavors and textures.

I had to know more. So I flew off to Kentucky for a ham picaresque in the dead of January, when the whole state was even freeze-butt-colder than my driveway in the Berkshires. And I discovered that not only are there ham-to-ham differences, there are also astounding differences among the artisanal producers.

Why Kentucky? One, the microclimates—they're more like those for European ham production: a little cooler that the rest of the South, then milder and drier in the right months. Two, the heritage cures that have been handed down for generations. And three, the bourbon.

Still, Kentucky is the forgotten stepsister at the country-ham ball. Virginia, North Carolina, Tennessee—they all have fancier suitors.

That wallflowerness sort of stands to reason, since Kentuckians themselves are quieter, less showy than other Southerners. First thing I noticed? They drive more deliberately. Not more slowly, just with turn signals and a proper distance between cars. As if distance itself were a virtue.

Which perhaps it is, but not in the Hi-How-Are-Yew-I-Luv-Yer-Hair part of the South where I grew up. I was used to back slaps, loud laughs, and Gospel tracts; I was ill-prepared for Bill Robertson, Jr., the curer at Finchville Farms.

Bill's the current incarnation of a three-generation business that's located in what was his family's general store, post office, and bank, out between Louisville and Lexington, where it's more horse than hills, more Derby than Appalachia. The Robertsons may have once owned Finchville, but you wouldn't know it from Bill. I came in with my hail-fellow Southernness—he simply sat down in his chair, the desk between us, and knocked a cigarette out of a pack.

Bill was making country ham old-school: solely with atmospherics. In the business, it's called an "ambient cure." Or economic suicide, what with global warming and the capital outlay for meat that's going to hang for months in barns, windows and beat-up fans the only climate-control strategy.

I thought I knew the business. I arrived armed with the facts, had read every article I could about country hams. I could recite the process: salt, resalt, wash, hang, smoke.

Turned out I knew nothing. Yes, Bill's salt cure included brown sugar as well as ground red and black pepper—which got churned up with the help of a cement mixer his father bought after a particularly successful night in the casino.

"So you salt the hams, set them aside, and then resalt a week or so later?" I asked.

"No. I don't fool with all that."

"You don't resalt the hams before you wash them?"

"Don't fool with washing either," he said, dangling his cigarette between his knees.

He explained he wrapped the salted hams in butcher paper, netted them in mesh bags, hung them off racks, and let the weather do the rest.

"It's how my family's done it. Three generations."

"You smoke them in butcher paper?"

"Don't smoke at all."

I gave up and listened.

"In April, it can be dry or it can be wet around here," he said. "Some days, the hams are bigger, soaking up more humidity. That paper's real wet. Some days, they're smaller. Then the paper's drier, of course. Back and forth. And you know what? I think that does something to the flavor."

"You're just playing a waiting game?"

"Yeah, just."

"For the weather?"

"For the salt to move through the meat. I also watch the temperature inside the hams. It has to stay right so the salt keeps going."

"And if it doesn't?"

"I pray. By mid-July, the hams should lose about twenty-four percent of their original weight."

"And then?"

"They're good to go."

We left his office to shiver in the cold and have

a look at the few hams left over from the holiday rush. He hauled open the door of an enormous shed and there they were: still wrapped in their ghostly white paper, hanging inside those netted bags.

He handed me a hunk of a cooked slice. It was mild, chewy, surprisingly complex, with distinct flavors of maple and nutmeg—although there was no maple or nutmeg in the cure. Smoky, too—although there was no smoke in the process. These all seemed feints and pulled punches.

Actually, they were complex chemistry at work: a series of amino acids and protein chains slowly breaking apart to form hundreds of new, unexpected flavors, tricks on the tongue, all held in suspension in a salty liquid that inhibited other microbial activity.

Finchville Farms's gentle, unsmoked, salty hamminess was also an excellent starting point for my tour—because deeper complexities lay ahead.

Stronger personalities, too. Early the next morning, I drove to the western end of Kentucky, beyond the hollers, where the land does its long, lazy downdog to the Mississippi River. By ten o'clock, I was in Princeton, a brick-front downtown made up of mostly gewgaw stores that had once been saloons. I had come to meet Nancy Newsom Mahaffey of Newsom's Country Hams.

I had also come at a bad time. She'd just received her first shipment of that year's hams. She was, to say the least, harried. Not that it really mattered. She'd be a gale-force wind even on temperate days: dark-haired, big-eyed, always moving, always talking (her accent thick and unabashed), ensconced in the business her grandfather had established—a country store that sold sorghum candy, mayhaw jelly, and those country hams "the Colonel" had once made for his family and friends. Nancy's the Colonel now. Or so she calls herself.

She came around the counter to give my hand a firm shake, then instantly set to complaining about her mailing list. "They call up and give me their customer numbers. I ask for a name. I'm not doing business with a number."

A true Southerner, she loved the niceties. We talked as she offered me tastes of various hams.

"I been doing this my whole life," she said. "Back in 1987, this business burned right to the ground and I didn't even look back. I knew I was going to rebuild. I put some potted plants in front of the burned-out building and someone stopped on the road to ask me if they were for sale. I didn't have time to think. I had to get back in business."

When I asked her how many hams a year she cured, she demurred. "You're not going to put that in your book, are you? Enough. I fulfill my orders and I . . ."

I couldn't let her go on. She had handed me a square of wax paper with some thin, ruby-pink slices on it. I had taken a bite of something that stopped me cold, made me pay attention. "What the hell's this?"

She flashed a wide grin. "My twenty-four month-prosciutto. Well, twenty-six-month now. It's been hanging a while."

It was like nothing I'd had in a long time, the meat aged until the fat melted at tongue temperature: soft, sweet, a little salty, smooth as a perfectly cooked duck breast, but with more tang, more spice.

"How'd you do this?" I asked.

"You wanna see?" She grabbed her purse and headed out to her car.

We drove over to her mother's modest house. A huge semitrailer sat in the driveway; the guys were off-loading hams that would be salted that day and laid on wooden racks for a couple weeks before heading to the smokehouse across the breezeway.

Nancy pulled open its blackened door, and the brassy, tannic odor of curing meat hit me. I shuddered.

"Something wrong?"

"No, no. That smell." I remembered it well from our own attempts to cure a ham.

Nancy's smokehouse wasn't just how the business got done; it was the business itself: gnarly, greasy-black, full of ambient molds—these were the backbone of that prosciutto I'd tasted.

"If we have to put climate controls in this place, I'm turning it over to my son," she said as we blinked back into the sunlight. "I wouldn't know what to do. I just do what I do. Natural cure. Salt and brown sugar. I don't fool with peppers or anything. Hang the meat up, let the air blow past it. It's what I know. And I don't want to change."

She may have to. Weather patterns are shifting, pork producers are consolidating, and consumers are pressing for convenience. There are problems aplenty.

I found one solution when I left her and drove up near Owensboro and the Ohio River, where the land was flatter and richer, the silts of the river providing a deep muck for farmers like Charlie Gatton, Jr., of Father's Country Hams, a big operation down a tangle of country roads.

Charlie was a squat barrel of a man, a two-generation curer, his tenor laugh puncturing his all-business approach. While Nancy held the past as her holy talisman, Charlie was something of a ham-trepreneur. We stood in his climate-controlled room surrounded by rolling bins of salted hams, while he donned a hairnet and rubber gloves, dropped a raw, pink joint into the sugary cure, and rubbed it into the meat.

Doing twenty things at once and without missing a beat, he outlined his process for me: "We cure them with salt, brown, and white sugar. Rub it in, just at the cut of meat and into the hock. We lay them down between thirty-seven and forty-two degrees Fahrenheit for four weeks, resalting after about ten days. Then we move the hams into a fifty-five-degree environment for four weeks. Then we hang them out back and smoke over hickory."

Food snobs, beware. The country-ham business can't get locked in nostalgia. With air pollution and ambient pesticide residues that kill the molds necessary for aging, there may be little to gain from romantic wistfulness. In fact, these newfangled scientific controls actually help Charlie hang on to tradition.

Like everyone else, he netted and hung the hams hocks down. Italians hang *prosciutto crudo* hock up. But with the hock down, the larger muscles up top slowly weigh the thing down and ball the meat around the bone so the hams end up in large, oval planes, perfect for slicing off ham steaks.

Charlie's hams were lean, the taste clean and bright with shadows of marmalade and toast. If Bill's were gentle on the tongue and Nancy's had deep flavors in the back of the mouth, Charlie's hit the upper palate. Excellent white wine, instead of red. A country ham for all takers: bright, bracing, quintessentially Southern. And a step into the modern world with traditions intact.

As the sky lapsed into its evening chromatics, I left Father's Country Hams and drove south into the deepening valleys on my way to my last stop: Scott Hams, the people who'd made the first country ham Bruce had tested. I found their house down a roller-coaster road that climbed straight up and plunged back down the hillocks with nary a curve or an embankment: a Thomas Hart Benton canvas come to life.

June Scott pulled some plastic chairs into their office in the barn, Leslie came out of the back room where he was cutting meat, and I asked them for their story—which they told in that way long-married couples do: "Go ahead—you tell this part. You will anyway."

Back in 1988, they entered their second national championship sponsored by the American Association of Meat Processors. The year before, they'd come in sixth.

"This time, we didn't even have money for the flight," June said. "We had to drive to Albuquerque."

"And then she didn't want to get out of bed for the judging that morning," Leslie added, thumbing at her. "She thought there was no use."

They won first place. And have done so repeatedly.

"She still does the hams," Leslie smirked. "I'm just the hired help. Hang 'em, help her get 'em on the hooks. Just salt and brown sugar in the cure. Nothing else."

"You do your part," she said.

"What you tell me."

It was like being with my grandparents: comfortable, relaxed, at ease. June hadn't even taken her hairnet off.

"I wanted to be a social worker," she said, the regret clutching at her words. "But Leslie wanted me home. So we started trying to make a go of it. But I really wanted a town job."

The disconnect rattled in my head. Success and regrets. "But you've won every national championship," I said. "And repeatedly."

"Uh-huh," she said.

"It's all trade-offs," Leslie added.

I could sense the silence of the empty space under the floorboards of my food-writing career. There's a depressing way "artisanal" gets romanticized, as if to imbue it with overtones of nobility. In truth, it's just hard work. Rewarding, sure. But the fetishization that creeps into any foodie discussion of artisanal products smears their true merit. May I never endure another waiter blathering on about how lucky we are to have this-and-that from here-and-there, which all adds up to how proud of ourselves we are to be eating such-and-so. May I never endure another hectoring food writer wagging a finger in my face and telling me how to be local or how I don't honor this or that tradition. May I instead remember and give thanks for people like the Scotts who work hard so that someone else can get dinner on the table.

Year after year, they crank out hams that are the quintessence of their craft: deeply flavored, lightly smoked (over green hickory and sassafras), aged about 10 months (or longer for prosciutto-style hams), quite meaty, tender but not soft, with a delicate tang to the fat belying inner depths.

Leslie took me back to the smoking racks while June filled an Internet order. He tapped me on the shoulder, pointed to the hooks in the ceiling. "You know, we was working in here once, late, maybe eight, eight-thirty one night, hanging the hams after we'd washed the cure off. I'd been up since long before dawn. Well, you work with someone a lot, your wife, and you kind of say things you oughtn't. I don't remember what it was. But she got down off the rack and told me to do the rest myself. She went on to the house. I finished up. I come in and she had my dinner on the table but she'd gone to bed. She set my breakfast out the next morning, too. Later in the day, she come out to me and said, 'You just had to say you're sorry. That's all I needed.' So I did. I said it. And learned something, too. Just say 'you're sorry,' kind of repent, and then go on."

And they have. On and on, gentle regrets in tow, just doing what they've done. Afterwards, they didn't even see me out as the sun set behind their house on its lonely bump of a hill. They just went back to work on their artisanal craft, long divorced from this overhyped, margin-driven, media-doped world.

THE BUTTON BUSTERS

Although many high-end markets carry American country hams, the selection can be limited. The best way to get this American delicacy may well be the way Bruce got ours: via mail-order. A web search will put you in touch with a host of producers, even the ones mentioned here. All will drop-ship right to your door.

Still, there's no preparing yourself for the moment when the UPS truck pulls into your driveway and the driver announces, "I've got your meat."

Having been thoroughly disoriented by this ham-in-the-mail scheme, you'll probably want the comfort of the classics.

So voilà.

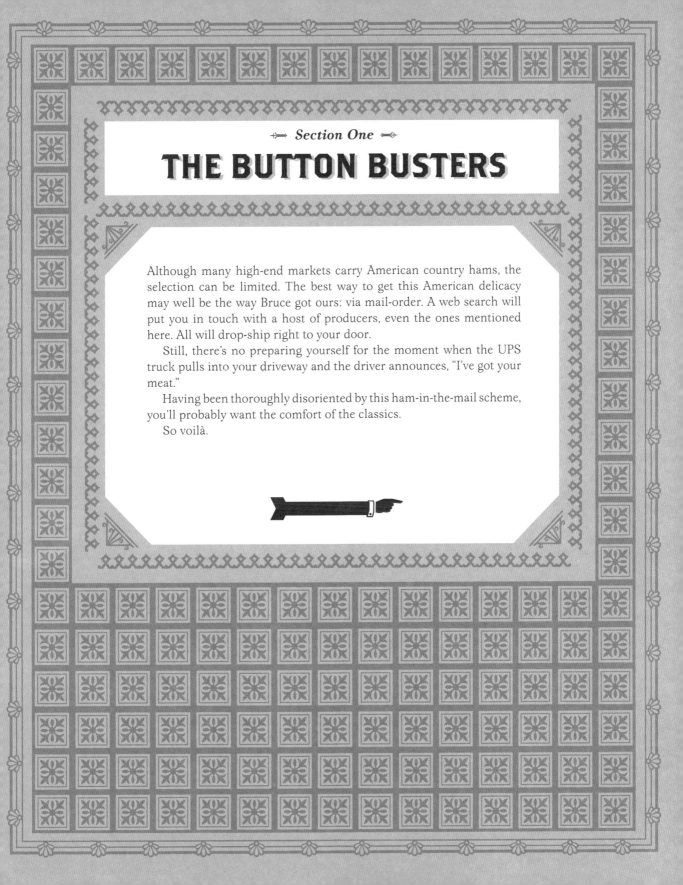

GLAZED AND ROASTED COUNTRY HAM

FEEDS 16 TO 26, DEPENDING ON HOW MANY BOWLS OF COLE SLAW, ROASTED ROOT VEGETABLES, AND MASHED SWEET POTATOES YOU'VE GOT ON HAND

You can't rush this titan: two days for soaking, many hours for roasting. If you're making country ham for a holiday meal, plan ahead; then set your alarm for 5:30 a.m. on the day of the feast. Otherwise, decide lunch is going to be, oh, late in the afternoon, the way it probably should be on a holiday anyway.

SLASH THE SHOPPING LIST

Frankly, an American country ham doesn't need a glaze at all. Feel free to skip step 10.

THE INGREDIENT SCOOP

While it's been salted to chemical stability, a **country ham** isn't meant to be aged in your home. If you've ordered the meat from a reputable supplier, they've released it after it's been properly aged. However, you can easily hang the thing from a nail for a month or so in a cool, dry place until you're ready to use it. You may get a few drips of grease on the floor, but you can solve that with a plate (or a nosy collie). If you're not going to use the ham within a month of purchase, freeze the whole thing, netted wrapping and all, for up to 6 months. Thaw it out in the refrigerator in that very wrapping, about 1 day for every 4 pounds. Never store a country ham wrapped in plastic; nasty gases can build up. Also never store it long-term in the refrigerator: The high humidity can begin to break the meat down.

One 12- to 16-pound bone-in American country ham

2 cups cider vinegar

One of the five glazes (see step 10)

1. Peel the ham out of all packaging, netting, and wrapping. Working in a cleaned sink, use warm water and a clean, supple brush or a brand-new sponge to wipe off any white or green mold that clings to the meat. Those colors come from various chemical and bacterial sources; almost all are similar to the molds found on aged cheeses. American country hams develop their flavors during aging as neutral-tasting proteins break down into glutamic acid (the chemical moniker for "meat taste") and flavor-packed tyrosine (an amino acid—aka the dusty white film). Even some of the meat's unsaturated fats break down to become new flavor compounds. In other words, that fuzz is the harbinger of flavor. No, you don't want to eat it, but its presence indicates that the complicated process of making meat tastier and more tender via dry-curing is under way.

2. Set the ham in a large tub or ice chest just slightly wider and longer than the joint itself. Fill this container with cool water, submerging the ham. Set aside in a cool place to soak for 12 hours.

One note: Do not store the soaking ham in the garage during the summer or winter, a place too hot or too cold for it. Instead, store the ham in its tub indoors, preferably in the basement where the temperature's a little more moderate and constant. Don't have a basement? Select one of the cooler parts of your house. A back bedroom closet, say. Just warn the kids that there's a big, soaking piece of meat back there. If not, you're setting them up for years of therapy.

3. After 12 hours, drain off all the water, replenish with fresh, cool water, and set aside for another 12 hours.

4. Do this two more times, soaking for 12 hours and changing out the water each time, for a total of 48 hours. By the way, you'll want to pour that soaking water down the drain. It's salty and hammy. Tossing it into the back yard will invite furry well-wishers.

5. Adjust the oven rack so the ham can fit inside with some head space to spare, then preheat the oven to 325°F. Meanwhile, transfer the ham to a large, high-sided roasting pan. A disposable, aluminum roasting pan can work, but it can also be awfully flimsy. Don't use your broiler pan. It's not deep enough.

6. Run cool tap water into the roasting pan until it comes about halfway up the sides, then pour in the vinegar. Cover the roasting pan tightly with its lid (if it has one) or seal tightly with aluminum foil. Bake until an instant-read meat thermometer inserted into the thickest part of the meat without touching bone registers 160°F, about 20 minutes per pound—in other words, about 4 hours for a 12-pound ham, 4 hours 40 minutes for a 14-pounder, or 5 hours 20 minutes for a 16-pounder.

7. Lift the ham onto a large cutting board. Although you can get the job done with two enormous spatulas and some helping hands, the easiest way is to wear silicone cooking mitts and manhandle the meat onto the board. Throw out all the liquid and any scum or impurities in the roasting pan.

8. Increase the oven's temperature to 375°F. Use a thin carving knife to slice the rind (that is, the skin) off the ham, leaving behind as much of the fat as possible. Throw out the rind.

9. Use that knife to score the fat in the classic crosshatch (or diamond) pattern. To do so, cut a series of diagonal lines across the top of the ham, then cut a second series at a ninety-degree angle, every line equidistant from those on either side. Don't cut down into the meat. Set the ham, crosshatch pattern up, in the roasting pan.

10. Whisk one of the following in a small bowl until smooth. Brush the ham with the glaze you choose.

ORANGE-BOURBON GLAZE

½ cup orange marmalade

2 tablespoons bourbon

PINEAPPLE-RUM GLAZE

½ cup pineapple jam

2 tablespoons dark rum

APPLE-HONEY GLAZE

½ cup honey

2 tablespoons apple juice concentrate
(thawed)

CRANBERRY-PORT GLAZE

½ cup canned smooth cranberry sauce

2 tablespoons Port

½ teaspoon ground cinnamon

¼ teaspoon ground allspice

¼ teaspoon ground cloves

CURRIED MANGO GLAZE

½ cup mango chutney

2 tablespoons orange juice concentrate
(thawed)

1 teaspoon bottled curry powder

11. Continue baking until the ham is golden brown and lacquered, shiny but still succulent, and an instant-read meat thermometer inserted into the thickest part of the meat without touching bone registers 170°F, about 1 hour.

12. Let the ham rest in its roasting pan at room temperature for 30 minutes before carving. Then lay the roasted ham, fat side up, on a carving board so that the thin, bony end (that is, the hock end) is pointed to the left if you're left-handed or to the right if you're right-handed. Position your knife near the hock end but far enough along the ham that you'll be cutting into a generous bit of meat. The knife's blade should be positioned so that it forms a 90-degree angle with the carving board below. Spear the ham with a meat fork, then make your first cut straight down toward the carving board. Now make a second cut about an inch away, even farther from the hock end, but this time at a 45-degree angle to the original cut, thereby cutting out a wedge of meat that you should set aside. Continue making very thin slices parallel to that 45-degree cut. There's an old tradition that country ham slices should be see-through. You needn't go nuts—but the thinner you slice it, the more tender it will be. Basically, you're carving parallel to the aitch bone (page 38), but you'll have to make your way through several hams before you're proficient in the anatomy. Once you're in the carving groove, you'll need to turn the ham over and repeat the process on the other side, always through the thickest part of the meat. By the time you've sliced off most of the center meat, you'll be left with the thick butt end of the ham and the thinner hock end. The butt end, home to a set of complicated bones, can later be carved into irregular chunks, these then diced for stir-fries, gratins, and other leftovers; the hock end should be saved back for soups and stews. For more on the rationale of roasting the hock still attached, see page 135.)

ROUND OUT THE MEAL

First, make a creamy slaw, but give it a twist: Grate up a peeled jicama and a cored and seeded red bell pepper with the cabbage. Keep these vegetables cold and covered in the refrigerator; at the last minute, toss them with a dressing made from mayonnaise and sour cream in a 2-to-1 ratio, as well as a little lemon juice, minced dill, salt, and pepper.

Also have some chile-braised black-eyed peas for a side dish. Mince up a small seeded and stemmed *serrano* pepper and cook it in a little oil along with some minced shallot. Add a couple cans of unseasoned drained and rinsed black-eyed peas and a little canned broth; bring to a low simmer. Cook just a few minutes, until most of the liquid has been absorbed and the black-eyed peas are heated through. Season with a pinch of ground cinnamon as well as salt and pepper.

For dessert, peel bananas and slit them in half lengthwise. Place these in a baking dish just large enough to hold them, then dot with unsalted butter and apricot jam before sprinkling with a little rum, a touch of vanilla extract, and a pinch of ground allspice. Cover and bake in a pre-heated 350°F oven until the sauce is thick and the bananas are tender, about 20 minutes. Serve in bowls with vanilla ice cream or frozen yogurt.

FRIED COUNTRY HAM STEAKS WITH RED-EYE GRAVY

MAKES 4 SERVINGS BUT CAN BE DOUBLED OR TRIPLED, PROVIDED YOU DOUBLE OR TRIPLE THE NUMBER OF SKILLETS IN USE

Charlie Gatton, Jr., of Father's Country Hams will be quick to tell you that the future lies in country ham steaks—and he's not wrong. These are slices off the ham, usually from the thickest bit of muscle, farthest from the hock. But read the label carefully: Some are precooked and ready-to-eat. Thus, they do not need to be soaked in advance (so skip steps 1 and 2 in this recipe).

Two ½-pound, ¼-inch-thick uncooked country ham steaks

2 tablespoons lard or solid vegetable shortening

⅓ cup plus 3 tablespoons water, plus additional for soaking the steaks

2 tablespoons espresso or very, very strong coffee

1. Place the ham steaks in a large baking pan, cover with water, and soak for 20 minutes at room temperature.

2. Drain the steaks; cut off the thick outer rind if there is one (but leave the fat for better protection and flavor); and pat dry.

3. Melt the lard or shortening in a large skillet over medium heat. Add the ham steaks, then pour in ⅓ cup water. Crank the heat to medium-high and bring the water to a boil. Turn the ham steaks once or twice as the water boils away.

4. Once the water is gone, continue cooking the steaks, frying them in the residual fat, until browned in splotchy patches, turning once, about 2 minutes per side. Transfer to a serving platter.

5. Pour the coffee and 3 tablespoons water into the skillet. As the mixture comes to a boil, scrape up any browned bits on the bottom of the skillet. Boil for 30 seconds, then pour into a small bowl. Use this red-eye gravy as a dip for the ham, a sop for biscuits, or a drizzle for accompanying eggs, particularly those served sunny side up.

TESTERS' NOTES

The debates about red-eye gravy rage. The name? Some say it refers to your red eyes at breakfast after a night of drinking. Other says that the little red circle in the creamy translucence gives rise to a vulgar name for a part of a woman's anatomy. (Shouldn't you then have two bowls of gravy?) But those debates are nothing compared to the ones about how the stuff should be made. Purists insist it's nothing but ham drippings, no additives; others, Alabaman in nature, that the gravy should be mixed with ketchup or even yellow mustard. In the end, we prefer the traditional Kentucky way: with coffee. But for the best taste, we use something no country restaurant would have on hand: espresso. If the gravy is too salty for your taste, calm it down with dashes of a hot red pepper sauce like Tabasco sauce.

GRILLED COUNTRY HAM STEAKS
WITH A PLUM GRILL-MOP

SERVES 4 BUT CAN BE DOUBLED, TRIPLED, OR MULTIPLIED ANY WAY YOU WANT

The recipe for this mop (a thick barbecue sauce) will make more than you'll need: Refrigerate the remainder in a glass jar or a plastic container for up to 2 weeks, or freeze for up to 1 year. Again, the recipe assumes you're working with uncooked, unsoaked slices of country ham. If you've got ready-to-eat, already soaked slices, skip step 3.

SLASH THE SHOPPING LIST

Omit the eleven ingredients in step 1 and instead use about ½ cup thick, fruit-based barbecue sauce—but be careful that it's not too spicy. Too much heat can knock a slice of American country ham senseless.

2 medium shallots, finely chopped

1¾ cups canned tomato sauce (about a 14-ounce can)

½ cup plum jam

½ cup beef broth

¼ cup dark rum

2 tablespoons Dijon mustard

2 tablespoons red wine vinegar

1 tablespoon Worcestershire sauce

1 tablespoon minced fresh peeled ginger

¼ teaspoon freshly ground black pepper

⅛ teaspoon ground cloves

Two ½-pound, ¼-inch-thick, uncooked country ham steaks

1. Stir the shallots, tomato sauce, jam, broth, rum, mustard, vinegar, Worcestershire sauce, ginger, pepper, and cloves in a medium saucepan over medium heat and bring the mixture to a simmer.

2. Knock the heat down to low; simmer slowly, uncovered, stirring occasionally, until the sauce has thickened a bit, about like loose ketchup, 15 to 20 minutes.

3. Meanwhile, place the ham steaks in a large baking pan and cover with cool water. Set aside to soak at room temperature for 20 minutes. Drain, cut off the steak's outer rind (leaving any fat in place), and pat dry.

4. Heat a gas grill to medium heat or prepare a medium-heat, well-ashed coal bed in a charcoal grill.

5. Set the soaked steaks on the grill grate right over the heat and spread about 2 tablespoons barbecue sauce on each. Close the grill and cook for 1 minute. Then open the grill, turn the steaks, and spread about 2 tablespoons barbecue sauce on the other side.

6. Continue turning, slathering with sauce without letting it burn but cooking with the grill's lid mostly closed, until the ham steaks are hot and cooked through, about 5 minutes. Serve at once, cutting each steak into chunky wedges.

SAVING THE HOCK

AN ARTISANAL COUNTRY HAM will come with its hock—that is, the joint where the meat narrows from the tibia/fibula to the trotter's metatarsals. Some culinary gurus insist that you remove the hock before roasting a country ham, arguing that you can save it for soups and stews without any glazes.

In so doing, you'd also be saving way too much salt; the reserved hock will eventually leach it into whatever you're making. Dead Sea Vegetable Soup, anyone?

So we soak and roast the hock on the ham. Later, when we're cleaning up, we take the hock off with a sharp cleaver or a clean, sterilized hacksaw. We remove any sticky, glazed fat, seal the hock in a zip-closed plastic bag, toss it in the freezer, and wait for the next pot of vegetable soup.

A NAUGHTY ★ ★ HAM ★ ★

A RECENT STUDY by Huanlu Song at Beijing Technology and Business University found the following flavors reported by American country ham tasters: chocolate, peanuts, popcorn, tortillas, butter, cheese, milk, mushrooms, melons, peaches, cucumbers, roses, coconuts, potatoes, burnt sugar, and cut grass.

Those perceived flavors aren't pretentious kookiness. There's a complex chemical structure to the taste, thanks in large part to the Strecker degradation, a process that occurs as the hams age: At least a third of the meat's rather tasteless amino acids are broken down into various smaller chemical bits (imines and ketones) that all add up to big flavors.

In addition, as the ham heats up in your oven, it undergoes a second bit of chemical wizardry: the Maillard reaction, named for Louis Camille Maillard (1878–1936), a French chemist who studied the interactions of amino acids and sugars until he shipped off to become a recluse in northern Africa.

Here's how the Maillard reaction works: A carbohydrate molecule will start a chemical dance with an amino acid when they are heated together. As they shake and shiver, various unstable compounds are flung out, break apart, and add up to hundreds of new flavors.

In common parlance, it's called "browning." Add that to the flavor storehouse already in the ham, and you have a complexity to rival fine wines and cheeses.

EAT COUNTRY HAM RAW?

THE QUESTION'S ACTUALLY NOT as far-fetched as you might think. After all, you eat Italian *prosciutto crudo* and Spanish *jamón Serrano*, which have been dry-cured, hung, aged, and not otherwise cooked.

So can you? Maybe.

But *should* you? That's another matter entirely.

Yes, country hams are bacteria-killing salt deserts, the water activity level well below dangerous levels (see page 110). Some producers will tell you can eat "raw" country ham if it's been aged at least 12 months. Others say 18 months. And still others, 24 months. (Note that all of these are getting up near the aging required for high-end European hams.)

In the end, the USDA remains mute on the matter, partly because no American producer has wanted to press it. Yes, old-timers eat paper-thin slices of ultrasalty, uncooked, even unsoaked country ham. But these people have lived so long (and drunk so much?) that they're probably bacteria-resistant on a host of fronts. Best to leave them to their vices and opt for safety.

NEW TAKES FOR COUNTRY HAM STEAKS

These recipes all use uncooked slices of American country ham, sometimes sold as steaks. Thus, almost all the recipes require that you soak the meat.

What's with all this soaking? Osmosis: the flow of a liquid caused by the difference in concentrations of various soluble components kept apart by a semipermeable membrane.

When an American country ham is soaked in water, cell membranes respond to the changing osmotic pressure—that is, the difference between the clean water outside the cells and the more salt-soaked liquid inside them. Under pressure, the clean water flows into the cells and carries out the salt until a new equilibrium is achieved. (That's why you have to change the water repeatedly when you're soaking a whole country ham—the osmotic pressure returns to an equilibrium with a good deal of the salt left in the meat.)

Some artisinal producers have helped shortcut this process by selling already soaked, ready-to-eat country ham steaks. Such slices must be refrigerated and should be used within a couple days of your getting them home. Or stick them in the freezer for up to 6 months.

Can you use leftover country ham for these recipes? Of course—but omit any soaking.

And can you use other types of ham? Well, yes. Any smoked ham will do, particularly a spiral-sliced, wet-cured ham, or even bits of a leftover smoked fresh ham (page 24). Again, omit the soaking. In addition, cut off any seasonings or sugary coatings. Ham may be wonderfully forgiving, but spice blends aren't.

COLLARDS AND COUNTRY HAM

MAKES 6 SERVINGS

There may be no more authentic Southern side dish made from left-over country ham. This one's spiked with heat and vinegar, a fine contrast to the salty meat.

2 tablespoons lard or solid vegetable shortening

4 ounces uncooked country ham steak, rind removed, the meat cut into ½-inch cubes

6 tablespoons chopped red onion (about a quarter of a large red onion)

1 medium garlic clove, minced

½ teaspoon red pepper flakes

1 pound cleaned, stemmed, chopped collard greens (about 8 cups), preferably still wet from their bath

2 cups water

¼ cup white wine vinegar

Freshly ground black pepper to taste

1. Melt the lard in a very large skillet over medium heat. Toss in the ham and onion. Cook until the meat's splotched with brown bits, about 3 minutes, stirring often.

2. Add the garlic and red pepper flakes. Cook until ridiculously aromatic, about 1 minute, stirring often.

3. Add the collards, toss well two or three times, then pour in the water and vinegar. Raise the heat to high and bring to a boil, stirring and tossing the greens until they wilt a bit. Without a doubt, the best tool is a pair of kitchen tongs that can grab the greens in a knot and turn them over. If you're working in a nonstick skillet, make sure the tongs have a surface designed not to scratch the nonstick coating.

4. Cover, reduce the heat to low, and simmer slowly just until the greens are tender, stirring occasionally, about 20 minutes. The liquid should simmer at the barest bubble; otherwise, you'll lose too much to evaporation. However, the simmer must be high enough to get the greens tender. Check the skillet occasionally to make sure it hasn't gone dry. If necessary, add a little more water, cover, and continue cooking.

5. Uncover and continue cooking until the liquid in the pan or skillet has reduced to a thick sauce, about like a glaze, perhaps 5 minutes more. Before serving, stir in a couple grinds of black pepper.

THE INGREDIENT SCOOP

Collards, like so many leafy greens, can be up to 70 percent air by volume when raw—thus you must buy a lot because they deflate (or wilt) over the heat. To clean the collards, place them in a cleaned sink, stopper it, and fill it with cool water. Give the leaves a little agitation, then leave them alone for a couple minutes while the grit sinks to the bottom. Fish the greens out, leaving the grit behind. No need to dry them, since any extra water on the leaves will simply aid their getting tender. However, do remove the fibrous, woody stems. If desired, freeze these stems and save them for the next time you make stock. (Don't you love it when cookbook authors write crap like that?) And one final note: The timing for cooked collards can be tricky. Those fresh in summer will take considerably less time than those long-stored in winter. Keep checking by tasting the greens—and be a little flexible with the timing. Of course, this extra patience works fine for adults but can be a disaster with five-year-olds. That said, if your five-year-old is eating collards, kudos to you.

COUNTRY CARBONARA

MAKES **2** HEART-STOPPING LUNCH SERVINGS OR **4** SMALL
FIRST-COURSE OFFERINGS

Carbonara is traditionally made with an Umbrian delicacy: cured pork jowl, or guanciale (Italian, gwan-CHAH-lay, from a word for "cheek"). That said, country ham gives the dish a perfect hominess. Even so, carbonara should never include cream; the richness must come entirely from the butter and egg yolks.

6 ounces uncooked country ham, any rind and its attendant fat removed

2 tablespoons unsalted butter

3 medium shallots, diced

½ pound dried spaghetti

2 large eggs, at room temperature, cracked into a small bowl and beaten with a whisk until uniformly creamy and yellow

2 ounces finely grated Parmigiano-Reggiano (see page 87)

Freshly ground black pepper to taste

1. Soak the ham in a large baking pan or bowl filled with cool water for 30 minutes at room temperature, then drain. If you're using leftover cooked country ham or other leftover ham bits, omit this step.

2. Cut the meat into thin little matchsticks so they'll match the spaghetti to come. They needn't (in fact, can't) be as long as the noodles, just the same width.

3. Melt the butter in a large skillet or sauté pan set over medium heat. Dump in those ham matchsticks and cook, stirring often, for 2 minutes.

4. Add the shallots and cook, stirring often, until softened and even a little browned, about 2 minutes. Take the skillet off the heat.

5. Bring a large pot of water to a boil over high heat. Add the spaghetti and cook until al dente (soft but with a little tooth at its center), about 6 minutes. Drain in a colander set in the sink but reserve up to ½ cup of the cooking water.

6. From here on out, kitchen tongs are the best tool. Set the skillet or sauté pan with the ham and shallots back over medium heat and bring back to a sizzle. Immediately drop the heat to low, add the pasta, and toss a few times.

7. Pour in ¹/₄ cup of the reserved cooking water, toss well, and then add the beaten eggs. Stir, stir, stir—quickly and constantly, tossing everything together so that you create a custard, not scrambled eggs. It also helps to lift the skillet or pan on and off the heat occasionally, so it doesn't get too hot. If the pasta starts to stick or the sauce gets too thick, add a little more of the cooking liquid to loosen it up, about 1 tablespoon at a time.

8. Once you've got a creamy sauce, take the skillet or pan off the heat. Stir in the cheese until melted; season with pepper to taste.

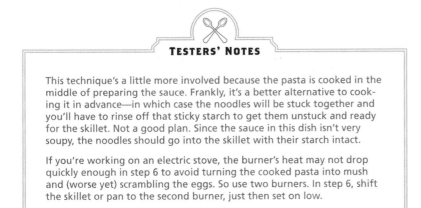

TESTERS' NOTES

This technique's a little more involved because the pasta is cooked in the middle of preparing the sauce. Frankly, it's a better alternative to cooking it in advance—in which case the noodles will be stuck together and you'll have to rinse off that sticky starch to get them unstuck and ready for the skillet. Not a good plan. Since the sauce in this dish isn't very soupy, the noodles should go into the skillet with their starch intact.

If you're working on an electric stove, the burner's heat may not drop quickly enough in step 6 to avoid turning the cooked pasta into mush and (worse yet) scrambling the eggs. So use two burners. In step 6, shift the skillet or pan to the second burner, just then set on low.

COUNTRY HAM, BUTTERNUT SQUASH, AND CHILE STEW

FEEDS ABOUT 6 HUNGRY PEOPLE

Bruce's first attempt at creating this hearty warmer was a bit of a bust—only because he didn't double the batch! I wanted some squirreled away in the freezer for future lunches. Again, if you're using ready-to-eat country ham steaks or wet-cured ham leftovers for this recipe, omit step 1.

1 pound thickly sliced uncooked country ham, preferably a couple country ham steaks, rind removed

2 dried New Mexican red chiles

1 dried ancho chile

1 dried chipotle chile

2 tablespoons peanut oil

1 medium yellow onion, chopped

1 medium green bell pepper, cored, seeded, and chopped

3 medium garlic cloves, minced

2 tablespoons honey

1 teaspoon ground cumin

1 teaspoon dried oregano

½ teaspoon ground cinnamon

3½ cups canned diced tomatoes (about one 28-ounce can)

1½ cups reduced-sodium, fat-free chicken broth

One 2-pound butternut squash, peeled, cut in half, seeded, the flesh cut into 1-inch cubes

1. Place the ham in a large baking dish or a shallow bowl. Cover with cool water and soak at room temperature for 1 hour, changing the water once during the soaking time. Drain.

2. Cut the meat into ¹/₂-inch cubes and set aside.

3. Stem all the chiles and break them open over the trash can, pulling out the inner membranes and discarding any seeds as well.

4. Place those chile pieces in a medium bowl and cover with boiling water. Set aside to soften for 30 minutes. If the chiles won't stay submerged, set a small plate on top to force them down.

5. Use kitchen tongs to take the chiles out of the water and load them into a food processor fitted with the chopping blade. Also add ¹/₃ cup of the soaking water. Process to a thick paste, scraping down the inside of the canister once or twice so that all the little bits of chile take a spin against the blades.

6. Heat a large pot over medium heat. Pour in the oil, then add the onion and bell pepper. Cook, stirring often, until softened, about 4 minutes.

7. Add the cubed ham and garlic. Cook, stirring constantly, for 30 seconds.

8. Stir in the honey, cumin, oregano, and cinnamon for about 30 seconds, until just aromatic; then add the pepper paste from the food processor, scraping it out with a rubber spatula so you get every little bit. Cook and stir until quite aromatic, about 1 minute.

9. Pour in the tomatoes, add the broth, and stir in the butternut squash. Bring everything to a simmer.

10. Cover, reduce the heat to low, and cook until the squash chunks are wonderfully tender, about 50 minutes.

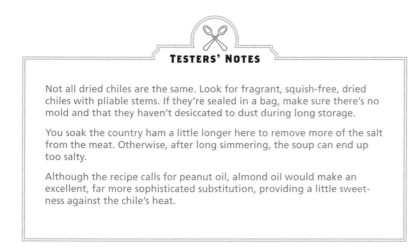

TESTERS' NOTES

Not all dried chiles are the same. Look for fragrant, squish-free, dried chiles with pliable stems. If they're sealed in a bag, make sure there's no mold and that they haven't desiccated to dust during long storage.

You soak the country ham a little longer here to remove more of the salt from the meat. Otherwise, after long simmering, the soup can end up too salty.

Although the recipe calls for peanut oil, almond oil would make an excellent, far more sophisticated substitution, providing a little sweetness against the chile's heat.

POTATO GRATIN ᴡɪᴛʜ COUNTRY HAM, BRUSSELS SPROUTS, AND LEEKS

FEEDS ABOUT 8

Buy fat, tubular russets to make the long, thin slices necessary for a successful gratin (a layered potato casserole), here a main course if you serve a salad on the side. There are two ways to get the potatoes sliced correctly. One: Lop off one end of each potato so they'll stand up on your cutting board, then cut paper-thin slices down the spuds with a sharp knife. Or two: Set a mandoline's blade to the ⅛-inch setting, then attach the potatoes one by one to the food guard and run them lengthwise down the ramp and over the blade, creating long, thin slices.

THE INGREDIENT SCOOP

Don't use any other potato varietal: Only **russets** are high enough in starch to thicken the liquid in the casserole while it bakes.

To shred **Brussels sprouts**, set them on your cutting board and make slices about ⅛ inch apart, parallel to the way the little stem would have stuck up if you hadn't already removed it. The bits should fall apart like shredded cabbage.

4 medium russet potatoes (about 2½ pounds), peeled and cut lengthwise into ⅛-inch slices

1¾ cups reduced-sodium, fat-free chicken broth

1 cup milk, preferably whole milk

7 tablespoons unsalted butter, plus additional for greasing the baking dish

8 ounces uncooked country ham steak, rind removed and discarded, the meat diced into ¼-inch cubes

1 large leek, white and pale-green part only, halved lengthwise, washed carefully to remove any grit, and thinly sliced

8 ounces Brussels sprouts, stems removed, the heads thinly sliced

2 teaspoons stemmed thyme leaves

½ teaspoon freshly ground black pepper

1 cup fresh bread crumbs

2 ounces Parmigiano-Reggiano (see page 87), finely grated

1. Place the potato slices, broth, and milk in a large saucepan. Bring to a low simmer over medium heat, stirring occasionally so the starchy slices don't stick. Cover, reduce the heat to very low, and simmer slowly just until the potato slices have turned tender, about 12 minutes. It's best if you rearrange the slices a couple times while they cook so they take turns closer to the heat without any sticking to the bottom of the pot.

2. Meanwhile, melt 3 tablespoons butter in a large skillet set over medium heat. Add the diced ham and cook, stirring often, until the ham is cooked through and even a little browned, about 4 minutes.

3. Add the leeks; cook, stirring often, until softened, about 4 minutes.

4. Stir in the shredded Brussels sprouts, thyme, and pepper. Keep stirring and cooking, just until the Brussels sprouts threads start to turn tender, about 3 minutes. The point here is not to overcook anything, because it still has a long time in the oven. Set the skillet aside.

5. Preheat the oven to 350°F. Use a little butter on a piece of wax paper or a paper towel to grease the inside of a 9-by-13-inch baking dish.

6. Now build the casserole. Use a slotted spoon to transfer about a third of the potato slices to the baking dish. Arrange them in an even pattern across the bottom, all pointing the same way and overlapping one another. Spoon and spread half the ham mixture evenly over the potato slices. Then make another layer of potatoes, all facing the same way and overlapping, using about half the remaining slices in the saucepan. Spoon and spread the rest of the ham mixture evenly over those potatoes, then perform the whole operation again with the remaining potatoes, creating a top layer. Drizzle the cooking liquid left in the saucepan evenly over the casserole.

7. Use a microwave or a small saucepan set over low heat to melt the remaining 4 tablespoons (¹/₂ stick) butter. Cool a couple minutes.

8. Mix the melted butter with the bread crumbs and cheese in a medium bowl. Sprinkle this mixture evenly over the casserole.

9. Bake uncovered until browned, bubbling, and utterly irresistible, about 30 minutes. Cool the casserole on a wire rack for 5 minutes before slicing into squares to serve.

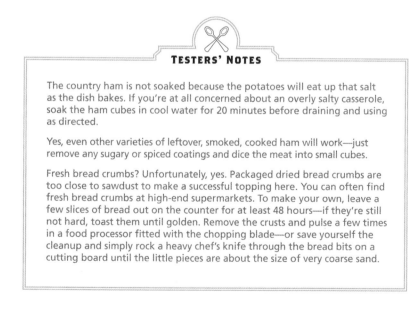

TESTERS' NOTES

The country ham is not soaked because the potatoes will eat up that salt as the dish bakes. If you're at all concerned about an overly salty casserole, soak the ham cubes in cool water for 20 minutes before draining and using as directed.

Yes, even other varieties of leftover, smoked, cooked ham will work—just remove any sugary or spiced coatings and dice the meat into small cubes.

Fresh bread crumbs? Unfortunately, yes. Packaged dried bread crumbs are too close to sawdust to make a successful topping here. You can often find fresh bread crumbs at high-end supermarkets. To make your own, leave a few slices of bread out on the counter for at least 48 hours—if they're still not hard, toast them until golden. Remove the crusts and pulse a few times in a food processor fitted with the chopping blade—or save yourself the cleanup and simply rock a heavy chef's knife through the bread bits on a cutting board until the little pieces are about the size of very coarse sand.

THE HISTORY OF AMERICAN COUNTRY HAM

BASICALLY, IT'S YET TO BE WRITTEN. Ask some country-ham producers, as I did, and you'll get lots of different stories. Nancy Newsom Mahaffey gives the colonial boilerplate: The English landed in Virginia and learned to cure meat from the Native Americans. And here's Bill Robertson: "The Chinese started this whole thing." June Scott just shrugs and says, "Everyone around here's always cured ham."

One story goes like this: Hernando de Soto, Spanish explorer and conquistador, brought a bunch of pigs to Florida, raised them, and let them run loose all over Christendom—until people had so many hogs, they had to start doing something with the meat.

And another: The Jamestown settlers brought so many pigs with them that the animals overran the colony and eventually had to be relegated to their own island, Hog Island, in the James River.

Truth be told, the first documented reference to an American country ham does not occur until 1944; it details how the hams were cured in Virginia, Kentucky, Tennessee, Georgia, and Vermont.

Vermont? Well, it just goes to show that dry-curing hams has been an *American* cottage industry for quite a while. Until fairly recently, country hams were actually considered the poor stepchildren of their fancier, wet-cured brethren.

But not anymore, particularly since certain European and Japanese chefs started using American country hams with abandon in the early 1990s and since the burgeoning Chinese market in America discovered the meat. One of America's great "undiscovered" products has become an international sensation—and deservedly so.

JINHUA HAMS

JINHUA HAMS (金華火腿, *jeen-hoo-ah hoo-oh tooee* in Mandarin) are air-dried, salted hams from the Zhejiang province. They are made from a breed of small pigs called "two black ends," a reference to the black hairs that sprout from their noses and rumps.

These hams are salted several times, dried, washed, and then trimmed to resemble furled bamboo leaves. There is no sugar in the cure, but some producers do add sodium nitrate.

The meat is then hung to dry for up to 10 months—by which time it is often covered with a fine film of yellow mold, the result of local spores and the Zhejiang microclimates.

Unfortunately, modern production sometimes short-circuits the process by injecting the hams with salt water, clipping the hanging time, and rubbing the meat with a yellow food dye to replicate the traditional appearance.

That said, artisanally made Jinhua hams have a flavor and texture very similar to American country hams, particularly the stronger, pungent, "moldy" taste associated with long-aged country hams. Jinhua hams have not yet cleared the necessary hurdles for import, mostly because producers have been caught spraying the hams with pesticides to prevent rot in the warmer months; thus, you'll often find American country hams hanging over the meat counter in Chinese markets.

One butcher in New York City even told us he preferred these American hams for soups and stir-fries. But he ducked his head, clearly embarrassed.

CHINESE-INSPIRED HAM AND WINTER MELON SOUP

MAKES 6 HEARTY SERVINGS

Bruce told me this recipe is just an excuse to make the best Chinese soup stock ever. If you should choose to make only the stock (that is, steps 1 through 4), store it in sealed containers in the freezer for up to 3 months. To make an easy soup from that stock, thaw one container overnight in the fridge, then heat it up in a pan with some sliced bok choy and peeled and deveined medium shrimp.

1 pound uncooked country ham, the rind and its attendant fat removed and discarded, the meat cut into ½-inch cubes

1 fresh ham hock (not smoked), or 1½ pounds pork bones

1 chicken back and 1 chicken neck, or 1½ pounds chicken bones and scraps

3 medium scallions, roughly chopped

Four 1-inch-long peeled fresh ginger pieces

12 cups water

1 pound peeled Chinese winter melon, seeded, the pale flesh cut into ½-inch cubes

SLASH THE SHOPPING LIST

Skip the first four steps and add 6 cups chicken broth and 1 teaspoon grated, peeled ginger to the other ingredients in step 5 (if you must—Bruce really doesn't approve).

THE INGREDIENT SCOOP

Winter melon (冬瓜, *dong gua* in Mandarin, but also called "fuzzy melon," "ash melon," and "hairy melon") is an enormous tubular or oblong gourd grown throughout India, Southwest Asia, and southern China. The skin is usually a pale, mottled green, the flesh a translucent white. The melon itself is so large you usually only buy a wedge, to which the seeds are attached by thin, fibrous membranes, like a honeydew on steroids. Pull off and discard those seeds, then scrape out their floppy filaments with a serrated grapefruit spoon. Finally, cut the flesh off the tough peel. Note that the winter melon's weight in the recipe is "peeled"—that is, not with the peel on. Consider buying about 1¼ pounds just to make sure.

1. Place the ham cubes in a large bowl, then cover with cool water. Set aside to soak at room temperature for 30 minutes. Drain in a colander set in the sink.

2. Stock a large pot with the hock, chicken, scallions, ginger, and half the soaked ham (that is, 8 ounces—cover and store the other half of the ham in the refrigerator until you're ready to use it in step 5).

3. Pour in the water and bring to a simmer over medium heat. Reduce the heat to low and cook at the lowest simmer possible, just a bubble or two at a time, uncovered, for 6 hours.

4. Set a strainer over a large bowl, then slowly pour the stock and all its contents from the pot into the strainer. Discard the stuff in the strainer; pour the stock back into the pot.

5. Add the remaining 8 ounces of ham along with the winter melon. Bring to a simmer, then reduce the heat and cook at a very low simmer for 15 minutes, just until the cubes of melon are meltingly tender.

JAPANESE-INSPIRED STICKY RICE WITH COUNTRY HAM, CHESTNUTS, AND SWEET POTATOES

FEEDS ABOUT 8, EVEN MORE IF YOU'VE GOT OTHER THINGS TO PASS AROUND

This dish is a tweak on "autumn rice," a Japanese comfort-food favorite made with the first rice of the new crop and often served as a breakfast dish. Bruce's version is a thoroughly American interpretation, a great side dish for almost anything off the grill. In this recipe, the country ham bits are not first soaked because they then lend necessary salt to the rice. (Bruce has also omitted any soy sauce to compensate for the saltier taste.) If you're concerned about too much sodium, soak the ham for 20 minutes in cool water before using. And if you're using presoaked ham steaks or bits of leftover smoked ham, then you're good to go from the start.

THE INGREDIENT SCOOP

Mirin (みりん, *meer-in*), a low-alcohol, high-sugar Japanese cooking wine made from rice, is available at almost all Asian markets as well as the Asian aisle of most supermarkets. Once opened, store in the refrigerator for up to 3 months.

2 cups sushi or short-grain white rice

8 ounces jarred steamed or roasted chestnuts, cut into ½-inch pieces

8 ounces sweet potatoes, peeled and cut into ¼-inch cubes

6 ounces uncooked country ham steak, rind removed, the meat chopped into ½-inch pieces

2½ cups reduced-sodium, fat-free chicken broth

¼ cup mirin

1 teaspoon dry ginger

1. Combine everything in a large saucepan and bring the mixture to a simmer over medium-high heat, stirring occasionally.

2. Cover, reduce the heat to low, and simmer slowly until the rice is almost tender, about 30 minutes. Set the pan off the heat, covered, for 10 minutes before serving.

GLORIOUS LEFTOVERS

No one can make a country ham without help in the eating department. Bruce and I are always up for a meal, but even the two of us can't sit down to a 16-pound country ham undaunted. So we conceptualized a set of recipes for the inevitable leftovers. Some of the preparations are involved and over-the-top; others, simple and accessible.

Fortunately, you don't have to wait until you have leftovers to make any of them. As we've said, you can get packaged, cooked, ready-to-eat country ham steaks from most producers.

And while we're at it, we'll admit that many of these will also work with leftovers from a smoked, wet-cured ham like a HoneyBaked®, or even the leftover bits from a smoked fresh ham (page 24).

CHIVE AND CHEDDAR HAM BISCUITS ⟨WITH⟩ HONEY MUSTARD

MAKES 16 STUFFED BISCUITS

Here's something of a Tidewater tradition, often served the morning after a big feast: little ham sandwiches made with homemade biscuits. The best are made with yeast but not raised, the yeast being just one of three leaveners.

SLASH THE SHOPPING LIST

If you'd prefer not to make your own honey mustard, omit step 1 and its five ingredients; simply use a high-quality bottled brand.

¼ cup smooth Dijon mustard

2 tablespoons coarse-grained mustard

2 tablespoons packed dark brown sugar

2 tablespoons honey

1½ teaspoons cider vinegar

2 tablespoons plus 1 teaspoon granulated white sugar

One ¼-ounce package or 2¼ teaspoons active dry yeast

¼ cup warmed water, between 105°F and 115°F

1½ cups cake flour

1 cup all-purpose flour, plus additional for dusting and more as necessary

1 teaspoon baking powder

1 teaspoon baking soda

½ teaspoon salt

½ cup solid vegetable shortening

2 ounces shredded Cheddar (about ½ cup)

2 tablespoons minced chives or the green parts of scallions

¾ cup plus 2 tablespoons regular or low-fat buttermilk

4 to 6 ounces cooked leftover country-style ham, sliced as thinly as possible and preferably warmed

1. Mix both mustards, the brown sugar, honey, and vinegar in a small bowl until spreadable but uniform. Set aside.

2. Sprinkle 1 teaspoon sugar and the yeast over the warm water in a medium bowl. Set aside until frothy, about 5 minutes. If for any reason the yeast mixture doesn't foam, throw it out and start again. Either the yeast had gone bad or the water wasn't the right temperature.

3. Meanwhile, set the rack in the center of the oven and heat it to 400°F.

4. Stir both flours, the baking powder, baking soda, salt, and the remaining 2 tablespoons sugar in a large bowl until you can't tell the sugar or baking powder from the other parts of the mixture.

5. Dollop the shortening into the bowl, then cut it into the mixture with a fork or a pastry cutter, pressing the shortening through the tines and into the flour mixture until it resembles coarse meal, with no big chunks of shortening anywhere and the dry ingredients uniform in texture.

6. Use a fork to stir in the cheese and chives, then the buttermilk and the foamy yeast mixture. Keep stirring until a soft dough forms, adding additional all-purpose flour as necessary to keep the dough pliable.

7. Dust a clean, dry work surface with a little flour; dump the dough onto it. Knead lightly just until smooth, about 1 minute. If you want to make the dough in advance, prepare it to this point, then seal in plastic wrap and place in the refrigerator for up to 1 week. Take out as little or as much as you need for any given moment, let that amount come near room temperature (about 20 minutes on the counter), then roll and bake as directed.

8. Lightly flour your work surface again; lightly flour the dough and a rolling pin. Roll to about $1/2$ inch thick; cut into 2-inch circles using a biscuit cutter, cookie cutter, or a thick-rimmed drinking glass.

9. Place the rounds at least 2 inches apart on a large baking sheet and bake until puffed and lightly browned, about 12 minutes. Cool on the baking tray for 2 minutes, then transfer to a wire rack and continue cooling for 5 minutes.

10. Split each biscuit in half, then spread a little honey mustard on the cut sides. Place a little ham on the cut side of the bottom half, then top with the other half of the biscuit.

JERK-STYLE COUNTRY HAM AND PINEAPPLE TAMALES

MAKES 20 TAMALES

Call this Bruce's culinary free-for-all: a Caribbean filling made with American country ham and served as a Tex-Mex delicacy in corn husks. There's not much more I can say, except they freeze well. Make them in advance, then wrap them individually in plastic and freeze for up to 3 months; thaw on the counter for 30 minutes before steaming as directed.

20 large, dry corn husks for tamales

6 ounces dried pineapple

10 ounces cooked country ham, rind removed and discarded, the meat cut into little cubes (a little less than ⅔ cup)

3 medium scallions, cut into 2-inch pieces

¼ cup dark rum such as Myers's

2 tablespoons minced peeled fresh ginger

2 tablespoons packed dark brown sugar

2 tablespoons red wine vinegar

2 teaspoons ground cumin

1 teaspoon ground coriander

1 teaspoon dried oregano

1 teaspoon dried thyme

½ teaspoon ground allspice

½ teaspoon ground cloves

½ teaspoon grated nutmeg

½ teaspoon cayenne

¼ teaspoon garlic powder

4 cups instant *masa harina*

3 cups very hot water

⅔ cup peanut oil

1 teaspoon onion powder

SLASH THE SHOPPING LIST

Omit 1 teaspoon cumin, the coriander, oregano, thyme, allspice, cloves, nutmeg, cayenne, and garlic powder in step 3 and replace them all with 2 tablespoons jerk seasoning mixture. (Note: You'll still need 1 teaspoon ground cumin for step 4.)

THE INGREDIENT SCOOP

Masa harina (Spanish, *MAH-sah hah-REEN-ah*, "dough flour") is the base ingredient for tortillas and tamales. It's made from dried corn kernels that have been cooked in limewater, then ground to a powder. Some *masa harinas* are labeled "for tamales," others are all-purpose. Either will work here, so long as you have the instant variety.

1. Put the corn husks in a large bowl and cover with boiling water. Set them aside to soak until soft, about 30 minutes. If they all won't stay submerged, place a little plate over them in the bowl to force them down into the hot water.

2. Meanwhile, put the dried pineapple in a medium bowl and cover with boiling water. Soak for 10 minutes, then drain in a colander set in the sink. Chop the pineapple into tiny bits.

3. Transfer those pineapple chunks to a food processor fitted with the chopping blade. Add the ham, scallions, rum, ginger, brown sugar, vinegar, 1 teaspoon cumin, the coriander, oregano, thyme, allspice, cloves, nutmeg, cayenne, and garlic powder. Pulse until well chopped and thoroughly blended but not pureed. This is the filling for the tamales, so you want some tooth in the thing—in other words, no baby food.

4. Mix the *masa*, hot water, oil, onion powder, and remaining 1 teaspoon ground cumin in a large bowl to make a wet dough.

5. Take a corn husk out of the hot water and spread it on your work surface so that its natural curl faces you. Spread a generous ¼ cup of the *masa* dough into the corn husk, smoothing it out but also keeping it near the thicker bottom of the husk, like a little bed of dough for the filling. Spread the dough out to the sides a bit so that when you roll the husk closed the long way, that dough will encircle and even cover the filling.

6. Place about 1½ tablespoons of the ham mixture in the center of the dough in the corn husk.

7. Fold the sides of the husk up and over the filling, thereby also bringing the *masa* dough up and around the filling inside. Make sure the sides overlap and fully close, holding the filling tightly inside. Fold the wider bottom up over the husk and do the same with the narrower top. Tie these in place with butchers' twine so the tamale will stay closed.

8. Repeat steps 5 through 7 with the remaining husks.

9. Set up some kind of steaming contraption: either a large vegetable steamer in a large saucepan with about an inch of so of water in the bottom, or a couple of bamboo steamers placed over a wok with a similar amount of water in it. Bring the water to a boil over high heat.

10. Stand the tamales up in the vegetable steamer or lay them in the bamboo steamers. Cover, reduce the heat, and steam for 40 minutes, checking the water occasionally and adding more if necessary. In no event should the water rise and come in contact with the tamales. You want the water gently simmering in the pan or wok but not boiling vigorously. Once steamed, set the tamales aside for 5 minutes before serving, just so no one gets a steam burn from the incredibly hot filling inside. And don't be a Gerald Ford. In the 1976 presidential race, he tried to eat a tamale still in the husk while campaigning in Texas. He lost the state. Unwrap the husk and fork out the tender filling inside.

ARUGULA SALAD with COUNTRY HAM, PEARS, AND HONEY VINAIGRETTE

MAKES ENOUGH FOR 2 FOR DINNER, OR UP TO 6 FOR A VERY LIGHT FIRST COURSE

Make sure you remove not only the inedible rind but also any excess fat from the cooked country ham. The profound taste of that fat is just too strong, a poor match for the pears.

¼ cup walnut pieces

⅔ pound baby arugula leaves (about 4 cups)

6 ounces cooked country ham, rind removed and discarded, the meat thinly sliced and cut into strips

1 large ripe Bartlett pear, peeled, cored, and thinly sliced

1 tablespoon lemon juice

1 tablespoon apple cider vinegar

1½ teaspoons honey

½ teaspoon Dijon mustard

3 tablespoons toasted walnut oil (see page 87)

1. Sprinkle the walnuts around a dry skillet set over medium-low heat. Leave them alone a couple minutes, then stir well and continue cooking, stirring occasionally, just until splotchy brown and fragrant. Pour them out onto a cutting board, cool for a few minutes, then chop into little bits.

2. Mix the arugula, ham, and pear pieces in a large bowl.

3. Whisk the lemon juice, vinegar, honey, and mustard in a small bowl, then whisk in the oil in a slow, steady stream until you've got a creamy, somewhat thick dressing.

4. Pour the dressing over the arugula mixture, then sprinkle the toasted walnut pieces on top.

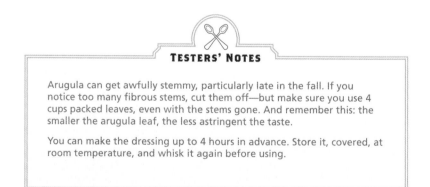

TESTERS' NOTES

Arugula can get awfully stemmy, particularly late in the fall. If you notice too many fibrous stems, cut them off—but make sure you use 4 cups packed leaves, even with the stems gone. And remember this: the smaller the arugula leaf, the less astringent the taste.

You can make the dressing up to 4 hours in advance. Store it, covered, at room temperature, and whisk it again before using.

NO-FRY EGG ROLLS
WITH COUNTRY HAM, GRUYÈRE, AND CHUTNEY

MAKES 24 APPETIZER POCKETS

These baked egg rolls are just as crunchy as the ones that come out of vats of fat and require a two-hour kitchen cleanup. But one warning: Since the chutney will directly affect their quality, try a hot tomato chutney or a deep, rich, berry-laced one. Any chunks of fruit in the chutney will need to be diced so the filling can easily be folded into the rolls.

1 pound cooked country ham, rind removed and discarded, the meat very finely chopped, even minced

8 ounces Gruyère, shredded through the large holes of a box grater

1 cup fruit chutney

1¼ cups toasted walnut pieces, finely chopped (for toasting and chopping instructions, see step 1, page 154)

1 teaspoon ground cinnamon

About ½ cup walnut oil, poured into a small bowl

24 sheets frozen phyllo dough, thawed according to the package instructions

1. Mix the ham, cheese, and chutney in a large bowl.

2. Mix the walnuts and cinnamon in a small bowl.

3. Position the rack in the center of the oven and preheat the oven to 375°F. Dab a little walnut oil on a wadded-up piece of paper towel, then grease a large, lipped baking sheet with some oil.

4. Place the phyllo sheets on your work surface and cover, first with plastic wrap and then with a clean kitchen towel. Wet your hand and sprinkle drops of water over the kitchen towel, making sure none gets on the counter. The towel should be barely damp, just enough to help keep the phyllo sheets underneath pliable.

5. Remove one sheet of dough and immediately re-cover the stack. Place the sheet on a clean, dry portion of your work surface so that one short end faces you on the counter. Use a pastry brush to smear a little walnut oil on the phyllo sheet.

6. Sprinkle 2 teaspoons of the walnut mixture evenly over the sheet, then place 2 tablespoons of the ham filling in a small, elongated mound at the end of the sheet facing you.

7. Starting at the short edge facing you, roll the sheet over once, just one flip to cover the ham filling. Fold the long sides over by about $1/2$ inch on each side—all the way up the sheet—so they fold in and cover the sides of the filling. Now roll the sheet up, starting with the filling and rolling the sheet away from you.

8. Brush the roll again with walnut oil and set it on the baking sheet. Repeat steps 5 through 8 until you've made 24 rolls, spacing them 1 inch apart on the tray. As you make more, keep them on the baking sheet covered with a kitchen towel.

9. Bake until lightly brown and crisp, about 25 minutes. Cool on the baking sheet for 2 or 3 minutes, then transfer to a wire rack to cool for a couple minutes more before serving.

TESTERS' NOTES

Working with phyllo dough is all about working quickly and efficiently. The parchment-paper sheets will dry out almost the moment you breathe on them. Keep the phyllo stack covered at all times—and get the individual sheets oiled up as quickly as possible. Our best advice? Get help. Pour a few drinks and get your guests making these with you.

HAM-AND-SHRIMP POTSTICKERS

MAKES 40 POTSTICKERS

Potstickers have to undergo a three-step cooking process: they are cooked, boiled, and crisped in one skillet. These may be a whimsical creation with country ham, but they're simply terrific with a pitcher of daiquiris.

1 pound peeled, deveined medium shrimp

4 ounces cooked country ham, rind and exterior fat cut off and discarded, the meat itself roughly chopped

2 medium scallions, cut into 2-inch pieces

2 tablespoons black vinegar

1 tablespoon minced, peeled fresh ginger

½ teaspoon five-spice powder (see page 50)

40 Chinese round dumpling wrappers

2 tablespoons sesame oil

1 cup water, plus more for sealing the dumpling wrappers

1. Put the shrimp, ham, scallions, vinegar, ginger, and five-spice powder into a large food processor fitted with the chopping blade. Pulse until a chunky paste, scraping down the insides of the canister occasionally with a rubber spatula to make sure everything's getting whacked up.

2. Lay a dumpling wrapper on a clean, dry work surface. Set a little bowl of water to one side. Put about 2 teaspoons of the ham filling into the center of the wrapper. Wet one finger and run it around the rim of the wrapper, then fold the wrapper over the filling so that the packet makes a half-moon, the wet parts adhering to each other. Dry your hand and pick up the dumpling. Crimp and pleat its edge closed by working your way around the arc, pinching a little bit together, folding it back over the part just before, and continuing around until you have a little pleated purse. Set aside under a clean kitchen towel, filling side down and pleats up, then continue making more.

3. Heat a large skillet, preferably nonstick, over medium heat. Swirl in the oil, then add the dumplings in one layer, filling side down. Cook for 4 minutes, browning the bottoms well.

4. Pour the water into the skillet, cover tightly, and turn the heat to high. Cook for 10 minutes.

5. Uncover the skillet and continue cooking until all the water has boiled away and the bottoms of the dumplings are again crisp, 3 to 4 minutes.

THE INGREDIENT SCOOP

Sesame oil is made from pressed sesame seeds. There are two varieties: regular and toasted (made, of course, from toasted sesame seeds). The latter is manhandled by heat and so is best as a light drizzle on cooked vegetables or finished stir-fries, a little added flavor to balance the other tastes. The former, untoasted variety is the only one called for in this book and is suitable as the oil used at the base of many dishes.

Black vinegar is a Chinese condiment made from fermented glutinous rice. It's sweetened and flavored with aromatics, usually star anise. It's available in gourmet and Asian markets, or from suppliers on the web. As a substitute for this recipe, use 1 tablespoon plus 1 teaspoon balsamic vinegar and 2 teaspoons Worcestershire sauce.

TESTERS' NOTES

While you're filling and sealing the dumplings, make sure you keep the counter dry. Wipe it down occasionally.

If desired, serve the dumplings at once with a side dipping sauce of equal parts soy sauce and rice vinegar.

PEKING HAM

MAKES 24 PANCAKES, ENOUGH FOR UP TO 8 FIRST-COURSE SERVINGS

THE INGREDIENT SCOOP

Hoisin sauce (海鲜, *hoy-sin*, "seafood" in Cantonese) is a thick, pasty condiment, considered by some the ketchup of China, familiar as the sauce served with mu shu pancakes and Peking duck. The sauce is traditionally made with sweet potatoes, but most bottlings today are made with soy beans, sugar, vinegar, and a wide range of flavorings and thickeners. Curiously, despite the name, there's no seafood in hoisin sauce.

TESTERS' NOTES

If you don't have a wok and a bamboo steamer, here's how you can improvise: Cut a baking potato into 3 or 4 columnar pieces about 2 inches long, then set them in a large pot such as a Dutch oven. Add tap water until it comes about halfway up those potato slices, then bring it to a boil over high heat. Reduce the heat and set a heat-safe plate in the pot on top of the potato pieces. Add the pancakes, cover, and steam as directed.

Admittedly, this recipe's a little far afield, but Bruce so loves Peking duck that he thought he'd try to replicate it with salty, smoky bits of country ham.

2 cups all-purpose flour

1 cup very hot water

2 tablespoons sesame oil (see page 159)

8 medium scallions, cut into thirds, then shredded lengthwise

½ cup hoisin sauce

18 ounces cooked American country ham, rind and exterior fat removed and discarded, the meat thinly sliced into matchsticks (about 1 cup plus 2 tablespoons)

1. Mix the flour and water in a large bowl to form a dough, then knead in the bowl for 2 to 3 minutes, adding a little more flour should the dough stick to your hands. Set aside for 20 minutes to allow the glutens to relax. Meanwhile, pour the sesame oil into a wide, shallow bowl.

2. Pinch off two balls from the dough, each about the size of a golf ball. Flatten both slightly, then dip the bottom of one in the sesame oil. Set it, oiled side down, on top of the other ball. Use a rolling pin to flatten the balls out, one on top of the other, until each is a circle about 6 inches in diameter. Repeat eleven more times to make 12 sets of two dough circles stuck together.

3. Heat a nonstick skillet over medium heat. Add several of the dough circles stuck together and cook about 4 minutes, turning once, until dry but very white. Don't brown, but do let them firm up in the skillet. Transfer to a wire rack and add more to the skillet in batches.

4. Once all the dough circles are on the wire rack and while they're still hot, peel them apart. (The recipe can be made up to this point about 1 hour in advance. Cover the pancakes with a clean kitchen towel and store at room temperature.)

5. Set a bamboo steamer over about 1 inch of simmering water in a wok. Set a heat-safe plate in the steamer, then place the pancakes on the plate. Cover and steam for 5 minutes to soften and warm the pancakes.

6. Spread each warm pancake with some of the shredded scallion, about 1 teaspoon hoisin sauce, and about ¾ ounce ham (a little less than 1 tablespoon). Fold closed like a soft taco and enjoy!

DELICATA SQUASH STUFFED ⟨with⟩ HAM AND APRICOTS

SERVES 4, ONE STUFFED SQUASH HALF APIECE

Ever since Bruce first turned me onto delicata squash, I've been a fan. With its creamy flesh and edible skin, it's a sweet fruit that's eaten as a vegetable. Here, he slices the squash lengthwise, cleans them out, and stuffs the little "boats."

⅓ cup chopped dried apricots

2 tablespoons bourbon

2 tablespoons unsalted butter, at room temperature

8 ounces finely chopped cooked country ham, rind removed and discarded (about 1 cup)

½ cup chopped walnut pieces

3 tablespoons packed dark brown sugar

1 tablespoon lemon juice

2 medium delicata squash, skins washed, halved lengthwise, any seeds and their attendant fibers scraped out (preferably with a serrated grapefruit spoon)

½ cup water

2 tablespoons apple cider vinegar

1. Stir the apricots and the bourbon in a large bowl, then set aside so the apricots can soak for 20 minutes. Meanwhile, preheat the oven to 350°F.

2. Stir the softened butter into the apricots and bourbon along with the ham, walnuts, brown sugar, and lemon juice.

3. Place the squash, cut side up, in a 9-by-13-inch baking dish or any baking dish into which they'll fit securely without crowding. Spoon the ham mixture into the hollowed-out grooves in the squash where the seeds used to be.

4. Pour the water and vinegar into the baking dish without pouring either directly on the squash halves. Cover tightly with aluminum foil and bake for 45 minutes. Every 15 minutes, uncover the dish and baste the squash and filling with the liquid in the baking dish.

5. Uncover and continue baking, basting every couple minutes with pan juices, until what's left as liquid in the dish becomes a thick glaze, 5 to 10 minutes more. Spoon this last bit up and onto the squash just before serving.

SPAETZLE *WITH* COUNTRY HAM AND MUSHROOMS

MAKES 6 COMFORT-FOOD-SIZE SERVINGS

Spaetzle *(German, SHPEH-tsluh, "little sparrows")* are Lilliputian dumplings, usually no more than an inch long, like thick threads of cooked dough. Although often sautéed with butter as a side dish, here they're gussied up to become a main course.

2¼ cups all-purpose flour

2 large eggs, at room temperature

¾ cup milk—whole, low-fat, or fat-free

Nonstick spray

3 tablespoons unsalted butter

2 large shallots, minced

1 medium red bell pepper, cored, seeded, and diced

8 ounces cooked country ham, rind removed, the meat diced

½ teaspoon caraway seeds

½ pound cremini mushrooms, thinly sliced

1 cup reduced-sodium, fat-free chicken broth

1 tablespoon Dijon mustard

1 tablespoon Worcestershire sauce

1. Mix the flour, eggs, and milk in a large bowl until you have a sticky, elastic, doughish batter.

2. Bring a large pot of water to a boil over high heat. It helps if it's a tall, thin pot so that the flat grater sits over its opening without your having to hold it in place.

3. Spray a flat grater with wide holes (see Testers' Notes) with nonstick spray, then set it over the pot. Scoop out some of the batter with a rubber spatula, maybe about ¼ cup, and then wipe it across the grater so that small, uneven bits of batter fall through the holes. Don't let any batter fall over the sides of the grater without going through the holes or these bits will be large, tough lumps. Work quickly and efficiently to get all the batter through the grater and into the water. Don't panic, but don't stop. If you find the batter sticking to the grater, give it another spritz with the nonstick spray.

4. Once all the batter is in little threads in the pot, reduce the heat to medium-low and cook at a simmer until the bits are tender, about 6 minutes. Drain in a colander set in the sink, then place the dough bits in a large bowl and cover with cool water while you make the sauce.

5. Melt the butter in a large skillet over medium heat. Add the shallots and bell pepper; cook, stirring often, until softened a bit, about 3 minutes.

6. Stir in the ham bits and the caraway seeds. Cook, stirring often, about 2 minutes, just until the ham is warmed through.

7. Add the mushrooms all at once. Continue cooking, stirring occasionally, until the mushrooms release their internal liquid and then that liquid reduces to a glaze, about 7 minutes in all. You'll notice a definite pickup of liquid in the skillet after a couple minutes. Just be patient until this turns into a thickened glaze—not like shellac, but like a well-tended reduction sauce.

8. Pour in the broth, then add the mustard and Worcestershire sauce. Bring to a simmer.

9. Drain the *Spaetzle* in a colander set in the sink, then add them to the skillet. Toss and cook to heat through, about 3 minutes. Serve at once

TESTERS' NOTES

Bruce is using a technique to make the *Spaetzle* familiar to many immigrants in America: the dough is wiped over a flat grater, one with holes about the size of the larger ones on a box grater. You can find this tool at most kitchenware stores or their online outlets. Of course, you can also use a fancier *Spaetzle* maker; follow the directions included with your model.

Want a richer dish? Cut the broth down to ½ cup and add ½ cup cream with the remaining broth.

The dish benefits from some garnish. Consider chopped parsley or even grated nutmeg in a small bowl at the table so everyone can add a pinch. At the very least, give each serving a few grinds of black pepper.

4

WET-CURED

HAM

4

Bruce refers to ham as "the most Christian of all meats." Maybe its religious association explains why in my childhood it always showed up at Easter, that most Christian of all holidays.

And funerals, too, which are kind of like Easter except without the hopeful part. Send a ham. It's the right thing to do.

"Flowers have to be watered," my mother once said, "and hams get to be eaten. You figure out which is better."

We tested her theory when my great aunt Viola passed away. Her other, zanier siblings had already gone to their reward. My grandmother, the kook, liked to take her car out to the red rust washes around Oklahoma City, shift into neutral, roll over the edge, and see how far she could get up the other side. My great-aunt Ruth, their sister, had been the urban sophisticate among the Methodists: She took her 7UP® with vodka. But Viola had greater dignity. She owned a Wurlitzer.

Which was an integral part of my summers in Oklahoma with my grandparents. Their conversation always went like this:

"Walter, maybe Mark should go over to Viola's and give a recital."

"Did you ask him if he wanted to?"

"No. But he does."

"How do you know?"

"Because *I* want to."

So I got chauffeured to Viola's for a luncheon concert of hymns. I pulled out the swell and gave rousing renditions of "The Old Rugged Cross" with bass-pedal obbligato.

At intermission, my grandparents and Viola headed off to the kitchen to make sandwiches from deli ham—which were served on TV tray tables for enjoyment during the second act. While they were away, I'd sneak in a little ragtime: Scott Joplin with the tremolo. It passed for rebellion.

Bruce and I weren't able to get away for Viola's funeral. I wanted to send something for the lunch afterwards—and remembered both my mother's dictum and Viola's sandwiches. So we sent a spiral-sliced, glazed, HoneyBaked® ham.

I didn't hear from my cousins for a few days. Oklahoma funerals, you know. So much potato salad, so little toilet paper. But I was worried the ham might not have shown up. So I called my mother.

"They got it?" I asked. (We dispensed with "hello" twenty years ago.)

"It was there when I arrived."

"Did they like it?"

"They loved it!"

"Great. I wanted to send one large enough so there were leftovers."

"Oh, they haven't eaten any."

"You said they loved it."

"They said you can't waste a ham like that on a funeral."

In many ways, we've saved the most popular American ham for the end of this journey: the wet-cured ham, sometimes sold spiral-sliced, most often the ham that shows up for picnics, socials, potlucks, weddings, and (so I thought) funerals.

Although wet-cured hams don't have the artisanal heritage that almost all dry-cured hams have, they nonetheless make up the bulk of the cured-ham market in North America. Some foodies call these "city hams," but very few people I met in the ham business used the term. They mostly called them "picnic hams" (although lately that term has been used to label the front shoulder, or Boston butt), "luncheon hams," or even "preacher hams" (a favorite term in western Kentucky).

To make a wet-cured ham, you either inject the meat with or soak it in some sort of brine (a salt solution). There may also be sugar, herbs, and even vinegar added to enhance the flavor. A few Brits use stout.

By using a brine, you're dramatically speeding

up the osmosis that happens when a country ham is soaked in water—only backward, as it were. This time, the salt lies outside the cells (that is, in the surrounding brine), not inside them (from the curing). If the pressure differences are correct, the "purer" water from inside the cells will be drawn out into the salt water, allowing the salt water back inside.

That salt then breaks down some of the natural proteins and peptides in the meat, and the liquid inside the cells gets thicker and denser. Although there's always a free exchange of water and smaller molecules like salt through the cell's semipermeable walls, those protein and peptide components, even broken apart, are too large to escape—which means things get tighter and tighter inside the cells, like Manhattan when the tourists arrive. Yes, when the ham is baked, it loses some liquid (the "juice" in the roasting pan)—but it by no means loses all of the liquid in the cells, given how much they've absorbed. Thus, you're assured a juicy roast every time. What's more, those broken-down peptides stay behind and increase the hammy flavor dramatically.

One warning: There are often nitrates or nitrites in the brine, because wet-cured hams are thought to be more appetizing if they remain pink after the cure. The best way to avoid this chemical fandango? Cure your own (see page 169).

A wet-cured ham can be smoked or not. Many deli hams have not been smoked. Others, particularly the whole joint for a holiday meal or the ones sold spiral-sliced, are indeed smoked, sometimes lightly, sometimes heavily. Some sort of sugary, spicy glaze is usually shellacked onto the smoked hams as they roast.

While it will never have the heritage or flavor development of certain dry-cured hams, a wet-cured ham, done properly, is a thing of beauty.

Or a horror. If you're anywhere near my age, you probably remember that quintessential American meat product from the convenience-dominated sixties: the congealed mass of livid, pink, wet-cured pork that was unlocked from its pear-shaped can by an attached key, the meat then slithering out onto a roasting pan. To get to this moment, the nitrate-doped meat—and it's not only ham but other pig parts as well (use your imagination)—has been mixed with gelatin to make sure the "roast" holds together. It is then extruded into the can, sealed, and steamed—if to 122°F, the thing can sit on the shelf for up to 2 years; if below 122°F, it must be refrigerated and sold within 9 months.

Forget the horror. There are terrific varieties of wet-cured ham available at your butcher counter, in the deli case, and from specialty-ham retailers. These tasty hams will keep you safely away from meat that needs to be unlocked and unmolded.

DO TRY THIS AT HOME

Sometime in late winter, I came downstairs to discover what was surely the most bizarre scene witnessed during all the recipe testing for his book: Bruce was trying to cram a raw, twelve-pound ham into a large soup pot. Straining, pushing, his knee on the thing, the pot on the floor. It was like trying to get me into last year's suit.

"What's up, Chef?" I asked.

"Just . . . trying . . . to get . . . a ham . . . brined."

"You really thought this out, didn't you?"

He stood up, a fine film of perspiration on his forehead. "I could have used one of those plastic office boxes—you know, for files."

I thought of various interactions between plastic and brine, none too savory. "What about a big ceramic flower pot? We could fill in the hole at the bottom."

"They're using food-safe glazes in Mexico?"

"OK, what about one of those giant bowls?"

He'd bought three beige bowls at an outlet mall: enormous things that seemed like a good buy at the time, until he got them home and realized he'd have to store them for years on end.

He dragged one of the bowls out of the pantry, set it on the counter, plopped the ham inside, and poured on the brine.

Which had to be salty enough to instigate osmosis right away. The meat cannot be brined too long or it will turn bloated and mushy.

So it went, our own wet-cured ham. But let me add this: It's important to have a plan worked out when you each grab a side of that big bowl to haul it from the counter to the fridge. Sticky brine all over the kitchen floor is a pain in the neck to clean up.

CIDER-CURED HAM

MAKES 16 SERVINGS, MAYBE UP TO 18

You can bake it, braise it, or smoke it—but any way you fix it, a wet-cured ham is like a pork version of corned beef: salty, sweet, and irresistible. Just one warning: This is a three-day recipe.

One 2-pound box kosher salt, plus a little more as necessary

12 cups apple cider

4 cups water

1½ cups honey

1 cup packed dark brown sugar

¼ cup unsulphured molasses (see page 180)

2 tablespoons allspice berries, crushed

2 tablespoons black peppercorns, crushed

½ tablespoon whole cloves

2 medium garlic cloves, peeled

1 medium yellow-fleshed or red-skinned potato

One 10- to 12-pound bone-in fresh ham, preferably the shank end, rind on

1. Stir the salt, cider, water, honey, brown sugar, molasses, allspice berries, peppercorns, whole cloves, and garlic cloves in a giant soup pot over medium-high heat until the brown sugar dissolves; then bring the mixture to a boil, stirring occasionally in case any sugar falls out of suspension and sticks to the bottom of the pot.

2. Remove the pot from the heat and cool, uncovered, to room temperature, about 3 hours.

3. There has to be enough salt in this marinade to cure the ham; the only way to judge this is to measure the liquid's viscosity. No, you don't need a fancy device. Just drop the potato into the cooled liquid. If the spud floats, there's enough salt. If it doesn't, remove it and stir in more kosher salt in ½-cup increments until that potato does indeed bob.

4. Immerse the ham in the cooled marinade in some large pot, bowl, or container. Cover and refrigerate for 48 to 60 hours (2 to 2½ days). If the ham in any way protrudes from the marinade, turn it every 8 hours or so to make sure the whole thing gets a good chance to drown in the brine.

5. Remove the ham from the marinade; rinse and pat dry. Cured, the meat will now stay in your refrigerator for up to 2 weeks. (Discard the brine.)

6. Before you cook the cider-cured ham, it must now be soaked to remove excess salt. Put the ham back in that giant pot or tub and fill with water until the meat is fully submerged. Refrigerate for 12 hours. Then drain again and pat dry.

TO BAKE:

1. Set the rack as high in the oven as you can while still affording the ham at least 3 inches of head space. Preheat the oven to 350°F.

2. Place the cured ham in a large roasting pan; cover tightly with the lid or with aluminum foil. Bake for 3 hours.

3. Uncover and continue baking until the ham is well browned and an instant-read meat thermometer inserted into the thickest part of the ham without touching bone registers 170°F, 2 to 2½ hours more. If you find the ham is browning too quickly, you can tent it loosely with foil.

4. Transfer the ham to a large cutting board and let stand at room temperature for 10 minutes. Peel off the rind, then carve the ham into slices the way you would carve a country ham (page 130), making slightly thicker slices through the meat.

TO BRAISE:

1 to 2 quarts apple cider
3 medium garlic cloves
One 4-inch cinnamon stick

1. Place the cured ham, thick fat up, in a large, flame-safe, covered roaster; a big Dutch oven; or a large, heavy French casserole oven. Add enough cider to come about halfway up the meat. Also toss in the garlic cloves and cinnamon stick.

2. Bring the cider to a simmer over medium-high heat. Then cover, reduce the heat to low, and braise at the merest bubble until an instant-read meat thermometer inserted into the center of the thickest part of the meat without touching bone registers 170°F, about 5½ hours. Check the pot occasionally; if the liquid has gotten too low, add a little more cider to compensate.

3. Transfer the ham from the pot to a large cutting board; let stand for 10 minutes. Peel off the rind, then carve the ham into ¼-inch-thick slices (see page 130).

TO SMOKE:

Wood chips, preferably mesquite, pecan, or hickory, soaked in water for 20 minutes

1. Either build a large, well-ashed coal bed in a charcoal grill and then rake the coals to the perimeter of their grate, or preheat one section of a gas grill to 325°F.

2. Set the ham either in the center of the rack on the charcoal grill, so it's not directly over the coals, or over the unheated section of the gas grill.

3. Either toss a few drained wood chips right on the coals in the charcoal grill, or place the chips in a smoker box or a metal disposable pan and set them over the heated burners of the gas grill. In any event, cover and smoke the ham, adding more charcoal briquettes occasionally to keep the temperature around 325°F, or adjusting the gas flame so the temperature remains constant but never directly under the ham. Also, add more drained chips occasionally to keep the smoke going. Keep roasting until an instant-read meat thermometer inserted into the thickest part of the ham without touching bone registers 170°F, about 8 hours. (Make sure you have enough gas in the tank to keep the flame going!)

4. Transfer the ham to a large cutting board and let it sit for about 10 minutes. Slice off and discard the rind, then carve the ham into thin rounds, working around the bone (as you would a country ham—see page 130).

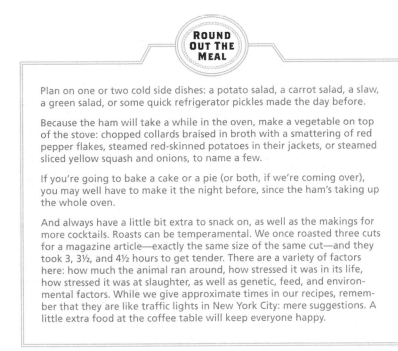

ROUND OUT THE MEAL

Plan on one or two cold side dishes: a potato salad, a carrot salad, a slaw, a green salad, or some quick refrigerator pickles made the day before.

Because the ham will take a while in the oven, make a vegetable on top of the stove: chopped collards braised in broth with a smattering of red pepper flakes, steamed red-skinned potatoes in their jackets, or steamed sliced yellow squash and onions, to name a few.

If you're going to bake a cake or a pie (or both, if we're coming over), you may well have to make it the night before, since the ham's taking up the whole oven.

And always have a little bit extra to snack on, as well as the makings for more cocktails. Roasts can be temperamental. We once roasted three cuts for a magazine article—exactly the same size of the same cut—and they took 3, 3½, and 4½ hours to get tender. There are a variety of factors here: how much the animal ran around, how stressed it was in its life, how stressed it was at slaughter, as well as genetic, feed, and environmental factors. While we give approximate times in our recipes, remember that they are like traffic lights in New York City: mere suggestions. A little extra food at the coffee table will keep everyone happy.

HAM SANDWICHES

MAKES AS MANY SANDWICHES AS YOU LIKE

Admittedly we're stepping into a muck of controversy, but the best ham sandwiches are made with wet-cured ham—or better yet, the leftovers from our cider-cured, braised version.

FOR A CLASSIC HAM SANDWICH, start with hearty white bread—not whipped bread but a country white. Slice the meat into thin bits—you'll need a sharp knife to get the slices as thin as possible. But slice up a load of them before measuring your mouth to determine how thick a sandwich you can handle. Stack up the ham on one slice of bread, then add some cole slaw as the only condiment you'll need: either radish slaw (page 92), jicama slaw (page 131), or a purchased cole slaw from the deli counter. For less mess, drain any excess juice off the cole slaw.

A GRILLED HAM AND CHEESE is not about the size of your mouth; it's about a thin layer of cheese and ham so that the heat gets all the way through the sandwich, warming both. We advocate for rye bread, a bit out of the norm. And we advocate for Gruyère, rather than the standard American slices. Use a cheese plane or a sharp knife to shave the Gruyère into thin slices, not see-through but certainly wobbly. Set a layer of cheese on one piece of rye bread, some thin slices of ham, and then another layer of cheese. Top with a slice of rye bread and make more sandwiches to your heart's content. Once done, melt a tablespoon or so of unsalted butter in a large skillet over medium heat, then slip in as many sandwiches as will fit. Set a second, smaller skillet or saucepan on top of the sandwiches to weigh them down (do not press down). Cook about 3 minutes, until golden brown and crisp; then remove the skillet or saucepan, turn the sandwiches with a spatula, set the cookware back on top, and continue cooking until brown and crisp on the other side, about 3 more minutes. Add additional unsalted butter to the skillet to make further batches.

TO MAKE A BARBECUED HAM SANDWICH, dice the sliced meat and mix it in a medium saucepan with purchased barbecue sauce, about 1/3 cup sauce for every 2 cups diced meat. Set the pan over medium heat while you prepare the sandwiches. Toast hamburger buns cut side down in an ungreased skillet or griddle over medium heat until lightly browned. Set them on plates, then top with the heated ham mixture as well as some thinly sliced red onion and some jarred pickle relish or pickled jalapeño rings.

HAM GRAVY FROM PAN DRIPPINGS

MAKES ABOUT 2½ CUPS

You can only make this gravy if you've first baked a wet-cured ham. But it will also work if you've bought a spiral-sliced ham and heated it to the proper temperature in the oven, using the pan drippings as the base for this gravy. In any event, you must use a heavy, flame-safe roasting pan, not a flimsy aluminum one.

The pan drippings from a wet-cured ham, particularly from the baked cider-cured ham (page 169)

1¼ cups water

¾ cup reduced-sodium, fat-free chicken broth

4 teaspoons all-purpose flour

2 teaspoons cider vinegar

2 teaspoons Dijon mustard

½ teaspoon rubbed sage

½ teaspoon dried thyme

TESTERS' NOTES

The roasting pan must be flame-safe to sit on top of the stove. Otherwise, pour everything into a saucepan to make the gravy. This will, however, squander some of the charred bits—the nuggets of true flavor—in the bottom of that roasting pan.

We first made this gravy with veal demi-glace—you know, the kind you get in little disk-like containers in the freezer section of high-end markets and have to reconstitute with water. Wow. Later, in the interest of accessibility, we retested the gravy with ordinary canned chicken broth. The results were fine, just not spectacular—like a college musical, rather than a Broadway show.

1. Skim the drippings of all fat. You can get the job done in one of three ways: (1) run a tablespoon along the surface of the drippings, pulling the fat to the side of the pan and lifting it out; (2) stick a bulb baster under the surface layer of fat, draw out the juices below, and squirt them into a separate bowl; or (3) use a fancy fat separator for gravies, available at kitchenware stores and their online outlets. In any case, you should end up with the fat gone from the roasting pan and the juices back inside.

2. Place the roasting pan over medium heat and stir in 1 cup water. Bring the mixture to a simmer, scraping up any browned bits as they loosen off the inner surface of the pan and begin to dissolve.

3. Stir in the broth and bring the mixture to a full boil.

4. Whisk the flour into the remaining ¼ cup water in a small bowl until smooth, then whisk this mixture into the boiling gravy just until thickened.

5. Whisk in the vinegar, mustard, sage, and thyme. Then remove the pan from the heat and pour the gravy into a gravy boat or serving bowl.

SMOKED

After we smoked our own wet-cured ham, Bruce had a refrigerator full of leftovers. His bliss, indeed: chunks of meat in zip-closed bags. We made fresh meals out of them for weeks. Hardly leftovers—more like extravagant dinners in themselves.

But don't wait for leftovers. Most supermarkets stock spiral-sliced smoked hams. Buy what you need and head to these recipes.

That said, here are at least two specialty, smoked, wet-cured British hams you have to try sometime if you can get your hands on them:

⇻ SUFFOLK HAM ⇺

The British have an established pig culture—and so myriad ways to prepare, cure, and even smoke ham. One of the best is this shellacked, mahogany-toned joint that has been wet-cured for six weeks in a pickling brine that includes stout, molasses, and spices. The ham is subsequently smoked and hung to age for about a month. The flavors are a little sour, a little sweet, and quite smoky. There are also varieties brined in a pickle made with port, yielding an even sweeter, stickier finish on the meat.

⇻ BRADENHAM HAM ⇺

From Wilshire, England, this ham actually rides the line between dry-cured and wet-cured. The ham is salted and air-dried for up to two weeks, then put into a wet cure laced with molasses, brown sugar, juniper berries, and other spices. The rind becomes shiny black; the meat turns sweet and aromatic, if a little pungent. The hams are hung to age for six months and then smoked.

DEVILED EGGS WITH HAM

MAKES 12 DEVILED EGG HALVES

Here's a meal in a bite. Bruce brought a tray to his knitting class in West Hartford. He said the women "fell upon them."

6 large eggs

4 ounces smoked, wet-cured ham, such as a spiral-sliced ham, any sugary coating removed, finely chopped into ¼-inch bits

1 medium scallion, minced

2 tablespoons mayonnaise (regular, low-fat, or fat-free)

2 tablespoons minced celery (about ½ a small rib)

2 teaspoons jarred white horseradish

1 teaspoon white vinegar

1 teaspoon minced tarragon leaves or ½ teaspoon dried tarragon

½ teaspoon dry mustard

¼ teaspoon cayenne, optional

Several dashes hot red pepper sauce, such as Tabasco sauce, to taste

1. Set the eggs in a large saucepan, cover them with cool water until the water stands about 1 inch over the eggs, and bring to a boil over high heat. Boil for 2 minutes, then cover the pan and set off the heat for 7 minutes.

2. Carefully drain the pan over the sink, leaving the eggs inside; then run lots of cold tap water into it to bring the eggs to room temperature. Peel off the shells.

3. Split the eggs in half lengthwise and use a little spoon to scoop the yellow yolks into a large bowl, taking care not to break or tear the whites. Save these back on a plate.

4. Mix the yolks with all the remaining ingredients. Using the back of a fork, mash the yolks fully into the mixture. Then use a small spoon to mound this mixture back into the indentations in the halved egg whites.

5. Place on a platter, cover with plastic wrap, and refrigerate for at least 3 hours or up to 24 hours so the flavors meld a bit.

BRIE, GRITS, HAM, AND APPLE CASSEROLE

MAKES 6 SERVINGS

Here's the perfect thing to serve when you want to give the friends a solid send-off the morning after a long weekend.

1 tablespoon unsalted butter, plus additional for greasing the baking dish

3 cups water

¾ cup quick-cooking grits

8 ounces smoked, wet-cured ham, diced

4 medium scallions, minced

1 medium tart apple such as a Granny Smith, a Rome, or an Empire, peeled, cored, and diced

6 ounces cold Brie, rind removed and discarded, the cheese inside diced

2 teaspoons minced marjoram leaves or 1 teaspoon dried marjoram

Several dashes hot red pepper sauce, to taste

2 large eggs, separated

1. Set the rack in the center of the oven and preheat the oven to 375°F. Put a dab of butter on a small piece of wax paper and use it to lightly grease the inside of a 10-inch-square or 6-cup oval baking dish.

2. Bring the water to a boil in a large saucepan over high heat. Whisk in the grits. Reduce the heat to medium so that the mixture simmers quickly, and continue whisking over the heat until thickened and mushy, about 5 minutes. Set aside.

3. Melt 1 tablespoon butter in a large skillet over medium heat, then add the ham, scallion, and apple. Cook, stirring often, until the scallion begins to soften and the apple bits turn golden, about 5 minutes.

4. Pour the contents of the skillet into the saucepan with the grits. Add the Brie, marjoram, and hot red pepper sauce; stir well until the mixture is fairly uniform, the ham and vegetables evenly distributed throughout. Mix in the egg yolks until well combined.

5. In the large bowl of an electric mixer, beat the egg whites at high speed until they're light and fluffy and form soft peaks when you dab the turned-off beaters in and out of them.

6. Use a rubber spatula to fold the beaten whites into the grits mixture, just until combined but not necessary dissolved. There may be some white streaks throughout.

7. Pour the grits mixture into the prepared baking dish. Smooth out the top and bake until lightly browned and set and the grits don't jiggle when the pan is tapped, about 40 minutes. Cool on a wire rack for 5 or 10 minutes before dishing up with a large spoon.

TESTERS' NOTES

If the Brie is even slightly warm, you'll never be able to dice it into little chunks. To ensure success, put it in the freezer for about 20 minutes before you begin the recipe.

If you've read enough recipes, "diced" might seem more like cliché than cooking instruction. In fact, it's a specific demarcation, a stop on a larger continuum and an aid to a successful dish. In general, the scheme for prepping ingredients goes something like this:

Roughly chopped: Uneven pieces up to 1 inch wide.

Chopped: Slightly smaller and more uniform pieces, about ¾ inch on each side.

Cubed: Small, ½-inch cubes.

Finely chopped: Smaller still but less uniform, about ¼-inch pieces.

Diced: A ¼-inch cube.

Minced: The smallest pieces of all, less than ⅛ inch, often made by rocking a knife through an ingredient.

BOURBON-SOAKED HAM AND BEANS

SERVES 6 OR 8

Unlike the wimpy, watery side dish that often passes for baked beans, this version is a real rib-sticker. With a salad, it's a full meal.

SLASH THE SHOPPING LIST

Substitute 1⅔ cups bottled barbecue sauce for these nine ingredients: chili sauce, broth, molasses, mustard, vinegar, paprika, Worcestershire sauce, cumin, and allspice.

THE INGREDIENT SCOOP

Molasses is a thick syrup made from sun-ripened sugar cane and prized for its aromatic, bright, sugary-but-still-slightly-sour taste. Sulphured varieties, never recommended, are made from immature canes from which the juice has been extracted by means of a noxious gas.

¼ cup almond or canola oil

1 large yellow onion, quartered and thinly sliced

1 large green bell pepper, cored, seeded, and thinly sliced

5¼ cups canned pinto beans, drained and rinsed (about three 15-ounce cans)

1 pound smoked, wet-cured ham, chopped

½ cup bourbon

½ cup bottled tomato-based chili sauce, such as Heinz

½ cup reduced-sodium beef broth

¼ cup molasses, preferably unsulphured

2 tablespoons Dijon mustard

2 tablespoons white wine vinegar

2 tablespoons mild paprika

1 tablespoon Worcestershire sauce

2 teaspoons ground cumin

½ teaspoon ground allspice

1. Heat a large saucepan over medium heat. Add the oil, then dump in the onion and green pepper. Cook, stirring often, just until both begin to soften a bit, about 4 minutes.

2. Stir in all remaining ingredients and bring to a simmer.

3. Cover, reduce the heat to low, and cook until somewhat thickened, 45 minutes to 1 hour.

TESTERS' NOTES

Canola oil, while an American standard, is admittedly a wasted bit of calories in a dish like this. Almond oil offers a little nutty sweetness underneath the other flavors.

For an even more toothsome and authentic dish, consider using 1 pound dried pinto beans instead of their canned kin. Soak the dried beans overnight in cool water, changing that water at least once. Drain the beans and place them in a large saucepan. Pour in cool water until it stands 3 inches over the beans. Bring to a boil over high heat, then cover with the lid partly askew until the beans are almost tender, with still a little give to the bite, about 1½ hours. Drain and add to the stew as you would the canned beans.

HAM-AND-CORN CHOWDER

MAKES 6 SERVINGS

Bruce thickened this soup with a beurre manié *(French,* burre man-YAY, *"kneaded butter"—that is, a mixture of mashed flour and butter), thereby avoiding that depressing wallpaper paste that often gets passed off as chowder.*

3 tablespoons unsalted butter, 2 tablespoons of it softened to room temperature

12 ounces smoked, wet-cured ham, chopped

3 cups fresh or frozen corn kernels

1 medium yellow onion, chopped

1 large Yukon Gold potato, chopped

2 teaspoons minced marjoram leaves or 1 teaspoon dried marjoram

1 teaspoon finely grated lemon zest

½ teaspoon celery seeds

3 cups reduced-sodium, fat-free chicken broth

1 cup dry white wine or dry vermouth

½ cup heavy or whipping cream

1 teaspoon salt, or to taste (the cured ham is quite salty)

1 teaspoon freshly ground pepper, preferably white pepper so little black specks don't float in the soup

2 tablespoons all-purpose flour

1. Melt 1 tablespoon unsoftened butter in a large soup pot or saucepan. Add the chopped ham and cook, stirring often, until frizzling and quite fragrant, about 3 minutes.

2. Stir in the corn, onion, and potato. Cook, stirring often, for 3 more minutes.

3. Add the marjoram, lemon zest, and celery seeds and continue cooking for about 20 seconds. Pour in the broth and wine. As the soup comes to a simmer, use a wooden spoon to scrape any browned bits off the interior surfaces of the pot.

4. Cover, reduce the heat to low, and simmer until the potato bits are meltingly tender, about 45 minutes.

5. Stir in the cream, salt, and pepper. As everything simmers for a couple minutes, use a fork to mash the flour with the 2 tablespoons softened butter in a small bowl until the mixture is quite uniform.

6. Stirring all the while, drop this butter mixture by dribs and drabs into the simmering soup, taking six to eight additions to get the whole paste added and stirring well after each before adding the next. The whole process should take about 3 minutes. Taste for salt, add more if necessary, then dish it up.

BLACK BEAN SOUP WITH A HAM BONE, ORANGE ZEST, AND ROOT VEGETABLES

MAKES 8 SERVINGS

Look no further for the best way to use that huge ham bone from your last spiral-sliced ham! Or if you're craving this soup right now, hie thee to a spiral-sliced-ham store or even the deli case in your market. At either one, you can often buy the bone from a smoked, wet-cured ham that's been used to make deli slices.

THE INGREDIENT SCOOP

Chipotles are smoked, dried jalapeños. They are sometimes canned in adobo sauce, a fiery mixture of tomatoes, garlic, vinegar, and spices. They pack a powerful punch of fiery capsaicin (the chemical compound that gives chiles their heat); wash your hands diligently with soap after working with the chiles.

1 pound dried black beans

2 tablespoons olive oil

1 medium acorn squash, peeled, seeded, and diced

1 medium celeriac (aka celery root), peeled and diced

2 medium green bell peppers, cored, seeded, and diced

1 medium yellow onion, diced

1 canned chipotle in adobo sauce, chopped

3 tablespoons finely grated orange zest

2 tablespoons minced oregano leaves or 1 tablespoon dried oregano

2 teaspoons ground cumin

1 tablespoon minced sage leaves or 2 teaspoons dried sage

½ teaspoon grated nutmeg

8 cups reduced-sodium, fat-free chicken broth

1 smoked, wet-cured ham bone, with the meat still attached

1 tablespoon thawed orange juice concentrate

2 teaspoons sherry vinegar

1 teaspoon salt

½ teaspoon freshly ground black pepper

1. Put the beans in a large bowl and pour in cool water until it stands about 1 inch over the beans. Set aside for 12 hours or overnight, changing the water once during soaking. Drain the beans in a colander set in the sink.

2. Heat a large soup pot over medium heat, then add the oil. Drop in the fresh vegetables—the acorn squash, the celeriac, the bell peppers, and the onion—and cook, stirring often, for 5 minutes.

3. Stir in the chipotle, orange zest, oregano, cumin, sage, and nutmeg. Cook, stirring constantly, until aromatic, about 20 seconds.

4. Pour in the broth and stir in the ham bone. Keep stirring over the heat as the soup comes to a full simmer, scraping up any browned bits that may be stuck to the bottom or sides of the pot.

5. Stir in the drained beans. Once the soup returns to a full simmer, cover, reduce the heat to low, and cook at a slow simmer until the meat is falling off the bones, 2½ to 3 hours.

6. Fish out the ham bone, set it on a cutting board, and slice off any remaining meat. Dice these bits—then also fish out and dice any large chunks of meat floating in the soup.

7. Stir the meat back into the soup, along with the orange juice concentrate, vinegar, salt, and pepper. Bring back to a simmer. If the beans are not tender, cover and continue simmering slowly until they are. But the soup will most likely be ready to serve once the meat has gone back in.

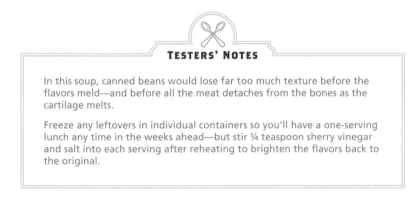

TESTERS' NOTES

In this soup, canned beans would lose far too much texture before the flavors meld—and before all the meat detaches from the bones as the cartilage melts.

Freeze any leftovers in individual containers so you'll have a one-serving lunch any time in the weeks ahead—but stir ¼ teaspoon sherry vinegar and salt into each serving after reheating to brighten the flavors back to the original.

STUFFED BAKED POTATOES ᴡɪᴛʜ HAM, MUSHROOMS, AND CHEDDAR

MAKES 4 STUFFED BAKED POTATOES

We're longtime fans of stuffed baked potatoes, sort of a single-serving-casserole-in-a-spud and a great meal at the end of the day. And there's no reason to stand on ceremony with the cheddar: substitute Colby, Gouda, Gruyère, or Havarti at will.

THE INGREDIENT SCOOP

How in the world do you know how much ½ **teaspoon of freshly ground black pepper** really is? By grinding it onto a cutting board and scooping it in a little measuring spoon, thereby wasting pepper and irritating yourself silly? Instead, do this one-time experiment. Make a small mark on your pepper mill. Starting at that mark, turn or crank the mill until you get ¼ teaspoon of pepper, counting each turn or crank. (Yes, this one time you'll have to scoop and measure with a little spoon.) You now know how many turns or cranks it takes to make ¼ teaspoon, and you can do the math for all the other permutations: two times that for ½ teaspoon, four times for 1 teaspoon, eight times for 2 teaspoons.

4 large russet or baking potatoes

2 tablespoons unsalted butter

8 ounces smoked, wet-cured ham, any sugary coating removed, the meat diced

2 medium shallots, minced

8 ounces cremini or white button mushrooms, thinly sliced

¼ cup brandy

½ cup heavy or whipping cream

2 teaspoons ground paprika

½ teaspoon garlic powder

½ teaspoon freshly ground black pepper

2 ounces Cheddar, finely grated (about ½ cup)

1. Position the rack in the center of the oven; preheat the oven to 350°F.

2. Don't prick or prod the potatoes. Just set them right on the oven rack to bake so that the bottoms get crunchy and concentrated. Bake until soft to the touch, about 75 minutes. Cool on a wire rack for at least 10 minutes. Meanwhile, raise the oven's temperature to 375°F.

3. Melt the butter in a large skillet over medium heat. Add the ham and cook, stirring often, until it's sizzling and lightly browned, about 4 minutes.

4. Toss in the shallots; cook, stirring often, just until those tiny bits start to soften, about 1 minute.

5. Add the mushrooms. Continue cooking until they give off most of their liquid and reduce in size by about half, and the liquid evaporates to a syrupy glaze, about 7 minutes.

6. Pour in the brandy and reduce it to a glaze as well. If the liquor ignites, cover the skillet and remove it from the heat for a couple minutes. Uncover and then continue with the recipe.

7. Pour in the cream; stir in paprika, garlic powder, and pepper. Set aside off the heat.

8. Cutting lengthwise, remove a slender top from each of the potatoes. Scoop the creamy flesh from both the main part of the potato and that little top, taking care not to prick or break the skin. Put the flesh in a large bowl and beat with an electric mixer at medium speed or with a hand masher until creamy.

9. Beat in the contents of the skillet as well as the cheese at low speed, until well combined. Spoon this mixture back into the larger sections of the potatoes, mounding it up in each. (You can discard those tops at this point.)

10. Set the potatoes, stuffing side up, in a 9-by-13-inch baking dish and bake until the cheese has melted and the filling is hot and creamy, about 15 minutes. Cool the potatoes on individual dinner plates for 5 minutes before serving.

TESTERS' NOTES

We've also tried this recipe successfully with dairy less heavy than the cream—with half-and-half, whole milk, or even low-fat milk. However, fat-free milk just doesn't give the filling enough richness.

SWEET POTATO HASH WITH HAM, PECANS, AND CRANBERRIES

SERVES 6 FOR DINNER, 8 FOR BREAKFAST

Hash is comfort food: a one-skillet, potato-based main course. Or try it for breakfast some weekend morning.

6 tablespoons untoasted sesame oil (see page 159)

1 pound sweet potatoes, peeled and cut into ¼-inch cubes

1 pound yellow-fleshed potatoes such as Yukon Golds, peeled and cut into ½-inch cubes

2 tablespoons unsalted butter

1 medium yellow onion, chopped

2 celery ribs, chopped

½ cup chopped pecan pieces

½ cup chopped dried cranberries

1 pound smoked, wet-cured ham, chopped

2 teaspoons minced sage leaves or 1 teaspoon dried sage

1½ teaspoons stemmed thyme leaves or 1 teaspoon dried thyme

6 tablespoons reduced-sodium, fat-free chicken broth

2 teaspoons apple cider vinegar

1 teaspoon salt

½ teaspoon freshly ground black pepper

1. Heat a very large skillet over medium heat, then swirl in the oil. Add the sweet potato and potato cubes; cook, stirring occasionally, until lightly browned on all sides, about 15 minutes.

2. Push the potato pieces to the perimeter of the skillet; melt the butter in the well you've created at its center.

3. Add the onion, celery, pecans, and dried cranberries to this well and cook, stirring occasionally, until the onions begin to turn translucent, about 4 minutes.

4. Stir the ham, sage, and thyme into the center well. Continue stirring for a few seconds without disturbing the potatoes.

5. Now pour in the broth and toss everything together, scraping up any browned bits on the interior of the skillet and getting the potatoes distributed evenly throughout it. If possible, use a big, flat, heat-safe spatula that you can slide under everything and toss it around without breaking up the potato cubes.

6. Everything should be just about ready to go. At the very last minute, once the potatoes are tender without being mushy, stir in the vinegar, salt, and pepper.

JAMBALAYA CROQUETTES

MAKES 16 CROQUETTES

The flavors of Creole jambalaya get recreated in these tasty croquettes.

¼ cup peanut oil, plus up to ½ cup more as needed for frying

3 tablespoons all-purpose flour

1 large yellow onion, chopped

2 green cubanel or bell peppers, stemmed, seeded, and chopped

2 celery ribs, chopped

2 medium garlic cloves, minced

1½ teaspoons stemmed thyme leaves or 1 teaspoon dried thyme

½ teaspoon cayenne

½ cup dry white wine or dry vermouth

3½ cups canned diced tomatoes

12 ounces smoked, wet-cured ham, chopped

1 cup arborio rice

½ pound medium or small shrimp, peeled and chopped

2 large eggs

THE INGREDIENT SCOOP

Cubanels (also spelled "cubanelles"), or Italian frying peppers, are long, green, fingerlike chiles, quite sweet and aromatic. In a pinch, you can substitute a small seeded, cored, and chopped green bell pepper combined with ⅛ teaspoon hot red pepper sauce (like Tabasco sauce) for the two cubanels.

1. Heat the oil in a large skillet over medium heat. Whisk in the flour, reduce the heat to low, and continue whisking, occasionally letting the whole thing alone for 10 or 15 seconds, until a milk-chocolate brown, about 10 minutes if the heat is low enough.

2. Add the onion, peppers, celery, and garlic all at once. Continue cooking, stirring almost constantly, until the vegetables are coated in the flour mixture and beginning to soften, about 5 minutes.

3. Stir in the thyme and cayenne, then pour in the wine, whisking constantly. Bring to a boil, whisking up any browned bits.

4. Pour in the tomatoes, then stir in the ham and rice. Bring back to a full simmer; then cover, reduce the heat to low, and simmer until the rice is cooked through, about 1 hour.

5. Uncover and let the mixture continue to sizzle and cook for about 10 minutes, until it's pretty dry; then stir in the shrimp. Cover and set aside to cool for 2 hours.

6. Whisk the eggs in a small bowl until creamy and pale yellow, then stir these into the cooled contents of the skillet.

7. Heat about 2 tablespoons peanut oil in a second large skillet set over medium heat, then scoop up the rice mixture in ⅓-cup increments and form it into patties. Place as many as will comfortably fit in the skillet without crowding and fry until brown, about 4 minutes. Turn and continue frying on the other side until crisp and brown, about 5 minutes more. Transfer to a plate, add more oil, and continue frying more.

SPLIT-PEA-AND-HAM BURGERS

MAKES 12 PATTIES

Serve these patties on buns with mayo and mustard on the side—or serve them atop a green salad with halved grapes and minced celery, all dressed in a lemony vinaigrette.

THE INGREDIENT SCOOP

What's the deal with the **reduced-sodium chicken broth**? First off, why let anyone else control the salt content of your meal? And second, inferior canned broths are sometimes doped with salt to make up for their watery taste. Buy a high-quality, good-tasting, reduced-sodium broth for the best results.

2½ cups reduced-sodium, fat-free chicken broth

1 cup dried split peas

6 tablespoons short-grain white rice such as sushi rice

12 ounces smoked, wet-cured ham, any sugary coating removed, the meat chopped

½ cup all-purpose flour

4 medium scallions, minced

½ teaspoon ground cumin

½ teaspoon ground coriander

½ teaspoon freshly ground black pepper

Up to ½ cup almond or peanut oil

1. Stir up the broth, split peas, and rice in a medium saucepan; bring to a boil over medium-high heat. Cover, reduce the heat to low, and simmer slowly until the rice is tender and the liquid has been absorbed, about 1 hour.

2. Transfer the split pea mixture to a large bowl. Stir in the ham, flour, scallions, cumin, coriander, and pepper. The mixture will be thick and pasty.

3. Heat about 2 tablespoons oil in a large skillet. Scoop up about 1/3 cup of the split pea mixture and form it into a patty. You may need to wet your hands to keep the mixture from sticking too much. Place three or four patties in the skillet—as many as will fit without crowding—and fry until brown and crisp, about 8 minutes, turning once with a flat spatula halfway through frying. Transfer these patties to a serving plate, add another couple tablespoons of oil to the skillet, and fry up more patties, repeating this process until you've used up all the split pea mixture.

MAC AND HAM AND CHEESE

**MAKES ABOUT 6 SERVINGS, IF YOU CAN FORCE PEOPLE TO
TAKE MANAGEABLE PORTIONS**

*This is admittedly a crazy, over-the-top rendition of the classic—and
one of the many reasons I love Bruce's creativity in the kitchen. Dishes
like this don't just make a book and a career; they also make a home.
Who could ask for anything more?*

4 tablespoons (½ stick) unsalted butter

¼ cup all-purpose flour

4 cups milk (whole or low-fat; do not use fat-free)

12 ounces Gruyère, finely grated

1 pound smoked, wet-cured ham, chopped

One 9-ounce package frozen artichoke hearts, thawed and squeezed of any excess moisture

1 tablespoon Dijon mustard

1 tablespoon mango chutney

1 tablespoon minced tarragon leaves or 1½ teaspoons dried tarragon

12 ounces dried ziti, cooked and drained according to the package instructions

1 ounce finely grated Parmigiano-Reggiano (see page 87)

THE INGREDIENT SCOOP

Gruyère is a cow's-milk cheese originally from Switzerland but now produced all over. Beloved for its nutty, sweet flavor, it's aged about 10 months, grates exceptionally well, and melts even better.

1. Position the rack in the center of the oven and preheat it to 350°F.

2. Melt the butter in a large saucepan over medium heat. Whisk in the flour, then whisk occasionally over the heat just until the mixture is bubbling and a very pale beige, about 2 minutes.

3. Whisk in the milk and continue whisking over the heat until thickened, about 4 minutes.

4. Drop the whisk and use a wooden spoon to stir in the Gruyère, ham, artichoke hearts, mustard, chutney, and tarragon. Remove the saucepan from the heat and stir in the cooked ziti.

5. Pour the contents of the pan into a 3-quart casserole dish, or even a 9-by-13-inch baking dish if you like more of the top exposed to the heat and many more crunchy bits as a result.

6. Sprinkle the Parmigiano-Reggiano over the casserole and bake until brown and bubbling, about 35 minutes. Cool on a wire rack for 5 minutes before serving.

TESTERS' NOTES

You don't want the ziti falling apart in the casserole. It's best to undercook it at first, so there's still a little crunch left at the center of the pasta, just 4 or 5 minutes. The only way to know? Take a piece out and taste it. When you drain the ziti, don't rinse it. Yes, it will turn into one big glob in the colander, but it will fall back apart when you stir it into the sauce; the pasta is then sticky enough to grab and hold that sauce.

NOT SMOKED

Not all wet-cured hams are smoked. In fact, many aren't. So these are recipes Bruce designed to highlight the more subtle flavors that smoke can mask. You'll need ready-to-eat, not-smoked, wet-cured ham in varying amounts. Either buy the requisite chunk from the deli counter or use leftover bits of a cider-cured ham (page 169). There are plenty of standard brands in the deli case at your market—you just might not have realized they weren't smoked until now. But beyond the usual fare, here are two specialty, wet-cured, not-smoked hams you might find:

➤ JAMBON DE PARIS ➤

This non-smoked, wet-cured ham (French, *zhahm-BONE duh pah-REE*, "ham from Paris") was once the standard across northern France. With its light, slightly minerally but still clean taste, it is used in everything from the simple jambon beurre (French, *zhahm-BONE burh*, "ham butter"—aka a sandwich of white bread, butter, and ham) to more complicated dishes like *jambon persillé* (see page 204). Unfortunately, there are many imitations made from extruded or pressed meat. The true *jambon de Paris* is a boneless ham, never rolled.

➤ PROSCUITTO COTTO ➤

As mentioned before, prosciutto simply means *ham* in Italian— which can explain the strange look you'll get if you walk into an Italian butcher shop and ask for "prosciutto." "Che tipo?" they'll ask. Cooked ham is *prosciutto cotto* (*proh-SHOO-toh COH-toh*)—a wet-cured ham that is then steamed, baked, or braised until it is soft and mellow, more like really good deli ham.

IBERIAN-INSPIRED FRITTATA

MAKES 2 TO 4 SERVINGS, DEPENDING ON WHAT YOU SERVE ON THE SIDE

We didn't put the names of all the ingredients in the title because you might have run away. Anchovies? Hazelnuts? Ham? Listen, this thing makes a dynamite brunch.

2 tablespoons olive oil

1 medium shallot, minced

2 jarred anchovies, minced

1 medium garlic clove, minced

2 teaspoons minced fresh rosemary leaves

6 ounces not-smoked, wet-cured ham, such as *prosciutto cotto*, diced

¼ cup chopped skinned hazelnuts

6 large eggs, at room temperature and well beaten in a large bowl

1. Heat a 9-inch skillet, preferably nonstick, over medium heat. Swirl in the oil, then add the shallot, anchovies, garlic, and rosemary. Cook, stirring constantly, just until the bits of shallot start to soften but not to brown, less than 1 minute.

2. Add the ham and hazelnuts. Cook for 1 minute.

3. Pour the eggs in all around the skillet, not in a lump in the center—then gently swirl the skillet so that they evenly coat the bottom, distributing the various ingredients evenly throughout the eggs.

4. Cover, reduce the heat to very low, and cook until the eggs have set and can be pulled back from the edge of the skillet with a heat-safe rubber spatula, about 14 minutes. Serve at once by loosening the frittata from the pan with the spatula, then sliding the frittata onto a serving platter before slicing it into piece-of-pie wedges.

CURRIED HAM SALAD

MAKES 6 HEARTY SERVINGS, ENOUGH FOR 6 FULL SANDWICHES

The only trick here is good knifework: Everything should be diced into fairly small, uniform bits so that you get lots of flavors in each bite.

1¼ pounds not-smoked, wet-cured ham, such as *prosciutto cotto*, diced

1 medium red bell pepper, cored, seeded, and diced

3 celery stalks, minced

1 medium shallot, minced

1 cup unsalted, roasted cashews, chopped

½ cup mayonnaise (regular, low-fat, or fat-free)

3 tablespoons mango chutney

2 tablespoons lime juice

2 tablespoons minced peeled fresh ginger

2 teaspoons bottled curry powder

1. Mix everything in a large bowl, cover, and refrigerate for a couple hours to blend the flavors. The ham salad can be stored, covered, in the refrigerator for up to 2 days.

TESTERS' NOTES

You needn't limit your choice of curry powders to the standard yellow variety. There are almost as many curry powders as there are cooks in India. You probably don't want to dump in a powder that's basically flavored cayenne (read the label carefully), but you can certainly go well beyond the average by choosing from the astounding array of powders at Indian markets or their online locations.

CROQUE-AMERICAIN

MAKES 2 SANDWICHES (BUT CAN BE DOUBLED OR TRIPLED, PROVIDED YOU
MAKE THE SANDWICHES TWO AT A TIME)

A croque-monsieur *(French,* croak-muh-SYUHR, *"crunchy mister"—
the exact origins of the name are lost in a haze of slang) is French bar
food: a fried ham-and-cheese sandwich, the cheese melted on top of the
bread rather than inside it. We mixed the classic up a bit and turned it
American. I suggested mixing blue cheese with mustard for the spread,
Bruce added two more cheeses, and the whole thing got turned into a
more substantial lunch, the cheeses now* inside *the sandwich, to make
it easier finger fare.*

½ ounce crumbled blue cheese (about
  1½ tablespoons)

2 teaspoons Dijon mustard

4 slices sourdough or rye bread

½ ounce Parmigiano-Reggiano (see
  page 87), shaved into thin strips

6 ounces thinly sliced not-smoked,
  wet-cured ham

1 small ripe pear, peeled, cored, and
  thinly sliced

2 ounces Gruyère (see page 191),
  shaved into thin strips

1 tablespoon unsalted butter

1. Mash the blue cheese and mustard in a small bowl with a fork until
it's a grainy paste. Spread this mixture onto one side of each of 2 pieces
of bread.

2. Top the mixture with the Parmigiano-Reggiano, ham, pear, and
Gruyère, in that order, dividing these ingredients evenly between the 2
slices of bread. Top each with a second slice of bread to make a sandwich.

3. Melt the butter in a large skillet over medium heat. Slip the sandwiches into the skillet, then weight them down by setting a second skillet or a small pot on top of them. Cook for 3 minutes, then remove the
second skillet and flip the sandwiches with a very large spatula. Set the
skillet back over them and continue frying until golden brown, about 3
minutes more.

MUSHROOM PÂTÉ WITH HAM

MAKES 8 TO 10 APPETIZER SERVINGS

Serve this pâté as an appetizer with cocktails, alongside rounds of crunchy baguette, as well as some grainy mustard, a little hot tomato chutney, and cornichons (sour, tiny pickles).

3 tablespoons unsalted butter

2 medium shallots, minced

1 pound cremini mushrooms, thinly sliced

1 teaspoon salt

2 teaspoons stemmed thyme leaves or 1 teaspoon dried thyme

½ teaspoon grated nutmeg

¼ cup sweet white wine such as a Riesling, Spätlese, Auslese, Port, or a late-harvest dessert wine

1 cup fresh bread crumbs (see page 143)

3 large egg yolks

8 ounces thin-cut bacon slices

8 ounces not-smoked, wet-cured ham such as *prosciutto cotto* or *jambon de Paris*, cut into ¼-inch-thick matchsticks

1. Melt the butter in a large skillet over medium heat, then add the shallots and cook, stirring often, until softened, about 3 minutes.

2. Dump in the mushrooms; sprinkle with salt. Continue cooking, stirring occasionally, until the mushrooms give off their liquid and it reduces to a glaze, 7 to 8 minutes.

3. Add the thyme and nutmeg; pour in the wine. Bring to a full simmer, scraping up any browned bits on the bottom of the skillet. Continue simmering until any liquid is a thick lacquer. Then remove the skillet from the heat and cool at room temperature for 30 minutes.

4. Scrape the contents of the skillet into a large food processor fitted with the chopping blade, add the bread crumbs and egg yolks, and process until smooth, scraping down the inside of the canister once or twice to make sure everything gets pureed.

5. Position the rack in the center of the oven and get it heated up to 325°F.

6. Overlap the bacon strips in a 1-quart loaf pan so that they completely coat its inside surfaces, the excess hanging over the edges (enough to later be folded back onto the top without necessarily covering it).

7. Spread a third of the mushroom mixture into the prepared pan, then line it with half the ham matchsticks. Top with half the remaining mushroom mixture, spreading it to the edges, then arrange the remainder of the ham matchsticks on top. Finally, smooth out the rest of the mushroom mixture so it completely covers the terrine. Fold any overhanging bacon slices over the top.

8. Bake the pâté for 1 hour. Drain off any fat that might skim or line the pan. Cool for 10 minutes on a wire rack, then weight down the top of the terrine and refrigerate for 24 hours. We used a second loaf pan, set right on top of the terrine and filled with dried beans. If you don't have a matching pan, consider covering the top of the pâté with plastic wrap, then setting some small cans on their sides right on top of the terrine—or perhaps a couple large baking potatoes. Don't worry about unmolding the pâté; just cut slices right out of the pan.

TESTERS' NOTES

This pâté is made in a rather esoteric loaf pan: a 1-quart pan, about 9½-by-4 inches. You can find these specialty loaf pans at most bakeware stores and their online outlets.

HAM AND POTATOES
SARLADAISE

MAKES ABOUT 8 SMALL APPETIZER SERVINGS

This dish (French, sahr-lah-DAYZ, "from Sarlat-la-Canéda, France") has become a cocktail party favorite at our house. It's traditionally made with potatoes and duck or goose confit, but one afternoon, when we had a house full of both weekend guests and leftover not-smoked, wet-cured ham, we tossed this version together and discovered that the ham gives the dish a lovely, silky finish, more American in taste and more economical to boot.

2 pounds russet potatoes

¼ cup lard or olive oil

1 pound not-smoked, wet-cured ham, such as *prosciutto cotto*, cut into ½-inch cubes

⅓ cup packed parsley leaves, chopped

4 medium garlic cloves, minced

1 teaspoon coarse-grained salt, such as kosher salt or sea salt

½ teaspoon freshly ground black pepper

TESTERS' NOTES

We tried this dish with a variety of potatoes: yellow-fleshed Yukon Golds, red-skinned (or so-called "new") potatoes, even yellow fingerlings. To be honest, russets worked best, offering up the creamiest finish, mostly because of their unique balance of starch and moisture. Plus, smaller potatoes were maddening to slice into thin strips.

1. Position the rack in the dead center of the oven and preheat it to 400°F.

2. Peel the potatoes, then use a very sharp, thin knife to cut them into ¼-inch-thick slices. It's easier to slice them the short way, thereby producing rounds, but they're more aesthetically pleasing sliced the long way for layering in the baking dish. However, it's troublesome to get those long slices. Best alternative? Slice a little off of one end, stand the potato up on your cutting board, and make the thin slices straight down.

3. Heat the lard in a very large skillet over medium-high heat. Test it with one potato slice to make sure the oil bubbles when the potato is added. But be careful: all that starch-laden water in the potato will pop and sputter in the hot oil. (You might consider using a splatter screen, available at cookware stores and their online outlets.) Add more slices in batches, and fry them until golden brown, turning occasionally, about 15 minutes per batch. As the potato slices are finished, transfer them to a 9-by-13-inch baking dish.

4. Once all the potatoes have been fried and are in the pan, sprinkle them with the remaining ingredients and toss well.

5. Bake, tossing two or three times, until everything is crisp and aromatic, about 20 minutes.

HAM AND SQUASH-NOODLE TETRAZZINI

MAKES 6 SERVINGS

Long strands of butternut squash act like noodles in this creamy, pasta-free version of the American casserole favorite.

One 2-pound butternut squash

¼ cup olive oil

2 large shallots, minced

12 ounces small Brussels sprouts, thinly sliced into shreds

1 medium garlic clove, minced

2 tablespoons all-purpose flour

1 cup white wine or dry vermouth

1 cup heavy or whipping cream

1 pound not-smoked, wet-cured ham, such as *prosciutto cotto*, chopped into ½-inch cubes

1 tablespoon Dijon mustard

2 teaspoons minced sage leaves or 1 teaspoon dried sage

½ teaspoon freshly ground black pepper

1. Slice the neck off the squash and peel it with a vegetable peeler. (Reserve the bulbous base for another use.) Then continue using the vegetable peeler to make long, thin strips of squash from the neck, sort of like really flat, wide noodles. Keep making these until you have about 4 cups.

2. Bring a large pot of water to a boil over high heat. Add the squash noodles; blanch for 1 minute. Drain in a colander placed in the sink.

3. Position the rack in the center of the oven and preheat it to 350°F.

4. Heat a very large skillet over medium heat, then pour in the oil. Add the shallots and cook, stirring often, until really frizzling and aromatic, about 1 minute.

5. Add the shredded Brussels sprouts and garlic; cook, tossing occasionally, to soften slightly, about 3 minutes.

6. Add the flour. Cook, stirring all the while, for 1 minute, to let the flour lose its raw taste without browning.

7. Whisk in the wine until the flour dissolves off the vegetables, then whisk in the cream and bring to a simmer.

8. Stir in the ham, mustard, sage, and pepper, then remove the skillet from the heat and stir in the blanched squash noodles. Pour the contents of the skillet into a 9-by-13-inch baking dish.

9. Bake until bubbling and browned, about 20 minutes. Let the dish stand at room temperature for 5 minutes before serving.

HAM POT PIE

MAKES **6** TO **8** SERVINGS, DEPENDING ON
HOW MUCH WILL-POWER EVERYONE HAS

The ultimate comfort food: a casserole of ham, veggies, cream, and puff pastry. Frankly, even smoked wet-cured ham will work here.

3 tablespoons unsalted butter

1 large yellow onion, chopped

2 medium carrots, chopped

2 celery ribs, chopped

1½ pounds not-smoked, wet-cured ham, cut into ½-inch cubes

2 tablespoons all-purpose flour

1 cup reduced-sodium, fat-free chicken broth

½ cup dry white wine or dry vermouth

2 tablespoons heavy or whipping cream

1 tablespoon Dijon mustard

1 tablespoon stemmed thyme leaves or 2 teaspoons dried thyme

1 tablespoon minced sage leaves or 2 teaspoons dried sage

½ teaspoon freshly ground black pepper

1 pound frozen puff pastry dough, thawed according to the package directions

SLASH THE SHOPPING LIST

Substitute 3 cups frozen mixed vegetables for the onion, carrot, and celery. No need to thaw them—just drop them in the skillet with the butter and cook them a minute or so longer.

THE INGREDIENT SCOOP

Puff pastry is a flaky pastry dough. Its exact science is quite complicated—suffice it to say that the dough is repeatedly folded and rolled so the fat gets dispersed in the flour in thousands of layers. As it is quite time-consuming to make, most home cooks buy puff pastry in the freezer section of the supermarket—but be forewarned: Quality varies dramatically. Read the label to ascertain the ingredients. The best puff pastry doughs are made with butter or lard, not hydrogenated fat and stabilizers.

1. Position the rack in the center of the oven and heat it to 350°F.

2. Melt the butter in a large skillet set over medium heat. Toss in the onion, carrots, and celery. Cook, stirring often, until everything starts to soften a bit but still has crunch, about 5 minutes.

3. Add the ham and cook for 3 minutes, stirring often.

4. Sprinkle the flour over the contents of the skillet, then stir well and continue cooking about 1 minute more, just so the flour coats everything but does not start to brown.

5. Pour in the chicken broth and wine. Stir constantly until the flour dissolves, the liquid comes to a simmer, and the sauce thickens up a bit.

6. Stir in the cream, mustard, thyme, sage, and pepper. Pour everything into a 9-by-13-inch baking dish.

7. Unfold the puff pastry, remove any paper, and set the pastry on top of the casserole. Tuck it into the sides and the corners, sealing the filling into the baking dish. Use a sharp knife to make a few slits across the top of the dough. You could even try a decorative pattern. Or your initials.

8. Bake until the dough is puffed and golden brown and the filling is bubbling around the edges, about 45 minutes. Cool the casserole on a wire rack for 10 minutes to let the flavors meld a bit before you dish it up.

HAM-STUFFED CABBAGE ROLLS

MAKES 8 ROLLS

Stuffed cabbage has always been our "welcome-home" meal: Whenever one of us is away, the other makes this hearty dish ahead and has it in the fridge to heat up for the first dinner back together. Ham adds a salty sweetness, a little bit of luxury in what's otherwise a fairly healthy dinner.

½ cup pearl barley

¾ cup water

8 large red cabbage leaves

12 ounces not-smoked, wet-cured ham

½ cup chopped dill pickles

2 tablespoons Dijon mustard

1 teaspoon caraway seeds

1 teaspoon celery seeds

½ teaspoon grated nutmeg

½ teaspoon freshly ground black pepper

2 tablespoons unsalted butter

1 large yellow onion, chopped

¼ cup red wine vinegar

2 tablespoons packed dark brown sugar

1¾ cups reduced sodium, fat-free beef broth

½ teaspoon ground allspice

½ teaspoon salt

1 bay leaf

1. Mix the barley and water in a small saucepan and bring to a boil over medium-high heat. Cover, reduce the heat to low, and simmer slowly for 20 minutes, or until most of the water has been absorbed.

2. Meanwhile, bring a large saucepan of water to a boil over high heat. Cut the triangular bit of tough stem out of each cabbage leaf, then immerse them two by two in the boiling water. Blanch just until tender, about 4 minutes. Remove the leaves with tongs when done, spreading them out on paper towels, and continue blanching more of the leaves.

3. The barley should only be partially cooked—it will cook more in the steps ahead. Drain away any remaining liquid in the pan and pour the barley into a large bowl. Stir in the ham, pickles, mustard, caraway seeds, celery seeds, nutmeg, and pepper.

4. Lay one cabbage leaf, veiny side down, on your work surface, then put a scant ½ cup of the ham filling in its center. Fold the sides closed, then roll the thing up like an egg roll. Set it aside, seam side down, and continue making more.

5. Melt the butter in a large sauté pan or high-sided skillet over medium heat. Add the onion and cook, stirring often, until it's translucent and smells really sweet, about 4 minutes.

6. Stir in the vinegar and brown sugar. Cook, stirring constantly, for 1 minute. Pour in the broth; add the ground allspice, salt, and bay leaf. Bring the whole thing to a simmer.

7. Place the rolls, seam side down, in the pan. You might have to squeeze them in a bit to fit.

8. Cover, reduce the heat to low, and simmer slowly for 45 minutes. If you want to make this recipe in advance, stop here. Cool the pan at room temperature for a few minutes, then cover and refrigerate for up to 2 days. To reheat, place the pan back over low heat, add 1/4 cup broth, and continue heating until the sauce is bubbling and the rolls are warmed through.

9. Transfer the rolls to a large serving platter. Remove and discard the bay leaf. Raise the heat to medium; boil the residual liquid in the pan until it's reduced to half its volume, about 2 minutes. Spoon this sauce over the rolls just before serving.

JAMBON PERSILLÉ:
HAM'S COUP DE GRÂCE

Do not use a smoked ham for this recipe. The meat must be moist but quite delicate, the ideal results from *jambon de Paris* (see page 192) or, failing that, a not-smoked, wet-cured ham. If you're getting it straight from the deli case of your market (rather than using up leftovers), taste the meat before you buy it. It can't be bland in any way; you need full-flavored ham to stand up to the aromatic aspic that holds the terrine together.

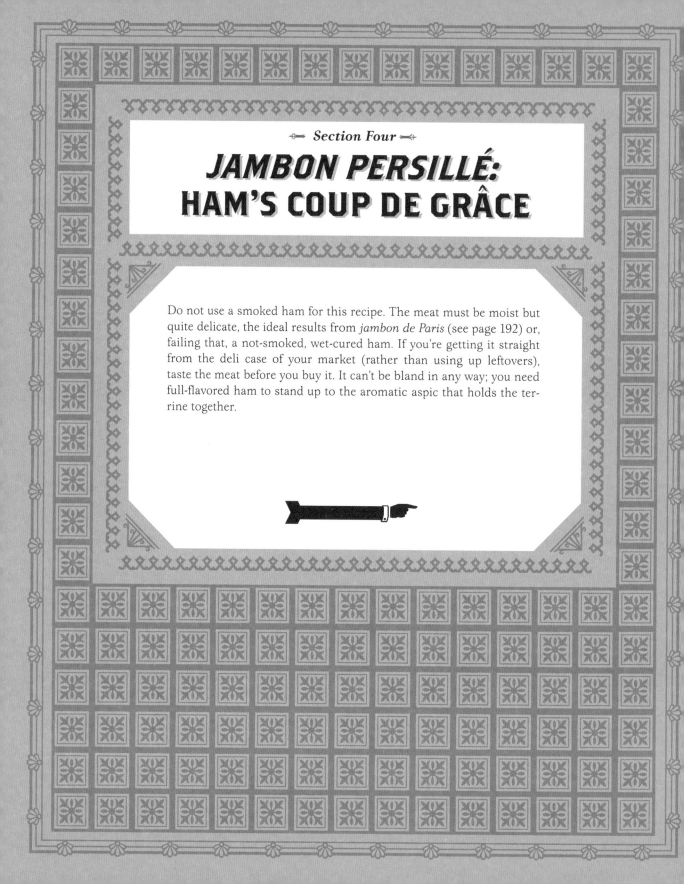

O f all the ways to work with and gussy up ham, none may be more dramatic than *jambon persillé* (French, *zhahm-BONE pair-see-YAY*, "parsleyed ham").

Basically, the preparation involves cubes of not-smoked, wet-cured ham (often *jambon de Paris*, page 192) suspended in a rich, aromatic aspic—one with no resemblance to that foofy stuff the old church ladies might have made. This one's a hearty, flavorful jelly that holds the bits of cured ham in place. Thus, *jambon persillé* is a fitting climax to our ham journey. No one fetishizes food like the French. This must be their *pièce de résistance*.

And Bruce's, too. When I first met him, he was a real New Yorker, the paradigm-made-flesh. He believed the world consisted of (1) the city, and (2) the Hamptons—with an unfortunate stretch of clogged expressway between.

I was more than prepared to remedy this catastrophic predicament. I took him to Paris, where we stayed in a workaday, two-star hotel run by a surly war widow. (But what war? This was 1996 and she was born years too late to have been married during World War II.)

All went as planned until Bruce saw his first butcher shop on the rue Cler—and the *jambon persillé* in the window.

"My two favorite food groups," he gasped. "Trayf and Jell-O."

He had the butcher lop off a hunk. We took it to the Parc du Champs de Mars, sat on the bench among more surly war widows (do they have an endless supply?), and ate it on a baguette with some nose-spanking mustard. That rich aspic and herbaceous parsley managed to foreground the tender bits of *jambon de Paris*.

In the years since, we've made many trips back to France. Our routine is always the same: Jet-lagged and bleary, Bruce bolts into the first butcher shop he can find to lay his hands on another slice of *jambon persillé*. He claims it's the cure for the indignities of coach travel.

So as the muddy starts of spring came to our house in the Connecticut woods and we neared the end of all things ham, he wanted to recreate that famed French dish for the American kitchen: a last hurrah, the *coup de grâce*.

But first off, a confession: A traditionally prepared *jambon persillé* is made by boiling down the pig's feet (the "trotters") until they yield a thick, protein-rich jelly. He figured no one we knew would go to all that trouble, even if they could lay their hands on trotters. So he streamlined the recipe a bit, the better to make it weekend party fare, meant to be served with retro cocktails. Gin fizzes, anyone?

Once we had the recipe nailed down, we did the unthinkable. We drove a *jambon persillé* down to Manhattan for a fussy cocktail party among the black-bedecked denizens of the city's arty set.

We learned one thing: Warn highbrow people before you bring in jiggly food. The aspic slid out of its terrine mold with the rudest noise.

"Thanks," said our hostess, a prim woman. She'd come from Wisconsin forty years earlier and had spent a lifetime trying to forget it.

We cut off a wedge and handed it to her.

She backed up. "Oh, I know this stuff," she said. "From Paris."

"Burgundy, originally," I chirped. "But like everything in France, it all ends up in Paris."

She wasn't a woman to be corrected. "Disgusting all the same."

Dismissed out of hand, our poor ham-in-aspic sat on the table a while, slowly losing its sheen as the jelly came to room temperature.

I panic easily. Call it the legacy of growing up under the imminent threat of the Rapture. I pulled Bruce aside. "That thing might liquefy!"

He brushed me off. "Have a bite. Give people the idea."

Sheesh, who was he kidding? I couldn't be seen diving into ham. Not at this weight.

Unbeknownst to us, there was a French couple in the room. They walked to the table, spotted our *jambon persillé*, and fell upon it.

"Where deed you get thees?" they asked our hostess.

She thumbed at us.

"I made it," Bruce said.

Ever the true foodies at any gathering, the French were enraptured. Pretty soon, they had most of the other guests wanting a slice, too. Our hostess eventually offered us the ultimate compliment: "I didn't think I could get it down, but . . ."

We didn't have to hear the rest. Because it's ham. Sure, all tarted up. But sweet or salty—there's something comforting about it. Something that says I came all the way to Manhattan but I haven't forgotten Kansas, North Dakota, Oklahoma, all of our rural roots—if not actually, then collectively. We all come from the land—even if in our distant past. And ham is the quintessence of that journey: humble meat that gets gussied up, only to remain true to its roots. It can even make the black-bedecked smile.

JAMBON PERSILLÉ

MAKES 1 TERRINE WITH ABOUT 10 SLICES

Traditional preparations often include garlic with the parsley. However, we feel its spike can be excessive, so we've used only a little bit as well as some shallots here, a softer hint with the ham and parsley. Be sure to mince that garlic into very fine bits so no one takes an unexpected hit.

4 cups reduced-sodium, fat-free chicken broth, plus a little more if necessary

4 medium carrots, peeled and cut into 2-inch pieces

2 medium celery stalks, cut into 2-inch pieces

1 medium yellow onion, peeled and quartered

2 teaspoons stemmed thyme leaves or 1 teaspoon dried thyme

8 whole cloves

2 bay leaves

3 teaspoons unflavored gelatin (about one and a half ¼-ounce packets)

2 tablespoons water

1½ cups packed parsley leaves, minced

3 medium shallots, minced

1 medium garlic clove, minced

1½ pounds not-smoked, wet-cured ham, such as *jambon de Paris*, diced

1. Bring the broth, carrots, celery, onion, thyme, cloves, and bay leaves to a boil in a medium saucepan set over high heat. Cover, reduce the heat to low, and cook very slowly for 35 minutes.

2. Uncover and continue cooking over a very low temperature for 10 minutes.

3. While the broth cooks, sprinkle the gelatin over the water in a small bowl and set aside to soften for 5 minutes.

4. Remove the saucepan from the heat, cool for a few minutes, and then strain the broth into a medium bowl, discarding all those solids. You should end up with 3 cups of liquid. If not, add a little more broth, just until you have the right amount.

5. Stir the softened gelatin and any residual water into the broth until the gelatin dissolves, then set aside to cool for 10 minutes. Meanwhile, mix the parsley, shallots, and garlic in a small bowl.

6. Make alternating layers of the ham pieces and the parsley mixture in a 6-cup loaf or pâté pan.

7. Gently pour the broth mixture over the ham pieces. Refrigerate for at least 24 hours, until the gelatin has set up the broth—but cover after a couple hours, once the mixture is chilled. If there's extra gelatinized broth left over, save it back in the freezer, adding it in dribs and drabs for extra richness to your next pots of soup.

8. To unmold, fill a large bowl with warm (not hot) water. Run a thin knife around the inner perimeter of the terrine or pan, then very briefly dip the mold into the hot water, just so it comes about three-quarters of the way up the side. Don't dip longer than a few seconds or the gelatin will start to melt! Turn upside down onto a serving platter, unmold (shake free if necessary), and serve slices with grainy, spicy mustard on the side.

THIS LITTLE PIGGY WENT ALL THE WAY HOME

ou haven't lived until you've tried to get a ham through airport security.

It was April, almost a full year of ham under our ever-more-ample belts, and we had one 14-pounder left from Wilbur, our pig.

"I'll bring it for Easter dinner," I told my mother.

It sounded pretty innocent in the thrum of long distance. It felt pretty innocent as we slung the frozen thing into a canvas bag and headed for the Hartford airport.

It *was* pretty innocent until we ended up at the X-ray machine with the ham and both our laptops dumped into various tubs.

I got stopped right away.

The agent was stern: pursed lips and bobbed hair. She snapped on her plastic gloves and reached into the bag. "Is this human?" she asked.

Yes, I wanted to say. It's a chunk of me. After the liposuction, I just couldn't part with myself. We've had such great times together: fresh hams, some even pan-fried, acres of *prosciutto crudo*, and the wet-cured one in the big bowl.

But I remembered those signs about jokes and terrorism. Was fat terrorism? Was ham? Maybe. Things were confusing in America.

"It's a ham," I said.

The woman didn't appear amused. "Why?"

Of all the questions, it's the one I least expected. "From our own pig," I said.

"Uh-huh. We had a turkey once." She narrowed her eyes. "I'll have to check."

Within minutes, the ham was out of its plastic bag. It was frosted and gray—not exactly at its best. She set it on that white folding table. A gaggle of TSA's finest gathered around. They waved wands. They swabbed. They opened manuals.

Finally, she walked back over, the glimmer of a smile around those thin lips. "You say it's from your own pig?"

"Absolutely."

If it had come from someone else's pig or (God forbid) the store, would it have made a difference?

"OK," she said. "You can go."

I slipped on my shoes and tried to get the ham and the laptops back into their respective bags.

"What were they doing?" Bruce asked when we met up again.

"The ham. They wanted to know what it was."

"You told them?"

"I hardly knew where to begin."

And so we flew to Texas, where Easter was already summer, its warmth the best antidote to the chill still padlocked onto Connecticut. We arrived with our ham in tow, a fitting end for the last bit of Wilbur. No longer a blank, this joint represented so much possibility, so much history, so many meals. It would soon be roasted and become, well, the very best thing of all, the exemplar of hope: dinner on the table.

SOURCE GUIDE

For dried spices or other esoteric ingredients to make the various spice rubs and combinations, try:

KALUSTYANS
www.kalustyans.com
212 685-3451 or 800 352 3451
123 Lexington Avenue
New York, NY 10016

PENZEY'S
www.penzeys.com
800 741-7787
For brick-and-mortar outlets near you, check out Penzey's website.

To locate an American country ham or order country ham steaks, check out the list of producers at their national organization:

THE NATIONAL COUNTRY HAM ASSOCIATION
www.countryham.org
800 820-4426
P. O. Box 948
Conover, North Carolina 28616

That said, here are the specific producers featured in this book:

NEWSOM'S COUNTRY HAMS
www.newsomscountryham.com
270 365-2482
208 East Main Street
Princeton, Kentucky 42445

FINCHVILLE FARMS
www.finchvillefarms.com
800 678-1521 or 502 834-7952
P. O. Box 56
Finchville, Kentucky 40022

SCOTT HAMS
www.scotthams.com
800 318-1353
1301 Scott Road
Greenville, Kentucky 42345

FATHER'S COUNTRY HAMS
www.fatherscountryhams.com
877 525-4267
P. O. Box 99
Bremen, Kentucky 42325

To order a whole, European, dry-cured ham like a prosciutto crudo *or a* jamón ibérico, *check out these websites:*

www.tienda.com
www.casaoliver.com
www.dartagnan.com

To take a culinary adventure in Spain, including trips out to the Dehesa to see the famed ibérico pigs, contact

A TASTE OF SPAIN
www.atasteofspain.com
Telephone to Barcelona: 34 856079626

And to follow us through our next project, to get daily recipes and lots of cooking tips, or to learn more about ham in all its incarnations, check out www.realfoodhascurves.com.

CONVERSION CHART

WEIGHT EQUIVALENTS: The metric weights given in this chart are not exact equivalents, but have been rounded up or down slightly to make measuring easier.

VOLUME EQUIVALENTS: These are not exact equivalents for American cups and spoons, but have been rounded up or down slightly to make measuring easier.

AVOIRDUPOIS	METRIC
¼ oz	7 g
½ oz	15 g
1 oz	30 g
2 oz	60 g
3 oz	90 g
4 oz	115 g
5 oz	150 g
6 oz	175 g
7 oz	200 g
8 oz (½ lb)	225 g
9 oz	250 g
10 oz	300 g
11 oz	325 g
12 oz	350 g
13 oz	375 g
14 oz	400 g
15 oz	425 g
16 oz (1 lb)	450 g
1 ½ lb	750 g
2 lb	900 g
2 ¼ lb	1 kg
3 lb	1.4 kg
4 lb	1.8 kg

AMERICAN	METRIC	IMPERIAL
¼ tsp	1.2 ml	
½ tsp	2.5 ml	
1 tsp	5.0 ml	
½ Tbsp (1.5 tsp)	7.5 ml	
1 Tbsp (3 tsp)	15 ml	
¼ cup (4 Tbsp)	60 ml	2 fl oz
⅓ cup (5 Tbsp)	75 ml	2.5 fl oz
½ cup (8 Tbsp)	125 ml	4 fl oz
⅔ cup (10 Tbsp)	150 ml	5 fl oz
¾ cup (12 Tbsp)	175 ml	6 fl oz
1 cup (16 Tbsp)	250 ml	8 fl oz
1¼ cups	300 ml	10 fl oz (½ pint)
1½ cups	350 ml	12 fl oz
2 cups (1 pint)	500 ml	16 fl oz
2½ cups	625 ml	20 fl oz (1 pint)
1 quart	1 liter	32 fl oz

OVEN MARK	F	C	GAS
Very cool	250–275	130–140	½–1
Cool	300	150	2
Warm	325	170	3
Moderate	350	180	4
Moderately hot	375	190	5
	400	200	6
Hot	425	220	7
	450	230	8
Very hot	475	250	9

ACKNOWLEDGMENTS

ANY BOOK HOLDS A MULTITUDE. THIS ONE INCLUDES:

The generous Kentuckians who gave me their time and stories as I toured the state's country ham trail—among them, **Nancy Newsom Mahaffey** of Newsom's Country Hams, **Bill Robertson and Tim Switzer** of Finchville Farms, **Leslie and June Scott** of Scott Hams, and **Charlie Gatton, Jr.,** of Father's Country Hams. **Nancy Newsom Mahaffey** provided the whole country ham used in the photos on page 10, **Charlie Gatton** provided us with county ham steaks for recipe testing, and **Tim Switzer** sent the steaks that made their way into the shot on page 133.

Dan and Tracy Hayhurst of Chubby Bunny Farm in Falls Village, Connecticut. They raised Wilbur on their land, gave us a lesson in animal slaughter we'll never forget, and provided us with so many meals over the years from their incredible CSA.

Allen and Robin Cockerline of Whippoorwill Farm in Salisbury, Connecticut, for listening to endless talk of curing ham. Plus, the pig shots in the book are all from their farm.

Miguel Ullibarri at A Taste of Spain, one of the country's premier culinary tour operators. Miguel may well be the world's foremost authority on *jamón ibérico*; he commented extensively on the full text of the dry-cured, European ham chapter, making it a far better piece than we could have produced alone.

The many people at Stewart, Tabori & Chang who made this book what it is: **Luisa Weiss**, our editor, who had the vision to acquire the book in these difficult times and is surely one of the most competent and professional people we've ever worked with; **Leslie Stoker**, our publisher, who continues to oversee the gorgeous books Stewart, Tabori & Chang is known for; **Alissa Faden** who came up with this kick-butt design that we loved at first sight; **Elizabeth Norment**, the finest copyeditor we've ever had; **Tina Cameron**, the production manager, who kept the book clicking along (even when we turned it in so early!); and **Claire Bamundo**, who's overseen the publicity for this single-subject wonder.

Marcus Nilsson, the photographer; **Angharad Bailey**, the prop stylist; and **Allison Attenborough**, the food stylist. We had so much fun during the three days they were at our house—and ate way, way, way too much ham.

Our two compatriots at Writers' House: **Susan Ginsburg**, our agent for more than a decade now and the only one who could place so many books in such a challenging climate; and **Bethany Strout**, a calming voice in the midst of writerly insecurities.

Alberto Solis at Fermin USA, who sent us the whole *jamón ibérico* for the photo shoot (the cover as well as pages 10 and 73). We debated doing a ritual dance around it. Then we just ate it.

Geoff Schwartz, Field Marketing Manager at HoneyBaked Ham®, who sent us two wet-cured hams for recipe-testing, hams that made us a favorite of friends for a couple weeks thereafter.

Jeffrey Elliot, who provided the beautiful and wonderful Staub cookware for the photo shoot.

Herb Eckhouse of La Quercia in Iowa who took time out of his busy day to talk about curing ham in the New World using Old World techniques.

Patricia Clough, ever a good friend, who did some behind-the-scenes snooping for us at the Fancy Food Show.

Steve Albert and **Jason Weiss**, who helped me with the pronunciation of the many foreign words in the manuscript.

INDEX

PAGE REFERENCES IN ITALIC REFER TO ILLUSTRATIONS

Published in 2010 by Stewart, Tabori & Chang
An imprint of ABRAMS

Text copyright © 2010 Bruce Weinstein and Mark Scarbrough
Photographs copyright © 2010 Marcus Nilsson
Photograph on page 77 copyright © 2010 Miguel Ullibarri

Library of Congress Cataloging-in-Publication Data
Weinstein, Bruce, 1960-
 Ham : an obsession with the hindquarter / Bruce Weinstein and Mark
Scarbrough.
   p. cm.
 ISBN 978-1-58479-832-3
 1. Cookery (Ham) 2. Ham. I. Scarbrough, Mark. II. Title.
 TX749.5.H35.W45 2010
 641.3 64--dc22
                         2009021451

Editor: Luisa Weiss
Designer: Alissa Faden
Production Manager: Tina Cameron

The text of this book was primarily composed in Brothers, Lomba, and Copperplate Gothic.

Printed and bound in China
10 9 8 7 6 5 4 3 2 1

THE ART OF BOOKS SINCE 1949

115 West 18th Street
New York, NY 10011
www.abramsbooks.com